Sex in Language

Also available from Bloomsbury

A Critical Introduction to Metaphor Studies, Andreas Musolff
The Bloomsbury Companion to Cognitive Linguistics,
edited by John R. Taylor and Jeannette Littlemore
The Sexual Politics of Meat, Carol J. Adams
Using Corpora to Analyze Gender, Paul Baker

Sex in Language:
Euphemistic and Dysphemistic Metaphors in Internet Forums

Eliecer Crespo-Fernández

Bloomsbury Academic
An imprint of Bloomsbury Publishing Plc

B L O O M S B U R Y
LONDON · OXFORD · NEW YORK · NEW DELHI · SYDNEY

Bloomsbury Academic
An imprint of Bloomsbury Publishing Plc

50 Bedford Square	1385 Broadway
London	New York
WC1B 3DP	NY 10018
UK	USA

www.bloomsbury.com

BLOOMSBURY and the Diana logo are trademarks of Bloomsbury Publishing Plc

First published 2015
Paperback edition first published 2017

© Eliecer Crespo-Fernández, 2015

Eliecer Crespo-Fernández has asserted his right under the Copyright, Designs and Patents Act, 1988, to be identified as the Author of this work.

All rights reserved. No part of this publication may be reproduced or transmitted in any form or by any means, electronic or mechanical, including photocopying, recording, or any information storage or retrieval system, without prior permission in writing from the publishers.

No responsibility for loss caused to any individual or organization acting on or refraining from action as a result of the material in this publication can be accepted by Bloomsbury or the author.

British Library Cataloguing-in-Publication Data
A catalogue record for this book is available from the British Library.

ISBN: HB: 978-1-4725-9652-9
PB: 978-1-3500-2426-7
ePDF: 978-1-4725-9655-0
ePub: 978-1-4725-9654-3

Library of Congress Cataloging-in-Publication Data
A catalog record for this book is available from the Library of Congress.

Typeset by Fakenham Prepress Solutions, Fakenham, Norfolk NR21 8NN

To my son Jaime, for his naughty smile

Contents

List of Illustrations and Tables	ix
Acknowledgements	x
Foreword	xi
Preface	xiv
Conventions in the text	xvi
Introduction	1

Part 1 Metaphor, Euphemism and Dysphemism

1	Cognitive and Pragmatic Issues	21
	1.1 Contemporary metaphor theory	21
	1.2 Metaphor–culture interface	35
	1.3 A relevance-theoretic view of metaphor interpretation	39
2	The Cognitive Dimension of Euphemism and Dysphemism	45
	2.1 Euphemism, dysphemism and metaphor	45
	2.2 Neutralization, contrast and displacement in X-phemistic naming	50
	2.3 Metaphor types and X-phemism	53
	2.4 The persuasive and evaluative function of X-phemistic metaphors	61
	2.5 Cognitive issues in the interpretation of X-phemistic metaphors	65

Part 2 Sex-Related Metaphors in Internet Forums

3	Euphemistic Metaphors	71
	3.1 Euphemistic sex-related domains	72
	3.2 Reaching the intended euphemistic meaning	127
4	Dysphemistic Metaphors	135
	4.1 Dysphemistic sex-related domains	135
	4.2 Reaching the intended dysphemistic meaning	175
	4.3 The evaluative function of dysphemistic metaphors	178

5 Conclusions and Final Remarks	187
Appendix I: Euphemistic metaphors classified by source domain	193
Appendix II: Dysphemistic metaphors classified by source domain	199
Notes	203
References	215
Index	227

List of Illustrations and Tables

Figure 2.1 X-phemistic Categories and Types of Taboo Naming   47

Figure 2.2 X-phemism, Face and Emotional Load   50

Figure 2.3 Metaphor Types and X-phemism   54

Figure 4.1 Evaluative Realizations in Sexist Dysphemism: *Starving lioness*   181

Figure 4.2 Evaluative Realizations in Homophobic Dysphemism: *Pansy*   183

Figure 4.3 Evaluative Realizations in Quasi-dysphemism: *Flame-throwing*   184

Table 1.1 Basic Metaphor Types in CMT   30

Table 3.1 Emotion Scenario for Sexual Passion in the HEAT Metaphor   80

Table 3.2 Metaphorical Mapping of LUST as an Emotion   117

Table 3.3 Inferential Process of Euphemistic Interpretation: *Play with herself*   129

Table 4.1 Inferential Process of Dysphemistic Interpretation: *Chick*   177

Acknowledgements

I would like to express my gratitude to the following people for their support and assistance in the production of this book.

Among linguists, I owe most to Professors Keith Allan, Kate Burridge, Miguel Casas and Pedro Chamizo, whose works have influenced these pages. Special thanks go to Professor Andreas Musolff for his generous helping of ideas during my stay as an academic visitor at the School of Language and Communication Studies, University of East Anglia (Norwich, UK) in 2014.

On an institutional level, I would like to express my gratitude to the Research Committee of the University of Castile-La Mancha, who granted me a semester leave to conduct research at the University of East Anglia, which is reflected in the pages of this book.

I also wish to thank Dr Francisco Yus for his useful feedback on relevant-theoretic issues.

Last, but certainly not least, I would like to thank Ana and Irene for their patience and understanding.

Foreword

Sex in Language is a book on linguistic pragmatics that seeks to explain cognitive aspects of taboo language by examining the metaphors and metonymies utilized by writers in the online message boards 'Female First Forum', 'Married Man Sex Life Forum', 'Sexual Disorders Forum' and 'Talk about Marriage'. Many people have written about sexual taboos but few have sought data from such dynamic contemporary sources as does author Eliecer Crespo-Fernández. Many writers have exemplified the figurative language used in speaking of tabooed topics but few have sought to unravel its structure in the way this book unravels it. The research reported here is undertaken in the spirit of cognitive linguistics and, in adopting and exploiting conceptual metaphor theory, *Sex in Language* extends earlier studies of metaphor and metonymy. Crespo-Fernández also appeals to, though he doesn't claim to develop, Relevance Theory, but there is nothing in the book to discomfort confirmed Griceans.

The focus on and analysis of metaphors used in speaking about sexual body parts, effluvia, acts and accessories is the main strength of the present work. Metaphor arises through the mapping of concepts from a source domain onto a target domain in order to achieve some narrative or other communicative goal. The goal may be wholly or partly interpersonal (e.g. to save embarrassment or, conversely, to cause offence) and/or contentful (e.g. to get the point across or to hold interest by using a colourful expression). Predictably, perhaps, what the data presented in this book reveal is that the vast majority of figures employed in online forums are commonplace and bereft of originality. Whereas a metaphor is a mapping between at least two domains, metonymy links two parts of a domain, typically part for whole (*cunt* for woman) or whole for part (*person* for penis). Needless to say, the distinction between metaphor and metonym is not uncontroversial since each subpart of a domain can be perceived as domain in its own right.

One finds different figures used in different languages because figurative language is culturally conditioned. That said, it is often the case that a figure in one language can be understood (i.e. be explicable) if translated literally into another language. X-phemisms like French *baiser* and English *screw* can both mean 'copulate', but the former is metonymic (part-for-whole, kiss for copulate), the latter metaphorical. Cognates have different dysphemistic force in different languages: the Polish exclamative *Cholera!* means much the same as the English exclamative *Damn!* and to castigate someone as *con* in French has much the same force as calling them an *idiot* in English – *con* has nothing like the force of English *cunt*, its cognate. Hence, the conclusions that one reaches with respect to sex in the minds of speakers of the English language will not necessarily correspond with what occurs in the minds of speakers of another language. A few mismatches between English and Spanish are noted in *Sex in Language*.

I'd like to take up a point about X-phemism and (im)politeness: the notion of the Middle Class Politeness Criterion (MCPC) first advanced in Allan and Burridge (1991) as a benchmark for politeness in Anglo societies. Allan (2014) refines and further explicates the notion, seeking to show how the criterion applies to everyone within Anglo communities and that counterparts to the MCPC must exist for other languages and cultures. Essentially, politeness is a demonstration of consideration for others (addressees, bystanders, what is spoken of). McGlone and Batchelor (2003) report an experiment in which pictures of dogs urinating and defecating were presented to young adult subjects (67 per cent of them female), who were instructed to describe what they saw in an email to another person. There was greater use of euphemism by those subjects who believed their identity would be revealed than by anonymous reporters, leading McGlone and Batchelor to claim that people use euphemism in the service of self-presentation rather than out of consideration for addressees. This certainly has some force, since politeness is intimately connected with the presentation of face and speakers normally seek to maintain their own face along with that of others. So the weighting of egocentrism as against altercentrism is under constant negotiation and adjustment in social encounters. I would guess that deliberate dysphemism works best where the speaker's identity is known, though I am not aware of any experimental evidence for this.

Sex in Language is entertaining to read. The analysis of metaphor is instructive. The criterion for judging the structures of metaphors that are proposed (e.g. ORGASM IS THE END OF A JOURNEY) has to be their plausibility. There is also the question of their value as providing insight into language use. These are things a reader should bear in mind. In the concluding chapter Crespo-Fernández admits that the dividing line between euphemism and dysphemism is blurred because of the contextual conditions on any particular use. What those contextual conditions do is enable appropriate interpretations to be placed on a given use. Readers should always ponder the importance of context when judging people's use of taboo terms in the data found in this book, as in real life.

Keith Allan
Sunshine Coast, Australia

References

Allan, Keith. 2014. 'A Benchmark for Politeness', in *Interdisciplinary Studies in Pragmatics, Culture and Society*, Jacob L. Mey and Alessandro Capone (eds). Cham: Springer.

Allan, Keith and Kate Burridge. 1991. *Euphemism and Dysphemism: Language Used as Shield and Weapon*. New York: Oxford University Press.

McGlone, Matthew S. and Jennifer A. Batchelor. 2003. 'Looking out for number one: Euphemism and face', *Journal of Communication* 53: 251–64.

Preface

It is not the purpose of this book to offer a theoretical approach to the contrasting phenomena of euphemism and dysphemism. This book is not intended as a comprehensive analysis of the taboo of sex, which would have called for a multi-faceted study combining different disciplines such as anthropology, psychology or sociology. Neither is it my intention to present an exhaustive study on language and cognition. This book is intended as a contribution within the field of cognitive linguistics to the antithetical mechanisms of verbal mitigation and offence – to the use of language as shield and weapon, as Keith Allan and Kate Burridge once put it – in a major and universal area of interdiction: sex. Simply put, this study makes use of cognitive tools to explore euphemistic and dysphemistic figurative language in the sexual taboo.

Given that euphemism and dysphemism are fully contextual phenomena which respond to particular communicative intentions, in order to offer a more fine-tuned picture of both processes I must go beyond a purely cognitive or lexically rooted analysis. With the purpose of explaining the factors other than word meaning that determine the use and interpretation of sex-related metaphors in naturally occurring communicative contexts, I will touch on the cultural and social factors governing the use of figurative language in discourse and step into those pragmatic issues which are pertinent for the question at hand. In fact, the interplay between cognition and pragmatics provides the basis for the euphemistic or dysphemistic force of metaphors in discourse. In this regard, this book takes a step in cognitive and relevance-theoretic issues with the intent of widening the field of study of euphemism and dysphemism in the vocabulary of sex.

In the present volume I turn to internet-derived data to explore how sex is actually talked about in a collection of texts taken from real-life communication. However, it is not only the use of real-life data that is relevant here. Working with a corpus of online current English provides a fresh insight into the sexual vocabulary used nowadays and adds a valuable element to the study of sexual metaphor by focusing on a discourse type which has become a popular and established form of collective communication.

I have written this book, first and foremost, because I find fascinating the way metaphor provides a way to speak about the unspeakable, about such a delicate issue as sex, which, as a heavily tabooed area, shapes human behaviour and communication. And, of course, because following the cognitive-linguistic approach to language, I believe that metaphor is a primary tool for understanding ourselves and the world that surrounds us. As Lakoff and Turner insightfully claimed, metaphor has four characteristics which make them a very valuable tool to verbalize our thoughts and reason about them: it is omnipresent, accessible to everyone, part of our everyday conventional thought, and has the capacity of allowing us to understand ourselves and our world effectively (1989: xi). From this standpoint, it is my contention in this study that an analysis of the figurative language that is used to cope with taboos can yield insights into the way a taboo topic is understood within a cultural group and allow us to have access to attitudes, value judgements and emotions which are communicated implicitly through metaphors.

I must make it clear that some of the material in parts of Chapter 2 first appeared in the articles 'Sex-related euphemism and dysphemism: An analysis in terms of conceptual metaphor theory', *Atlantis*, 30 (2) (December 2008) and 'Conceptual metaphors in taboo-induced lexical variation', *Alicante Journal of English Studies*, 24 (November 2011).

Insofar as this book is concerned with human communication, sex and cognition, I hope it should prove valuable to researchers in a range of disciplines, including cognitive linguistics, discourse analysis, gender and sexuality studies or pragmatics, as well as to students of linguistic courses. And, of course, it may be of interest to anyone interested in getting to know how the metaphors we live by are used nowadays to talk and reason about such a (still) heavily taboo area as sex.

The author
Norwich, April 2014

Conventions in the text

Following the conventions used in contemporary metaphor research, metaphorical concepts, source and target domains, conceptual metaphors and image schemas are indicated by small capitals.

Linguistic metaphors, i.e. metaphorical terms and expressions as realizations of conceptual metaphors, are indicated by italics.

An asterisk indicates that the concept I am referring to is *ad hoc* or pragmatically inferred in the interpretative process.

Meanings are constrained within single quotes.

Introduction

The power of taboo and the power of metaphor

As usually happens with most things dangerous or censored, taboos[1] are tempting and fascinating for us. Judging from the endless series of mild and abusive references to forbidden concepts, it seems obvious that taboo is not indifferent to human beings. As Burridge (2004: 199) puts it, 'what is taboo is revolting, untouchable, filthy, unmentionable, dangerous, disturbing, thrilling – but above all powerful'. And this powerful influence of taboo makes it a universal phenomenon which is consubstantial with human beings. Precisely for this reason, it is far from being just a relic of the Dark Ages of the past; rather, taboo keeps its force intact in our so-called modern and industrialized societies. That this is so can be gathered from Horlacher (2010: 3):

> Both temporarily and geographically, the phenomena of taboo and transgression can be considered omnipresent, that is, existent in all societies and cultures and at all times. If the ubiquity of taboos and their influence on social structures is generally accepted with regard to the past ... what is remarkable is the fact that taboos not only continue to exist but they can actually be said to be flourishing.

It is generally assumed that every historical period and society develops and cultivates its own taboos, which can be considered as symptoms of the customs, censorships and bad habits of the society. The degree to which a topic is prohibited or considered distasteful does not only vary from one society to another; there are also significant differences within the same communities and even across individuals on account of age, education, etc. Although taboo is deeply woven into every culture and society, the fact remains that from a purely linguistic viewpoint, taboo-induced lexical variation is a topic that, curiously enough, has received little attention in scholarly literature (see Chamizo Domínguez, 2009: 430). A case in point is Hock's *Principles of Historical Linguistics*, published in the last decade of the twentieth century, a time when censorships were supposed to have already diminished. In this book, taboo only covers nine out of 679 pages. And this happens, curiously enough, despite the fact that Hock (1991: 294) talks about a 'chain of ever-changing replacements' triggered by taboo which, in his own words, 'can lead to a constant turnover in vocabulary'.

As Hock notes, the power of taboo is reflected on language. Taboo keeps language users from avoiding the forbidden concept and compels them to preserve or violate it, which leads to endless series of *cross-varietal synonyms*[2] for the verbalization of forbidden concepts. As Burridge (2004: 212) argues, taboo 'provides a fertile seedbed for words to flourish – and the more potent the taboo, the richer the growth'. This is part of the paradoxical nature of taboo: we need to refer to the concepts themselves, no matter how much they are forbidden. Or precisely because they are forbidden and socially sanctioned, taboo areas constitute the raw material of much of the so-called bad language people use every day. This ambivalent nature of taboo derives from the Freudian theory of emotional ambivalence. Freud (1967) uses the notion of ambivalence to refer to contradictory inner wishes and impulses to both preserve and violate the taboo, a struggle between fear and desire which lives on in the unconscious. Benveniste (1974: 255) applied this theory to the linguistic taboo: 'A given word must not be spoken. It is simply removed from the language, expunged from use, it must no longer exist. However, and that is precisely the paradoxical condition of taboo itself, that term must exist even though it is forbidden' (my translation).

In the reference to taboos, language users resort either to *euphemism* (i.e. the process whereby the taboo is stripped of its most explicit or obscene overtones) or to *dysphemism* (i.e. the process whereby the most pejorative traits of the taboo are highlighted with an offensive aim to the addressee or to the concept itself). From this viewpoint, euphemism and dysphemism are not merely a response to a forbidden subject; rather, these processes provide a way to speak about the taboo, that is, about the unspeakable, about those concepts banned from public domain and removed from our consciousness, either with the aim of preserving or violating the proscription imposed by society or by ourselves.

Given that metaphor stands out as one of the most prolific linguistic devices of lexical creativity and a potent source for euphemistic and dysphemistic reference (see note 5, Chapter 2), it is hardly surprising that speakers turn to metaphor as a means of coping with taboo topics. Metaphor includes other types of figurative language devices that involve, to a greater or lesser extent, the axiology of the word: metonymy, synecdoche, irony or litotes (see Chamizo Domínguez, 2005: 17) as well as circumlocution, hyperbole or antonomasia (see Casas Gómez, 1986: 218). As Lakoff and Johnson (1980: 3) point out, metaphors pervade everyday life, not only as far as language is concerned, but also in our thoughts and actions. In fact, metaphorical language plays a crucial role in the way we manage taboo topics: it is at the user's disposal to model the distasteful concept and present it without its pejorative overtones or, by contrast, with an intensification of its most unacceptable conceptual traits. Metaphor thus stands out as a major device in structuring euphemism and dysphemism conceptually, as we will see in the course of the analysis.

Sex: The ultimate taboo

Among those subjects traditionally banned from the public domain, sex has usually met the strongest interdiction. Whether owing to modesty, shame, social impositions or on account of the guilt that most religions have associated with sexual pleasure, sex has traditionally been considered taboo. Although every historical period develops its own taboos and taboo subjects can vary widely and change along with our social attitudes and beliefs, the fact remains that sex has shown remarkable staying power. This is the reason why sexuality (together with its less physical counterpart, eroticism) is still considered taboo by many people in contemporary Western communities and cultures. Sexuality deserves the consideration of 'multifaceted' taboo in that it is an area of human experience in which psychological, religious and social interdictions coexist. As Santaemilia (2005: 3) argues, the taboo of sex:

> ... stands at the crossroads of at least two compelling forces: on the one hand, a private and intimate experience which articulates our voices and our desires; and on the other hand, a complex process of discursive construction ... profoundly ideological and highly dependent on the morality of each historical period, on the changeable dialectics between individual values and social discipline.

The public and private interdictions Santaemilia points out explain the deep imprints that the sexual taboo has left on people's mind and language. Despite the fact that the censorship surrounding sex has progressively relaxed, especially since the 1960s when people began to change their perceptions of sexuality, prudish sensibility and religious intransigence still hold out in some places and social groups nowadays in which interdictions surrounding sex are still alive. Although religion and sexuality do not have to be mutually exclusive, the departure from sexual interdictions, especially in Western democratic societies, is partly due to increasing secularism in the Western world.

Although the taboo of sex still imposes certain restrictions in our time and is not an easy subject to discuss openly, sex is by no means limited to implicit, vague or indirect references; indeed, an explicit treatment of this taboo coexists with implicit allusions to sexual issues in present-day communication. The public use of terms referring to sexual organs and sexual play has become relatively common nowadays, even in print where the greater degree of formality is supposed – at least in theory – to erect certain barriers against bawdy language. Following Epstein (1986: 57), Western permissive societies have abandoned the silence on sexual topics for an explicit reference to the taboo of sex:

> Silence on the subject of sex has been broken, and it is unlikely to be restored. Sex throughout history has been on most people's minds, but in this century it has increasingly been on almost everyone's tongue as well.

Sex, as a major concern in human life and a multifaceted index of identity, gives rise to a great deal of figurative language which performs a twofold (euphemistic and dysphemistic) purpose, as we will see throughout the book. This stands as proof of the ambivalent response of human nature to taboos: no matter how much certain subjects are forbidden, we feel the need to refer to them in one way or another.

The force of the sexual taboo and its pervasiveness in everyday life is reflected in the tremendously high degree of synonymy in the vocabulary for genitalia and copulation in English. Sex is, indeed, an area of interdiction particularly fruitful in lexical generation. According to Allan and Burridge (1991: 96), there exist approximately 1,200 terms for *vagina*, 1,000 for *penis* and 800 for *copulation*, combining all types of X-phemistic (i.e. euphemistic and dysphemistic) naming one may find in the wide range of sex-related fields.[3] Judging from the endless series of mild and abusive references to sexual concepts, it seems obvious that sex is not indifferent to human beings. The sexual taboo both avoids and demands the emergence of words which are at both extremes of the axiological scale, from 'pure' euphemism to 'straight' dysphemism, with different axiological subcategories between these two basic modalities of taboo naming, as we will see in the course of the analysis.

I cannot go any further without stating how sex is approached in this book. I take sex and sexuality in a broad sense. All types of erotic desires and sexual practices, together with issues related to sexual orientation, fall within the scope of this book. What I consider by sex here goes beyond a purely sociological, biological or erotic dimension, since all these aspects make up a whole in people's experiences related with sex, which range from physiological dysfunctions to sadomasochistic scenes, from 'dirty' jokes to prostitution, from sexual games to pornography. In this respect, I agree with Cameron and Kulick (2003: xi), who conceive sexuality and the way it should be dealt with in a linguistic study as follows:

> All kinds of erotic desires and practices fall within the scope of the term [sexuality], and to the extent that those desires and practices depend on language for their conception and expression, they should also fall within the scope of an inquiry into language and sexuality.

Aims, theoretical frames and scope of the study

In the present volume metaphor is taken as a bridge that brings together the study of language and the study of conceptual interdiction. The main concern of this study is to demonstrate that many euphemistic and dysphemistic references to taboo subjects are based on underlying metaphor systems within the well-known framework of conceptual metaphor theory, initially proposed by Lakoff and Johnson (1980), later redefined by the contemporary theory of metaphor (Lakoff 1993) and improved by subsequent works that I will refer to in Chapter 1. In this regard, I adopt the view of metaphor and metonymy as basic tools to conceptualize the world, as proposed by the Lakoffian tradition of metaphor research. In so doing, I attempt to gain an insight into the conceptual nature of sex-related verbal mitigation and offence and the way these processes fulfil their communicative and social goals in discourse.

In order to offer a full picture of the conceptual processes underlying euphemistic and dysphemistic use and interpretation, the present study is also embedded in relevance theory, a pragmatic theory with strong explanatory power in the inferential process of metaphor interpretation initially developed by Sperber and Wilson (1986). This theory is especially useful for a cognitively related analysis of metaphorical euphemism and dysphemism, as it attempts to explain the differences existing between literal and non-literal interpretation of metaphorical utterances and how these differences contribute to the recognition of the speaker's intention. In this regard, I will analyse the way hearers infer the intended euphemistic or dysphemistic meaning from sex-related metaphors and, therefore, how the intention of the speaker to be respectful or offensive projects in discourse. Together with the relevance-theoretic framework, other pragmatic issues will be addressed, like Grice's cooperative principle and the so-called conversational maxims, as well as politeness and face concerns.

Given that much dysphemistic language carries evaluative meaning, I will also make use of the achievements of appraisal theory, a relatively recent development of the Hallidayan framework of systemic functional linguistics concerned with the language of evaluation, attitude and emotion used to express (and react to) personal views and ideological positions. Developed, among others, by Martin (2000) and Martin and White (2005), this framework is especially suited to gain an insight into the figurative language identified in the sample consulted for blaming, accusing or name-calling; indeed, dysphemism involves expressing negative evaluation of behaviours through emotionally loaded and offensive language. In this regard, this book takes a critical approach by considering to what extent metaphors are used with an evaluative function, i.e. as a means to criticize and condemn people (mostly women and male homosexuals) who do not conform to conventional gender roles.

Having these research frameworks in mind, I will analyse linguistic metaphors and patterns of conceptual networks in euphemistic and dysphemistic language in an area of interdiction which constitutes a fascinating storehouse for metaphors of attenuation and offence: sex. The task undertaken here seems to prove a worthy enterprise, because while there has been substantial body of research on metaphor since Lakoff and Johnson's seminal book *Metaphors We Live By* (1980), to the best of my knowledge little attention has been paid to conceptual metaphor as a purely euphemistic or dysphemistic device.[4] Indeed, very few attempts have been undertaken to describe and explain the use of euphemism and dysphemism in communication from a cognitive standpoint and even fewer studies have dealt with sex-related euphemistic and dysphemistic processes. It is true that a considerable number of scholarly studies have been devoted to sexual metaphors along cognitive lines (Kövecses, 1986, 1988; Hines, 1996, 1999, 2000; Deignan, 1997, 2005; Murphy, 2001, among others). These works, however valuable they are, do not approach metaphorically motivated expressions as manifestations of X-phemistic processes. Apart from my own contributions to the subject (Crespo-Fernández, 2008, 2011), to the best of my knowledge only Chamizo Domínguez and Sánchez Benedito (2000) and Chamizo Domínguez (2009) have analysed sexual euphemism and dysphemism along cognitive lines. The present book adds a new element to these studies by looking at euphemistic and dysphemistic metaphors in a sample of naturally occurring language, which allows me to reflect on the social and communicative functions that X-phemistic metaphors perform.

The analyses that I present in this book are basically devoted to *conventional* metaphors. X-phemistic units are mostly motivated by conventional or semi-lexicalized metaphors, i.e. those that are established within a language and can suit the purpose of euphemism and dysphemism particularly well by conceptualizing a given entity in particular terms. Conventional metaphors are deeply entrenched in the language; their metaphoricity may go unnoticed and is commonly used unconsciously. This unmarkedness of metaphor, however, reflects the importance of metaphor in language and communication. As Gibbs (cited in Deignan, 2005: 15) argues, 'those things that are most alive, and most deeply entrenched, efficient and powerful are so automatic as to be unconscious and effortless'. Conventional metaphors are indeed 'alive' in that they reflect active schemes of metaphorical thought and constitute highly potent means of organizing experience. *Creative* or novel metaphors – i.e. those that draw on uncommon source concepts with respect to the target domain – are dealt with to a lesser extent, as these metaphors are highly specific, even one-shot occurrences of figurative thought and therefore are not representative of the way people conceptualize reality. Lexicalized (also called 'dead') metaphors are not perceived as having a literal counterpart and thus the connection between the metaphorical item and its original source domain is difficult (if not impossible) to establish. Despite this, the analysis of some of these dead metaphors may add valuable insights into the way certain sexual topics are verbalized in the sample consulted. In consequence, when these metaphors perform a euphemistic or dysphemistic function connected to their metaphorical origin, I decided it could be interesting to look at them and derive some cognitive implications from their use in present-day English. After all, as Kittay (1989: 89) claims, 'no matter how "dead" or conventionalized, metaphors are metaphors none the less'.

As cannot be otherwise in a study of such socially sensitive issues as euphemism and dysphemism, I take into account the role of conceptual metaphors in discourse, that is, their use in naturally occurring contexts, and not only at an abstract, cognitive level. Following Caballero and Ibarretxe-Antuñano, I start from the basic assumption that analysing metaphors in real contexts of language use involves exploring both the role of metaphor in cognition and the use of metaphors in communication, which inevitably leads to considering the cultural factors that affect the communicative act:

> Metaphor is both a conceptual and a socialization tool, and one that is partly acquired and effectively put to work through discourse interaction. Hence, there is a need to incorporate the cognitive, linguistic, and cultural aspects of figurative phenomena in research aimed at explaining why and how people interact through metaphor. (Caballero and Ibarretxe-Antuñano, 2009: 272)

This threefold dimension of metaphors makes it necessary to combine both a cognitive and a discourse view of metaphorical language. Take, for example, DEATH IS A REST. This metaphor fulfils a particular function in discourse: to provide a socially acceptable way to talk about such a delicate topic as death and, by so doing, provide some comfort and consolation to those left alive. Its main role in discourse is not, strictly speaking, cognitive (i.e. to provide an ontological status to the target domain of death) but to use a source domain like REST with a consolatory purpose in a real communicative context. In other words, this conceptual metaphor is only meaningful insofar as it fulfils a communicative need (cf. Caballero, 2006: 76): that of evaluating a taboo concept as positive and, in so doing, being able to euphemistically refer to it in communication.

Corpus data

Granted that euphemism and dysphemism are socially and culturally sensitive phenomena and, as such, highly dependent on context, this study is not based on isolated words, but on coherent and contextualized discourses excerpted from a sample of real language use. Corpora here are used as sources of evidence to explore how the taboo of sex is conceptually structured in contemporary English. In the selection of the corpus, I decided that it was interesting to focus on a sample of language in naturally occurring contexts in the taboo area under scrutiny, avoiding thus an approach to metaphorical language with examples constructed by the author or excerpted from lexicographic sources, which, however interesting they may be, lack authenticity.

The corpus for the present study has been excerpted from public internet discussion boards (often referred to as *forums*). Here the web is thus used as a source for the compilation of language data through messages posted in online forums which are freely available to the public in general. Internet message boards as a public form of computer-mediated communication have become increasingly popular in the last decades. They are an established form of collective communication in which participants use public message boards in order to exchange views, regardless of their separation in space and time, on a variety of topics, ranging from the more private to the more public (Claridge, 2007). Given that more and more people use the internet to communicate and exchange views on a wide range of topics, online forums constitute a form of collective and public communication in which, despite their public and free access, private and intimate topics are discussed. This is why message-board communication is a hybrid between interpersonal and mass communication in which private issues like sex are discussed in a public domain (Marcoccia, 2004: 118).

The sample of postings used in the book covers a time span of three years, from January 2011 to December 2013. It amounts to a total of 188 postings in which 240 X-phemistic metaphorical items have been encountered. All of them (included in their corresponding source domain) are listed in the appendices that close the book. As the reader will surely notice, the number of postings provided as examples is greater for the year 2013. The reason for this is that in some online forums the least recent postings are gradually deleted and only the most recent ones are available. However, this relative imbalance in the distribution of the data over the three-year period consulted does not affect the representativeness and value of the sample.

I should make it clear that the present study can make no claim to being complete or exhaustive. This is not a large-scale corpus study typical of corpus linguistics analysis in which the frequency of occurrence of metaphorical senses is given. I have not used any large collection of authentic machine-readable texts as object of research, as is the case in 'proper' corpus linguistics. Relying on relatively small data samples does not allow valid conclusions to be drawn in quantitative terms. This does not mean, however, that the data are gained by personal intuition (i.e. introspection) or from anecdotal or non-systematic evidence. In fact, the sample of internet postings consulted meets some basic requirements for analysis in discourse studies (Caballero and Ibarretxe-Antuñano, 2009): first, it deals with real language use; second, it guarantees that the author has considered a sufficient (i.e. not anecdotal) range of realizations of the research issue; and third, it ensures that the issue under analysis is used in certain communities and discourse types. Despite the relatively small amount of language data that constitutes this investigation, I believe that the sample consulted allows me to consider metaphor as a way of reasoning about sex nowadays in accordance with cognitive metaphor theory.

This approach obviously has its limitations, as compared to the data-driven approach, in which researchers work with an extensive and non-selective corpus of data, although they are not so much concerned with suggesting global cognitive structures to explain the data. Although it goes without saying that an extensive corpus is needed to reach valid conclusions in quantitative terms, I have adopted here a qualitative approach as I am primarily concerned with cognitive structures on the basis of an incomplete (although representative) set of language data.

By choosing internet-derived data, I focus on present-day English. Adopting a synchronic approach to current language data has some limitations. I had to leave out certain metaphorical conceptualizations like SEX IS DEATH or SEX IS KNOWLEDGE which, although widely used to talk about sexual issues in the past and recorded as such in lexicographic sources (Neaman and Silver, 1990; Holder, 2003; Sánchez Benedito, 2009), have not been detected in the sample consulted. However, working with a corpus of online current English has many advantages: apart from providing a fresh insight into the sexual vocabulary used nowadays in one of the most popular forms of communication, it is especially useful for studying real-language phenomena like euphemism and dysphemism.

Although in the collection of the language data for the present research I draw from written records, I am aware of the fact that some euphemistic and dysphemistic items usually blossom in the spoken language. To opt for a sample of online communication seems to overcome this limitation. In fact, the dialogic and interactive nature of discussion boards leads to analyse forum language with a view to oral linguistic features (Claridge, 2007: 88) in spite of the fact that, after all, it is a sample of written language. This language variant is therefore particularly interesting for my purpose here because it is close to the patterns that one expects to find in spontaneous and spoken communication (O'Keefe, 2012: 451). Indeed, the internet-derived data consulted are excerpted from informal and spontaneously created messages, in contrast with other more consciously or carefully constructed texts like, for example, political speeches.

The restriction of the language data to internet forums is especially useful to approach the linguistic study of sexual matters. Indeed, internet forums in which sexual issues are discussed are not only a breeding ground for metaphorical euphemism, as can naturally be expected; they are also a fertile ground for sex-related dysphemism for several reasons. In forum language, strict conventions in writing are not observed in the same way as in other more formal text types in which sex-related topics must be dealt with within the constraints imposed by sociocultural norms of polite behaviour. In addition, the anonymity of online communication plays a role in the way sexual issues are approached: people openly touch embarrassing topics and feel free to speak about feelings, desires and conflicts without concerns about how doing so might negatively affect their private lives or social images (Yus Ramos, 2005: 149). Furthermore, as the risk of face loss in internet forums is much lower than in face-to-face communication, online discussions seem to induce participants to be less sensitive towards the face wants of their addressees (Kleinke, 2008: 75), which ultimately leads to the appearance of sex-related language expressions which would otherwise have been difficult to find in a real communicative context.

Granted that, obviously enough, the sources used for any empirical analysis depend on the nature of the research being carried out, the discussion boards consulted are devoted to the subject of sex from different perspectives (marital intimacy, medical advice, sexual addictions, sadomasochism, pornography, etc.). The internet forums used as data sources for the present study are the following:

- *Female First Forum* (henceforth FFF)
  http://www.femalefirst.co.uk/board/
- *Married Man Sex Life Forum* (henceforth MMSL)
  http://marriedmansexlife.vanillaforums.com/
- *Sexual Disorders Forum* (henceforth SDF)
  http://www.psychforums.com/sexual-disorders/
- *Talk about Marriage* (henceforth TAM)
  http://talkaboutmarriage.com/sex-marriage/

As the names of the forums indicate, not all of them are addressed to the same type of participants: the potential members of FFF are women, TAM is oriented to married couples and MMSL mostly to married men. The sample involves both same-sex and mixed groups, as both males and females participate in the forums. By exclusively gathering data from sex-related forums, I believe that basic principles of data compilation such as the representativeness of the sample and its thematic coherence are followed. For the sake of minimizing variables and constructing a homogeneous sample of language data, I decided to focus on sexual metaphors used by heterosexual men and women. This does not imply, of course, that the postings related to homosexual issues encountered were not considered. It simply means that I did not take as data source any forum used exclusively by gays or lesbians. The reason for this is that the linguistic manifestations of homosexuality deserve a separate analysis, as (although not a homogenous community) many homosexuals have a distinctive language use, whether owing to the long-standing stigma of homosexuality or on account of their own sexual behaviour or practices.[5]

It is worth noting that the online forums consulted deal with sexual issues from different perspectives and with different purposes. For instance, in the threads of TAM sexual and marriage advice as well as relationship help are offered, whereas SDF is a subforum devoted to different types of sexual addictions and disorders within the 'PsychForums', a general psychology and mental health forum. Therefore, the degree of formality and the register of language employed to approach certain sexual topics may be expected to vary. It is also of note that the forums consulted are not thematically restricted, as different sexual topics are discussed in each of the subforums into which the main forums are divided.

As one can naturally expect, these forums bridge people from different cultures and countries who interact, share and discuss sexual issues with the rest of the participants, despite distance and sometimes time. The only thing that all participants in the discussion boards share is the language – the vast majority of them are native speakers of English – and their openness and readiness to discuss sexual issues and get ideas, support and advice from the different threads opened. Therefore, the fact that some of the forums used as source for language data are British (FFF and SDF) and others are American (TAM and MMSL) is totally irrelevant.

It is important to say that in the postings provided as examples to illustrate the analysis, the messages have been copied verbatim from the originals. This means that any erroneous spelling or mistakes in capitalization, punctuation or grammar remain exactly as found in the original source. In order to conceal the participants' identities in the forums I omit the usernames of the posters of the messages taken as examples.

Although this book is focused on metaphorical euphemism and dysphemism in English, some examples from other languages, namely Spanish, are used to describe and exemplify the various axiological categories of sex-related metaphors. However, my intention is not to check if a concept is verbalized in the same way in different languages. I merely attempt to provide additional examples that could enrich and complement the different linguistic manifestations of the cognitive structures discussed.

Contextual issues

There is an observation that should be made when dealing with research on phenomena of real language use in social contexts like euphemism and euphemism. A given word or expression is not expected to be euphemistic or dysphemistic *per se*; rather, its attenuating or offensive quality depends, if not totally, to a considerable extent on the context in which it is used. As Allan and Burridge (1991: 4) maintain, dysphemism, and its counterpart euphemism, 'are determined by the choice of expression within a given context: both the world spoken **of**, and the world spoken **in**' [in bold in the original].[6] The context of communication, together with the recognition of the speaker's intention, lead the hearer to grasp the speaker's intended meaning and thus identify the communicative force of the euphemistic or dysphemistic item. This helps to explain why the boundaries between euphemism and dysphemism are rather blurred. In fact, a given word or expression can only be understood properly as euphemistic or dysphemistic if we consider contextual issues, which includes the participants involved in the communicative act, the speaker's purpose, the hearer's world knowledge, and many other contextually related factors.[7]

To complicate matters, the axiological value of a word may change with the passing of time. What today is widely regarded as euphemism, with the passing of time and the erosion caused by its continuous use in the reference to forbidden concepts, may lead to dysphemism. This process, called 'euphemistic treadmill' by Pinker (2002), culminates in the lexicalization with the taboo sense of the once euphemistic word or expression, which is deprived of its capacity to mitigate the taboo, and fades from euphemism to dysphemism, requiring thus another euphemistic locution which could actually tone down the concept. It is a kind of 'euphemism carousel', as Keyes (2010: 13–15) puts it, which explains why a heavily tabooed word in current English like *pussy* 'vagina' first appeared as a euphemistic term to refer to female genitals (Chamizo Domínguez and Sánchez Benedito, 2000: 7).

Given the lack of stability of euphemistic (and for the same matter dysphemistic) labels, Allan and Burridge (2006) coined the cover term *X-phemism* to account for the set union of euphemistic, dysphemistic and orthophemistic, i.e. straight talking, using neutral terms from an axiological point of view, verbal realizations. From this perspective, X-phemisms constitute cross-varietal synonyms for a given concept in which the connotations obviously differ and suppose a means to manage taboo topics in communication depending on the context of use and the speaker's intention to be respectful or offensive towards the interlocutor or the topic being dealt with. As Allan and Burridge (2006: 47) write:

> X-phemisms are cross-varietal synonyms because an X-phemism, such as *shit*, means the same as another expression, in this case the orthophemism *faeces* and the euphemism *poo*; the three are typically used in different contexts, perhaps in different varieties or dialects of the language. Cross-varietal synonyms share the same denotation but differ in connotation.

We should also bear in mind that using taboo topics in real discourse may lead to the emergence of axiological categories in which the locution (i.e. the form of words) does not coincide with the illocution (i.e. the aim of a speaker in making an utterance) in a given communicative context and are thus felt halfway between euphemism and dysphemism. I refer to these axiological categories – which basically correspond with Allan and Burridge's (1991, 2006) 'dysphemistic euphemism' and 'euphemistic dysphemism' – as *quasi-euphemism* and *quasi-dysphemism* (see 2.1). Different X-phemistic types which come to be included in the aforementioned axiological categories – ludic, derogatory, provocative, uplifting, dirty, praising or cohesive X-phemisms – are also discussed in the course of the analysis. Therefore, in this study I use the label 'X-phemism' to refer to the processes of euphemism, dysphemism, quasi-euphemism and quasi-dysphemism, leaving out the category of orthophemism, which typically involves direct and literal language. The possible metaphorical origin of standard orthophemistic lexical units (like *intercourse*, for instance) will be considered in the analysis of the data, however, if cognitive implications may be derived from their use in the forums consulted.

Contextual issues play a crucial role in linguistic interdiction; indeed, the choice between X-phemistic alternatives depends almost entirely on context. Because of this, it is difficult to categorize linguistic units in terms of their axiological value, as already said. This led Allan and Burridge (1991, 2006) to propose what they called the *middle-class politeness criterion*, or MCPC, later redefined by Allan (2014), as a cultural frame devised to account for the evaluation of orthophemistic, euphemistic and dysphemistic language as the product of (im)polite behaviour. Allan maintains that MCPC functions as a benchmark for politeness within Anglo communities in that it guides the speaker's intuitions regarding the X-phemistic quality of a language expression in a particular context. By virtue of the MCPC, certain words are considered to be typically polite and therefore more apt to act considerately towards the interlocutor in a formal communicative situation.

However, the X-phemistic value of a particular language expression goes beyond considerations of politeness. In this respect, Allan (2014: 12) adopts Watt's term of *politic behaviour* to account for the fact that that different contexts impose different standards of appropriateness. For example, a typically dysphemistic term like *cunt* may admit a positive, i.e. quasi-euphemistic, use as a way to sexually arouse the partner during (or as a prelude to) coition. In this context, *cunt* is an example of politic behaviour: it is appropriate in this particular situation and for this purpose. However, obviously enough, it cannot be labelled as polite. This type of language exchanges offers the most evident default conditions for the MCPC.

Methodology

The method used to retrieve metaphorical expressions from the sample has been manual searching: I have carefully read throughout the forums searching for linguistic metaphors that contain specific target (i.e. sexual) domain vocabulary. Although this searching strategy certainly limits the potential size of the corpus, it allows for a comprehensive search and considerably reduces the risk of missing significant cases of metaphorical language used in the sample consulted. The analysis of metaphorical units also involves the description and explanation of metaphors on the basis of their degree of conventionality, as explained earlier.

In order to identify metaphorically used words in the corpus, I have relied on the so-called Metaphor Identification Procedure, or MIP, a method for linguistic metaphor detection in natural discourse developed by the Pragglejaz Group (2007). This method can be summarized in the following steps: first, reading the entire text and understanding the general context; second, establishing the contextual meaning for the lexical unit in the text; third, determining if the lexical unit in question has a more basic current-contemporary meaning in other contexts; and fourth, deciding whether the contextual meaning contrasts with a more basic meaning but can be understood by some form of familiarity with it. If this is the case, the lexical unit is identified as metaphorically used. After having marked a lexical unit as metaphorical, I moved on to uncover the underlying conceptual metaphor. To this end, I determined which source domain the lexical unit belongs to and described and characterized aspects of this domain in order to account for the mitigating or offensive value of the sex-related metaphorical item.[8] Finally, I checked the ways the X-phemistic meaning intended is captured by the participants in the forums.

This type of analysis is inductive: I start from the language data and it is only at a later stage that conceptual metaphors are derived from the linguistic metaphors previously marked as metaphorically used. The research methodology followed corresponds to the 'bottom-up' approach to describe and analyse metaphors in discourse, as opposed to the 'top-down' approach in which the researcher presumes the existence of conceptual metaphors and then searches the text for linguistic metaphors that are compatible with them (see Krennmayr, 2013). As Kövecses (2008: 132) argues, both approaches have limitations: 'Figuratively speaking, top-down researchers do not see the trees for the forest, and bottom-up researchers do not see the forest for the trees.' Here I decided that it was important to look through the online forums first, allow the metaphorical expressions to 'speak for themselves' and so uncover the conceptual structures underlying sexual language from the identification of the linguistic metaphors found in the data.

As said earlier, I have adopted a synchronic perspective in order to analyse the different sex-related metaphors, as, on most occasions, diachronic information is not very relevant for the description of the way the English-speaking community manages taboo topics nowadays. However, I will offer information about the semantic evolution of a word or expression if it provides us with valuable additions to the discussion.

Following Deignan (1999: 182), there are three main problems which arise in an investigation on metaphor in a sample of real language use, as is the case here. First, identifying dead metaphors as cases of literal rather than figurative language use (as already commented); second, dealing with cases of metaphors that occur in fixed collocations and can be described as idioms; and third, distinguishing between metaphor and metonymy (as I will explain in 1.1.3). To these, I would add the difficulty of establishing a dividing line between the different X-phemistic axiological categories in which metaphorical sex-related X-phemism may be included, as said before. Concerning the difference between metaphor and idioms, I follow Kövecses, who claims that 'the meaning of many … idioms depends on, and is inseparable from, the (metaphorical) conceptual system' (2002: 236). Simply put, in the present book I consider linguistic metaphors, metonymies and metaphorical idiomatic expressions as instances of figurative language and realizations of particular X-phemistic conceptualizations that serve the purpose of talking about sex in particular terms and reflect the ways we think and conceive sexuality.

Organization of the text

I have divided the book's contents into two main parts, the first one devoted to theoretical issues and the second one to the analyses of X-phemistic metaphors in discourse. These parts are in turn subdivided into five chapters. Chapter 1 ('Cognitive and Pragmatic Issues') clears the field for the analysis undertaken in the subsequent chapters and raises several key notions addressed in the book. In order to frame the analysis, this first chapter provides an overview of the essentials of the Lakoffian tradition of metaphor research and of the improvements of this cognitive-linguistic framework which are especially pertinent for the study. Furthermore, it addresses the cultural issues that participate in the metaphorical structuring of abstract concepts and briefly presents the relevance-theoretic view of metaphor interpretation. Chapter 2 ('The Cognitive Dimension of Euphemism and Dysphemism') advocates the usefulness of a cognitive approach to the analysis of linguistic interdiction and discusses some relevant issues that arise from studying euphemism and dysphemism along a cognitive standpoint, including the effect of lexicalization in conceptual metaphors, the partial utilization of source domains in metaphorical X-phemism and the notions of neutralization, contrast and displacement in X-phemistic naming, among others. The next two chapters, which constitute the core of the book, analyse the way euphemistic and dysphemistic metaphors are used to deal with sexual issues in a sample of real language use. Chapter 3 ('Euphemistic Metaphors') is focused on the analysis of the patterns of conceptual spheres that sexual euphemism can be fitted into and their communicative effects as encountered in internet forums. Following a similar structure, Chapter 4 ('Dysphemistic Metaphors') is devoted to the use and interpretation of dysphemistic metaphorical language in the taboo of sex. A summary of the conclusions and some final remarks that derive from the analyses carried out will bring this book to an end in Chapter 5 ('Conclusions and Final Remarks'). I finish this chapter by enumerating some guidelines for future research on conceptual euphemism and dysphemism in the field of sex.

For ease of reference, the book closes with two appendices listing the different X-phemistic linguistic metaphors which have appeared in the course of the analysis, organized according to their source domains. In each of these appendices I offer the source concepts within each domain and their linguistic realizations as detected in the corpus, together with the sexual topic(s) they target. Following the structure presented in the book, Appendix I lists the euphemistic metaphors and Appendix II is devoted to the dysphemistic ones.

Part One

Metaphor, Euphemism and Dysphemism

1

Cognitive and Pragmatic Issues

1.1 Contemporary metaphor theory

The theoretical assumptions on which the present study relies are derived from the well-known research framework of conceptual metaphor theory, as pioneered by Lakoff and Johnson in their seminal work *Metaphors We Live By* (1980), an innovative study which paved the way for the so-called contemporary theory of metaphor (1993). After so many years since these theories – which I will refer to as 'contemporary metaphor theory' (CMT) – came out, they still play a crucial role in the study of figurative language in a wide range of fields like (critical) discourse analysis, language learning and acquisition, translation studies, literary criticism or psychotherapy, just to mention a few (Taylor and Littlemore, 2014: 19–20). Despite the enthusiasm CMT has aroused in linguistic theory, the standard cognitive approach to metaphor has been subject to criticism, redefinition and improvement over the years. Different works, which I will refer to in 1.1.4, have extended beyond CMT, challenged some of its main assumptions and complemented this research framework in ways which are of most interest for the understanding of metaphors and their communicative impact in real-world discourse.

I will follow here the main tenets postulated by traditional CMT and make use of those redefinitions and improvements of the standard cognitive approach to metaphor that may aid in understanding sex-based euphemism and dysphemism, the main concern of this study.

1.1.1 Basic principles and key notions

Broadly speaking, CMT claims that metaphor is a device with the capacity to structure our conceptual system, providing, at the same time, a particular understanding of the world and a way to make sense of our experience. Metaphor permeates our daily experiences, not only through systems of language, but also in terms of the way we think and act. Lakoff and Johnson argue that we talk about things the way we conceive of them, and this is grounded in our experience and culture. From this standpoint, metaphor is defined as 'a cross-domain mapping in the conceptual system' (Lakoff, 1993: 203), that is, a mapping or set of conceptual correspondences from a source domain (the realm of the physical or more concrete reality) to a target domain (the more abstract entity). Simply put, according to Lakoff and Johnson (1980: 5), metaphor involves 'understanding one thing in terms of another', that is, the process whereby an abstract concept is understood in terms of another concept more accessible to sense perception. In this regard, within the cognitive-linguistic tradition, metaphor is considered as a device with the capacity to structure our conceptual system, providing, at the same time, a particular understanding of the world and a way to make sense of our experience. Hence, rather than a linguistic expression or a figure of speech with an aesthetic value, metaphor is a mode of thought and reason. As Lakoff (1993: 28) puts it:

> [T]he metaphor is not just a matter of language, but of thought and reason. The language is secondary. The mapping is primary, in that it sanctions the use of source domain language and inference patterns for target domain concepts.

To consider metaphor as a mode of thought rather than as a matter of language has important implications. Lakoff and Johnson introduced the notion of conceptual metaphor to distinguish it from the prior tradition of literary metaphor and, by so doing, emphasized the key notion that conceptual metaphors are, first and foremost, a matter of cognition. From the cognitive standpoint, the conceptual nature of a metaphor is more important than its linguistic materialization: '[M]etaphorical thought, in the form of cross-domain mappings is primary; metaphorical language is secondary' (Lakoff and Johnson, 1999: 23). The view of metaphor as a cross-domain mapping in conceptual structure provides for two levels of metaphor, i.e. conceptual metaphor and linguistic metaphor, which correspond to the concepts of 'metaphor' and 'metaphorical expression' respectively (Lakoff, 1993). The former, as already said, constitutes semantic mappings that take the form of TARGET DOMAIN/SOURCE DOMAIN, whereas linguistic metaphors are the surface realizations of the cross-domain mappings that constitute conceptual metaphors. For example, the conceptual metaphor SEX (i.e. target domain) IS WORK (i.e. source domain) motivates linguistic metaphors like *on the job*, *hand job* or *business*. These expressions are linguistic occurrences of the same metaphor (i.e. of the same mapping of conceptual domains) which operates at the conceptual level.

In this two-model of metaphor there is a projection of semantic components from a source domain onto a target domain, and the associations that constitute this metaphor map our perception about the most concrete domain onto our perception about the most abstract domain or the domain we want to categorize and verbalize. The source domain is therefore used to understand, structure and – depending on the speaker's intention – mitigate or reinforce the associations of a negative kind of the target domain, which is of crucial importance for a study of the X-phemistic nature of conceptual metaphors. This implies one of the basic tenets of CMT, the *principle of unidirectionality*, according to which the associative process goes from the more abstract concept to the more concrete reality. That this is so can be gathered from Barcelona (2003: 214): '[M]apping in metaphor is always *unidirectional*: only the source is projected onto the target domain, and the target domain is not at the same time mapped onto the source domain.' Metaphorical mappings are thus characterized by submappings or sets of ontological correspondences between the source and target domains as a result of reasoning about the latter using the knowledge we have about the former. For instance, in the metaphor SEX IS A JOURNEY there is a conceptual mapping from the more 'tangible' source domain of JOURNEYS to the more abstract target domain of SEX. The mapping tells us how sex is being conceptualized as a journey through a set of correspondences that characterize it, namely the lovers correspond to travellers, the sexual relationship corresponds to the journey and the sexual climax corresponds to the final destination of the journey.[1]

Despite the emphasis that mainstream CMT puts on the role of metaphor to conceptualize the abstract in terms of the concrete, metaphorical mappings do not always involve abstract targets, as the source domain is not always more accessible to sense perception or closer to our everyday experience than the target domain. In this respect, Szwedek (2011) provides evidence for the fact that the associative process between source and target domains does not invariably go from the more abstract concept to the more concrete reality, as sometimes abstract and non-physical concepts are used to reason about other abstract concepts or less abstract ones. In this sense, the metaphorical process may reflect the development of concrete-to-abstract thought, giving way to both concrete-to-abstract and abstract-to-concrete metaphors to refer to abstract entities. However, as Forceville (2006: 387-8) notes, a metaphor can also conceptualize the concrete in terms of the concrete 'once we leave the realm of the purely verbal'. For example, in advertising, he argues, metaphorical targets usually coincide with promoted products which are, rather obviously, concrete. Another case in point can be found in architectural metaphors, where visual metaphors map physical sources onto physical targets, as happens in *blind building*, a phrase used to refer to a spatial structure without windows (Caballero and Ibarretxe-Antuñano, 2009).

A key notion within CMT is that of *embodiment*. A basic claim of the cognitive approach to metaphor research is that metaphor is motivated by our interaction with the world. In the transfer of semantic components from source to target domains, the human body plays a crucial role: our bodily experiences determine the structure and grounding of our conceptual systems (Johnson, 1987, 1997; Lakoff and Johnson, 1999). Embodiment operates at two levels. First, it determines the nature of our reasoning. As Lakoff and Johnson (1999: 4) argue, 'the same neural and cognitive mechanisms that allow us to perceive and move around also create our conceptual systems and modes of reason'. Second, and as a consequence of this 'embodied reason', many of the metaphors we use to communicate are grounded in our bodily experience. In Johnson's (1997: 154) words:

> The nature of our embodied experience motivates and constraints how things are meaningful to us. But besides being embodied, meaning is also imaginative, in that it involves image schemas, metaphors, cognitive prototypes, metonymies, and other types of imaginative structures out of which our world is worked.

This view of embodiment gives rise to the notion of *image schemas*[2] within the conceptual system (Johnson, 1987; Lakoff, 1987a: 271–8). Granted that the features and functioning of our bodies determine the structure of our conceptual system, Johnson (1987: 29) defines image schemas as 'meaningful structures for us chiefly at the level of our bodily movements through space, our manipulation of objects, and our perceptual interactions'. In other words, image schemas are recurrent structures that emerge from our sensory and perceptual experiences in particular environments, that is, they are motivated by preconceptual structural correlations in experience. In this respect, Lakoff (1987a) claims that image schemas do not only structure our experience of space (image schemas have an inherent spatial structure), but also structure our concepts in abstract domains. The fact that everything we do is located in a point of time and space provides a metaphorical basis for its linguistic expression. Viewed this way, our daily experiences can be understood in terms of spatial dimensions (UP–DOWN, IN–OUT, CENTRE–PERIPHERY, etc.) that allow us to deal with abstract concepts in particular terms.

From this standpoint, Lakoff argues that concepts are structured in terms of *spatial* image schemas by virtue of the 'spatialization of form hypothesis'. In Lakoff's (1987a: 283) words, this hypothesis:

> ... requires a metaphorical mapping from physical space into a 'conceptual space'. Under this mapping, spatial structured is mapped into conceptual structure. More specifically, image schemas (which structure space) are mapped into the corresponding abstract configurations (which structure concepts).

Image schemas like CONTAINER, SOURCE-PATH-GOAL and UP-DOWN are crucial for the grounding of conceptual metaphors insofar as they establish patterns of understanding and reasoning about a given concept, which is of utmost importance for structuring taboo topics conceptually. Therefore, many abstract concepts arise from metaphorical mappings of spatial concepts, i.e. abstract reasoning derives from metaphorical mappings of image-schemas. Yu (1998: 28) puts the point as follows: '[M]etaphors based on image schemas give rise to abstract reasoning and abstract reasoning is based on spatial reasoning via metaphorical projection of image schemas.' The fact that abstract concepts (time, causes, changes, states, etc.) are understood in terms of spatial concepts which are structured by image schemas led Lakoff (1993: 229) to claim that 'abstract reasoning is image-based reasoning under metaphorical projections to abstract domains'. Not only does physical configuration play a role in embodiment, however. As we will see in 1.2, embodiment is also determined by cultural and social aspects which motivate human cognition and metaphorical conceptualizations.

The main idea behind CMT is that source domains are used to reason and talk about target domains. However, not all the components of the source domain are actually mapped onto the target. That metaphor offers a partial way of looking at reality derives from one of the features of general cognition that pervades language: we tend to perceive some aspects of reality as more relevant (i.e. salient) than others. In this way, when speakers intend to direct hearers' attention to a particular aspect of the denotatum, they appeal to a *salient* reference point that provides the perspective through which the reality being referred to is perceived (see Taylor and Littlemore, 2014: 7-8). This feature of cognition helps to explain the fact that the metaphorical utilization of the source domain is always *partial* (Lakoff and Johnson, 1980: 10-14; Kövecses, 2006a: 214): in the transfer of semantic components from the source to the target domain some aspects of the source are highlighted while others are ignored or disregarded (see 2.1). This partial nature of metaphorical mappings led Kövecses to propose the notions of metaphorical 'highlighting' and 'hiding' to account for the fact that not all aspects of the source domain are mapped onto the target domain. This metaphorical 'utilization', as Kövecses (2006a: 214) argues, involves that only certain components of the source domain are employed in the metaphorical projection from source to target, while the rest remain hidden.[3]

Related to the partial use of source domains is the notion of *metaphorical entailment*, i.e. the knowledge about the source domain that is transferred to the target domain. According to Kövecses (2002: 104), source domains have a 'metaphorical entailment potential', i.e. source domains can potentially lead to a number of metaphorical entailments to be applied to target concepts which derive from our everyday, folk understanding of the domain. However, this entailment potential is not always fully utilized in the metaphor: only some of the entailments that a source domain could give rise to are actually mapped onto the target domain. The reason why not all the possible entailments of a source domain are mapped onto the target can be explained on the basis of the invariance principle, according to which only those elements of the source domain that are coherent with the schematic structure of the target domain can be utilized in the metaphorical projection: 'Metaphorical mappings preserve the cognitive typology (that is, the image-schema structure) of the source domain, in a way consistent with the inherent structure of the target domain' (Lakoff, 1993: 215). Kövecses (2002: 103-4) gives a good example of incoherence between source and target domains in the metaphor LIFE IS A JOURNEY:

> In the source domain of a journey, the 'road' is preserved as I walk along it. This is why I can change my mind and backtrack and go the other way. But in the target of life, often the road is destroyed after I have made a choice and I cannot undo what I previously chose to do. As a consequence this feature of the source is prevented from being mapped onto the target.

The source domain of JOURNEYS is not fully exploited to comprehend the target domain of LIFE as the fixity of the road in the source cannot be transferred to the target. This phenomenon is called 'target domain overrides' as the schematic structure of the target rejects – or overrides – a metaphorical entailment from the source.

In the section that follows I will present the main metaphor types within CMT, which will allow me to step into aspects of the utmost importance for a cognitive approach to metaphor, such as Grady's theory of primary metaphor, among others.

1.1.2 Conceptual metaphor taxonomies

Metaphor is not a black-and-white phenomenon. Although all metaphors function according to the cognitive view of metaphor outlined in the preceding section, the wide range of metaphorical processes involved in conceptual structuring has led scholars to attempt to categorize the different types of metaphors existing. This is not an easy task whatsoever, since, as Lakoff and Turner (1989: 55) point out, the different metaphor types present fuzzy boundaries and the difference is, in many cases, a matter of degree. It is not my intention here to classify the different types of knowledge which are projected across domains (for a comprehensive classification of metaphor types, see Caballero, 2006: 75–8), but to briefly present the main metaphor types that may aid in categorizing the figurative language used to verbalize and reason about the sexual taboo.

In terms of the nature of the source domain involved and the cognitive function that metaphors fulfil, Lakoff and Johnson (1980) distinguish three basic types of metaphors, namely ontological, structural and orientational. *Ontological* metaphors provide ways to reason about abstract targets like feelings, emotions or ideas by viewing them as objects, substances or containers, which makes it easier to talk about, quantify and categorize them. As these metaphors, unlike the structural ones, do not have a well-defined target domain, our understanding of them is limited and incomplete (Lakoff and Johnson, 1980: 25). An example of ontological metaphor is LOVE IS A PHYSICAL FORCE, responsible for cases like 'I feel attracted to you' in which human (sexual) attraction and a mechanical, physical force are associated (see 3.1.7).

Structural metaphors enable speakers to understand an abstract concept through a set of conceptual correspondences between elements of both source and target domains. These metaphors project a whole structural system to talk about a topic. The target domain is therefore understood through the complex and detailed knowledge we have of the source domain (see Kövecses, 2002: 33). This is the case in SEX IS A JOURNEY, a metaphor which presents a well-defined source domain that allows us to speak of sex as a journey in different ways thanks to our everyday knowledge of this domain. In this metaphor there is a set of correspondences between different aspects of both domains involved – for example, the lovers are travellers, the sexual encounter is a journey, the orgasm is the destination, etc. From this perspective, structural metaphors exploit a richer and far more complex conceptual structure than orientational or ontological ones, and the amount of information mapped is richer than that involved in these metaphor types. This metaphorical structuring, however, can only be partial. Indeed, when considering a concept such as sex in terms of a journey, some aspects of that concept are hidden, whereas others are highlighted in the source–target pairing. For this reason, structural metaphors are particularly suited for euphemistic and dysphemistic reference respectively. (I will deal with the hiding–highlighting property of metaphors and its relationship with X-phemism in 2.1.)

As metaphors are grounded in our bodily and social experiences, there exist kinesthetic image-schemas into which our experience is organized, that is, recurring structures coming from our perceptions and bodily functioning. This leads to the emergence of a third type of metaphors grounded in our physical experience called *orientational* metaphors. In these metaphors, based on our experiences of the physical space we have and on how we physically interact in a specific environment, a concept is given a spatial orientation. For instance, in 'Anna fell asleep' the spatial orientation UP–DOWN provides the experiential basis for the orientational metaphor DEATH IS DOWN, based on the VERTICAL PATH image schema which is grounded in our physical experience: dead people are lying down. Orientational metaphors are thus related to spatial orientations and considered a subcase of metaphors based on image schemas (Ruiz de Mendoza Ibáñez and Pérez Hernández, 2003: 30).

The problem with this early classification derives from the fact that it largely ignores the function of these metaphor types in communication (indeed, this is one of the main weaknesses of standard CMT). From this viewpoint, as Caballero (2006: 76) argues, the main role of an ontological metaphor like PEOPLE ARE ANIMALS is not 'to provide an ontological status to target entities, but, rather, to highlight some of their properties. Thus, even if these properties may be regarded as being endowed with ontological status, the whole process is essentially attributive'. Therefore, by saying 'Jimmy is a lion in love' we ascribe the most salient features of the source domain involved, i.e. the fierce and aggressiveness of the lion, to Jimmy, who is therefore considered as being fierce and aggressive when involved in a sexual encounter. This attribution is only meaningful in actual communicative use, in which the realization of the metaphor performs a communicative need: to praise Jimmy's sexual qualities.

There are other metaphor types that emerge from Lakoff and Johnson's model. One of the most influential typologies is the one proposed by Grady (1997), who, in a groundbreaking essay on metaphor, put forward his primary metaphor theory. Although the traditional cognitive view of metaphor states that conceptualizations are grounded in our embodied experience, Grady claimed that many metaphors do not have an experiential basis. *Complex* (or compound) metaphors are not directly motivated by correlations in experience. Instead, they are the combination of *primary* (or primitive) metaphors, i.e. those deriving from the correlations that arise from our basic and physical experiences in our world. For example 'Anna is very close to me' is a linguistic realization of a primary metaphor (INTIMACY IS CLOSENESS) that expresses recurrent correlation in our embodied experiences: intimacy co-occurs with physical closeness. Similarly, AFFECTION IS WARMTH stems from a physical and universally applicable experience to motivate utterances like 'Anna is a cold person' meaning 'Anna is very distant'. On the other hand, a complex metaphor like A PURPOSEFUL LIFE IS A JOURNEY is not the product of a straightforward connection between both experiential domains, that is, it cannot be proven experimentally; rather, it is the product of combining primary metaphors together like PURPOSES ARE DESTINATIONS and ACTIONS ARE MOTIONS, together with a cultural belief according to which people are supposed to have destinations in life and move in such a way as to reach those destinations. There is no grounding for complex metaphors, as they are constructed by primary metaphors which *are* grounded. In Grady's view, complex metaphors are made up of primary metaphors that develop through *conflation*, as the concepts represented by the source and target domains tend to co-occur in experience, while they are differentiated at a later stage (see Ruiz de Mendoza Ibáñez, 2011). Complex metaphors reveal that social and cultural issues are important in redefining the connection between the source and target domains of primary metaphors in cultural terms.

In terms of the nature of the correspondences established, Grady (1999) made an additional distinction between *correlation* and *resemblance* metaphors. The former are based upon correlation between experiential domains, that is, they are experientially motivated, like MORE IS UP, a metaphor which is taken as a paradigmatic example of how the process of mapping operates in primary metaphors: two phenomena in different experiential domains – quantity increase and vertical elevation – conflate. On the other hand, the mapping of resemblance metaphors does not involve such correlation. They are based upon the non-literal perception of some shared features between the source and target domains. For example, in 'Anna is a tigress' the assumption that both tigresses and Anna are dangerous and voracious motivates the metaphorical expression.

Lakoff and Turner provided an additional classification of metaphors. These scholars considered the degree of generality of the information which is mapped from one domain onto the other to distinguish between *generic-level* and *specific-level* metaphors. Generic-level metaphors are not specific insofar as 'they lack specificity in two respects: they do not have fixed source and target domains, and they do not have fixed lists of entities specified in the mapping' (Lakoff and Turner, 1989: 81), as happens in the metaphor EVENTS ARE ACTIONS. However, the specific-level metaphor DEATH IS DEPARTURE is a particular instantiation of the generic-level metaphor EVENTS ARE ACTIONS (Yu, 1998: 31–2). In a specific-level metaphor the source and target domains are clearly specified, whereas in a generic-level one like EVENTS ARE ACTIONS events are represented as undetermined actions performed by unspecified agents. In terms of the degree of generality of metaphors and the functions they serve, Caballero (2006: 77) attempts to categorize these two basic metaphor types as follows:

> We may build a sort of functional hierarchy concerning metaphor: you need generic-level metaphor in order to understand specific-level metaphors ... whereas specific-level metaphors are used to understand abstract domains.

Finally, Ruiz de Mendoza Ibáñez (2000) took account of the nature of the mapping system to establish an additional and complementary division between *one-correspondence* and *many-correspondence* metaphors. In the former, closely connected with ontological and orientational metaphors, just one 'central correspondence' and just one 'central implication' between the target and the source domain are put into operation, the rest of the conceptual structure of the source-target domain being irrelevant, as in PEOPLE ARE ANIMALS. However, in the case of many-correspondence metaphors a whole system of correspondences is

Table 1.1 Basic Metaphor Types in CMT

Author	Metaphor types	Example
Lakoff and Johnson (1980) and Lakoff (1987a)	Ontological	LOVE IS A PHYSICAL FORCE
	Structural	SEX IS A JOURNEY
	Orientational	DEATH IS DOWN
Grady (1997)	Primary	INTIMACY IS CLOSENESS
	Complex	A PURPOSEFUL LIFE IS A JOURNEY
Grady (1999)	Correlation	MORE IS UP
	Resemblance	PEOPLE ARE ANIMALS
Lakoff and Turner (1989)	Generic-level	EVENTS ARE ACTIONS
	Specific-level	DEATH IS DEPARTURE
Ruiz de Mendoza Ibáñez (2000)	One-correspondence	PEOPLE ARE ANIMALS
	Many-correspondence	SEX IS A JOURNEY
Radden (2000)	Metonymy-based	INACTIVE IS DEATH

exploited, with several central mappings (consider the conceptual correspondences established in the structural metaphor SEX IS A JOURNEY).

The metaphor types commented are summarized in Table 1.1 (adapted from Caballero, 2006: 75). This classification is by no means comprehensive. It is merely intended as a basic typology to approach X-phemistic conceptual metaphors in CMT. It must be noted that some of the metaphors proposed may appear in more than one category, depending on the point of view adopted in each case.

I cannot go any further without dealing with the role of metonymy as a resource of figurative language that combines and interacts with metaphor in the conceptualization of sexual topics.

1.1.3 Conceptual metonymy

Metonymy is a pervasive cognitive strategy to conceptualize experience. In the tradition of cognitive linguistics, metonymy is considered as a mental mechanism that underlies many aspects of human conceptualization – rather than as a mere figure of speech – and, in this sense, comparable to metaphor. In fact, in the initial version of CMT, Lakoff and Johnson (1980: 35) defined metonymy as a mechanism capable of reasoning about reality in particular terms: 'Metonymic concepts allow us to conceptualize one thing by means of its relation to something else.' In this way, metonymy, the same as metaphor, is not merely a device with a referential function; it is considered as a way to provide understanding.

Despite the close links between metaphor and metonymy, the cognitive strategies of knowledge organization that these devices entail are not identical whatsoever. The main difference between both processes lies in the fact that conceptual metonymies do not involve two domains, one of which more abstract than the other, in a relation of resemblance, as is the case with metaphors. Rather, metonymies operate within a single domain. Ruiz de Mendoza Ibáñez (2000: 115) maintains that metonymies are cases of 'one-correspondence mappings within a domain' in a relation of contiguity whereby a part of a concept stands for the whole, the cause for the effect, the result for the action and so on. Following Kövecses (2000: 5), 'metonymy, unlike metaphor, is a "stand-for" relation (i.e. a part stands for the whole or a part stands for another part) within a single domain'. Croft (2003: 192–3) contrasts metaphor with metonymy by claiming that metonymy is an instance of *domain highlighting*, i.e. mental activation of a secondary (sub)domain by a source domain within the same domain matrix, whereas *domain mapping*, i.e. projection of the structure of one domain onto another, corresponds to metaphors. According to Ruiz de Mendoza Ibáñez (2011: 116), the only significant distinction between metaphor and metonymy is the domain-external nature of metaphor versus the domain-internal nature of metonymy. This author argues for the existence of a special domain-inclusion relationship between the subdomains source and target in metonymic projections as the basis for the distinction between two metonymy types that I adopt in the present study: *target-in-source* metonymies (i.e. those in which the target domain is included in the source), in which we have a cognitive operation of domain reduction; and *source-in-target* metonymies (i.e. the source domain is a subdomain of the target), which involve a domain expansion operation.

Given the close links between both devices of figurative language, it comes as no surprise that both metaphor and metonymy coexist and interact in the conceptualization of abstract concepts.[4] In fact, Goossens (2003), significantly enough, coins the cover term *metaphtonymy* (including the types 'metaphor from metonymy' and 'metonymy within metaphor/metaphor within metonymy' to account for the interaction between metaphor and metonymy.[5] As both semantic resources are so closely connected, a large number of conceptual metaphors have a metonymic basis. In this respect, Radden (2000: 93) argues for the existence of what he calls 'metonymy-based' metaphors that he defines as 'mapping[s] involving two conceptual domains which are grounded in, or can be traced back to, one conceptual domain' like INACTIVE IS DEATH, which derives from the experiential correlation between death and inactivity. This correlation leads to considering a metonymic relationship involved in the metaphorical mapping, given that inactivity is one of the most characteristic effects of death. In the same vein, Barcelona (2011: 38) maintains that there are two types of interaction between metaphor and metonymy: the metonymic motivation of metaphor and the metaphorical motivation of metonymy. Let us see a linguistic metaphor with a metonymic basis that this author provides as an example. In 'Mike is in low spirits', *low* is included in the conceptualization SADNESS IS DOWN. The mapping here is metonymic and not metaphorical, as part of the domain of SADNESS (one of the effects of sadness consists in a dropping bodily posture) would be mapped onto the overall domain of SADNESS, leading thus to a PART FOR WHOLE metonymy.

In summary, the distinction between metaphor and metonymy boils down to a question of degree and type of resemblance or contiguity that takes place in each expression of figurative language, as Barnden (2010: 25–7) argues.

Consequently, rather than focusing on the analysis of metaphor and metonymy as separate mechanisms, I will consider them as devices of figurative language that serve the purpose of conceptualizing sex in particular terms and explore how metonymy interacts with metaphor in the sexual vocabulary encountered in the forums.

1.1.4 Developments and redefinitions

The framework of CMT has been subject to redefinition and improvement over the years. Different studies have complemented the framework in significant ways by proposing a more dynamical and multidisciplinary approach than that originally envisaged by Lakoff and Johnson in the early eighties. In what follows, I will discuss those improvements and redefinitions of CMT that are especially pertinent to study X-phemistic conceptualizations in discourse, in particular those which have considered the communicative impact of metaphors and their function in culture and society. Indeed, in order to better assess the role that conceptual metaphors play in language and thus study such culturally sensitive phenomena as euphemism and dysphemism, a more comprehensive and usage-based approach to metaphor than that outlined in traditional CMT seems necessary.

One of the most influential redefinitions of CMT is that proposed by Steen (2011). This scholar moves away from a strictly cognitive-scientific approach to language in order to account for the communicative impact of metaphors in action. Steen proposes a comprehensive approach to metaphor by considering not only the linguistic and cognitive perspectives, but also the sociocultural dimension of figurative language. He argues that metaphor is not primarily a matter of thought rather than a matter of language, as the traditional cognitive view of metaphor maintained. In order to explain how metaphors work in real communicative use, Steen (2011: 59) proposes a three-dimensional model in which cultural and social aspects play a central role. He claims that metaphor performs three functions in discourse, namely *linguistic* (i.e. naming), *conceptual* (i.e. framing) and *communicative* (i.e. changing), which basically correspond to the three dimensions of metaphor in language: language, thought and communication: '[M]etaphor may be theoretically defined as a matter of conceptual structure, but in empirical practice it works its wonders in language, communication, or thought.' Steen calls this three-dimensional model of metaphor 'discourse-analytical', a label which places metaphor within the current trends of metaphor research in which the study of figurative language goes beyond a purely lexically rooted perspective to approach social, political and cultural issues in different discourse types (see Musolff, 2004, 2010; Charteris-Black, 2004, 2005; Caballero, 2006; Semino, 2008).

Steen's approach to discourse metaphor allows for a deeper insight into the deliberate use of metaphors in communication. As many metaphors do not work unconsciously and serve specific communicative goals in discourse, this scholar looks at the question of the deliberate use of metaphors from a rhetorical perspective. In Steen's (2011: 59) own words, 'metaphor may manifest itself when it is used in communication when it is used deliberately, and then it is a matter of conscious thought by challengeable metaphorical models with a predominantly social function'. This means that when people are aware that they are using a linguistic expression which derives from a given conceptual metaphor, their primary intention is to induce a change in the addressee's perspective on the target domain that is being communicated. To this end, the perspective of the source domain 'is deliberately exploited as an alien perspective to generate new information about the target domain for a wide range of genre-specific discourse purposes' (Steen, 2014: 132).

For his part, Gibbs considers that to approach metaphorical mappings in real discourse requires serious modifications to the standard version of CMT. He examines the mental processes that take place in metaphor use to account for the interaction of brain, body and world that simultaneously operate in the metaphorical structuring of abstract concepts. From this standpoint, Gibbs (2011: 551) defines conceptual metaphors 'as basins of attraction ... in the phase space of the talking and thinking of a discourse community, which emerge from many different forces, operating along different time scales'. This dynamical view of metaphor, he claims, is best suited to describe how metaphor use and understanding is determined by different constraints ranging 'from historical and cultural knowledge to the fast firing of neurons'. Gibbs's psychological approach to metaphor aims to provide a comprehensive view of conceptual metaphors in real communicative use in order to better assess the role that they play in language, thought and culture.

As issues of metaphor comprehension and recognition of the speaker's intention cannot be excluded from a cognitive-linguistic approach to metaphor, some scholars have combined cognitive assumptions with relevance-theoretic notions to offer a comprehensive view of metaphor and explain its working mechanisms within the field of inferential pragmatics. In this regard, Tendhal (2009) proposes a 'hybrid theory of metaphor' that incorporates assumptions both from CMT and from relevance theory in order to analyse how people get implications from a metaphorical utterance by inferring what is behind the words. Tendhal accounts for the interaction between metaphor in thought and metaphor in communication that arises in real contexts of language use, in the line of other works which have combined both approaches to study the process of metaphor comprehension within a theoretic-relevance perspective (Ruiz de Mendoza Ibáñez and Pérez Hernández, 2003; Herrero Ruiz, 2009).

1.2 Metaphor–culture interface

Steen's and Gibbs's redefinitions of traditional CMT outlined in the preceding section take account of the central role cultural and social issues play in the structuring of metaphorical conceptualizations. As Kövecses (2006a: 2) claims, metaphors are an inherent part of culture: metaphorical language represents the ways in which a community thinks and acts, which is grounded in specific kinds of culturally organized experiences. In other words, metaphors are both grounded in the nature of our bodies and brains and culturally constructed: the body, as a universal source for metaphorical conceptualizations, coexists with cultural factors to explain how metaphorical mappings emerge and function in discourse. As Yu (2008: 247) explains:

> Conceptual metaphors emerge from the interaction between body and culture. While the body is a potentially universal source for emerging metaphors, culture functions as a filter that selects aspects of sensorimotor experience and connects them with subjective experiences and judgments for metaphorical mappings. That is, metaphors are grounded in bodily experience but shaped by cultural understanding. Put differently, metaphors are embodied in their cultural environment.

The consideration of the cultural forces and social constraints that govern human interaction as essential elements in metaphor use and understanding has led to improvements of the CMT framework which are especially pertinent here. In this regard, the connection between metaphor and culture emerges within CMT as a potent source when it comes to structuring abstract concepts conceptually. In fact, metaphorical language does contribute to comprehend culture: it reflects the social values and beliefs that define cultural groups.

In this respect, the notion of *idealized cognitive models*, initially developed by Lakoff (1987a), reflects the crucial role that cultural models play in metaphorical conceptualization. An idealized cognitive model (ICM) is a cognitive structure which is idealized in order to represent reality from a certain perspective. ICMs are mental structures that shape the way we see the world and offer a particular mental representation of an area of experience that does not usually match reality. Therefore, the meaning of a word depends on the kind of mental representation that we use to reason about it, which is an inherently subjective and culture-dependent process (Kövecses, 2006a: 63–9). ICMs are closely related to social and cultural issues and, therefore, to a view of cognition linked to real communicative use. As Cienki (2007: 170) points out, 'ICMs and domains all derive from an approach to language as a system of communication that reflects the world as it is construed by humans, rather than as it might be represented from some god's-eye point of view'. Consequently, ICMs do not represent an objective state of affairs in the world and are idealized in different ways. A typical example of ICM is the concept BACHELOR. The frame for this concept represents an idealized version of reality ('adult unmarried male') which does not include every real-life situation, affected by sociocultural constraints, in which *bachelor* may occur.

Granted the crucial role that culture plays in the conceptual organization of our knowledge about the world, different works have applied cognitive theories and notions to corpus data in the area of (inter)cultural communication. Kövecses (2005, 2010), Yu (2008) and Shariffian (2009, 2011), among others, have gone beyond a purely cognitive-linguistic approach to metaphor by exploring the relationship between body, language, culture and cognition that takes place when using metaphor in real-world discourse. Kövecses's work on the influence of the cultural component in the production and understanding of metaphors is especially useful for my purpose here. This scholar claims that the influence of universal embodiment coexists with the pressure of the cultural environment in the process of conceptualization. In this vein, he includes the notion of *local context* as an inevitable component in metaphorical structuring:

> Our effort to be coherent with the local context may be an important tool in understanding the use of metaphors in natural discourse. This aspect of metaphor use has so far remained outside the interest and, indeed, the competence of 'traditional' conceptual metaphor theory. (2010: 206)[6]

The consideration of the local context as a basic element in the production and understanding of metaphorical conceptualizations leads to two kinds of metaphor variation: cross-cultural variation and within-culture variation (Kövecses, 2010: 208–10).

Allied to this view of context as a basic component in the emergence of metaphors in discourse, Kövecses proposes several key notions to approach metaphors from a sociocultural angle within the cognitive-linguistic tradition, namely *main meaning focus, central mapping* and *differential experiential focus*. These concepts focus on the mapping potential of a given source domain and are especially useful to approach the implications of X-phemistic conceptualization, which is based on highlighting or disregarding (depending on the speaker's intention) particular aspects of the target domain through the source domains used to talk about it (see 2.1). Kövecses (2005: 12) considers that a metaphorical conceptualization is based on what he calls *main meaning focus* or major theme of the source domain, which he defines as 'the basic and central knowledge about the source domain, inherited by the target, that is widely shared in a community'. For example, the main meaning focus of FIRE as a source domain is INTENSITY and that of the domain of JOURNEY is PROGRESS. The major theme of a given source domain consists of predetermined conceptual materials which are applied regardless of the target domain; that is, the major theme of the source domain of JOURNEY is the idea of progress, which may be applied to conceptualize different target domains like sex, life or death. This meaning focus characterizes source domains: it represents the social values and cultural knowledge shared by members of a society that are preserved for the metaphorical structuring of the target. The notion of main meaning focus is at the core of Kövecses's version of CMT:

> The main driving force in the construction of the sentence meaning is provided by the notion of the main meaning focus. This is what characterizes source domains and what is carried over from the source to the target domains in the standard CMT view. (2011: 21)

Closely connected with this notion of main meaning focus is that of *central mapping*, i.e. a submapping in a metaphor that projects the main meaning focus of the source. Following Kövecses (2000: 84–9), a central mapping reflects major human concerns relative to the topic being dealt with, it is motivated experientially – culturally or physically – and gives rise to metaphorical linguistic expressions that characterize a given metaphor. For example, in FIRE metaphors, in which the main meaning focus is INTENSITY, the central mapping is INTENSITY IS HEAT. The other key notion put forward by Kövecses, *differential experiential focus*, accounts for the fact that the embodiment associated with a target domain consists of several components that are given a different priority in different cultures. What this process involves, in Kövecses's words, is that:

> … different peoples may be attuned to different aspects of their bodily functioning in relation to a target domain, or that they can ignore or downplay

certain aspects of their bodily functioning as regards the metaphorical conceptualization of a particular target domain. (2005: 246)

Given that this process focuses on the priority given to some elements of the source domain over others, it has important implications for the way we think about the entities we want to categorize. Indeed, conceptual metaphors are based on particular components of the domain chosen to talk about a given concept which may vary according to different factors in the surrounding context.

These notions proposed by Kövecses are useful to account for the cultural belief that contributes to establish the connection between source and target domains. This cultural belief applies to complex metaphors on account of its characteristic 'culture-sensitivity'. In fact, complex metaphors are especially relevant for cultural issues and perform a crucial cultural role in discourse, unlike primary metaphors, which are based on common, universal bodily experience. Take, for example, the complex metaphor A PURPOSEFUL LIFE IS A JOURNEY, a combination of the primary metaphors PURPOSES ARE DESTINATIONS and ACTIONS ARE MOTIONS. As Yu (2008: 251) maintains, 'its validity in a particular culture depends on this culture's holding the combination of the two propositions PEOPLE SHOULD HAVE PURPOSES IN LIFE and PEOPLE SHOULD ACT SO AS TO ACHIEVE THEIR PURPOSES and the two primary metaphors'. Therefore, complex metaphors can be said to be culturally embedded.

Shariffian's studies on metaphor in culture are also worthy of mention. This author proposes what he calls 'the theoretical model of cultural conceptualizations' in order to describe how language, cognition and culture interact with each other. As Shariffian (2009: 168) puts it:

... the lexicon of a language is perhaps the most direct link with cultural conceptualizations in the sense that lexical items largely acts as labels, and hence 'memory banks' for conceptualizations that are culturally constructed.

Given that a large proportion of conceptualizations emerge as cultural cognitions, Shariffian (2011: 5) proposes the notion of *cultural conceptualization*, i.e. a cultural schema and category that emerges in cultural groups where people have similar cognitive systems of values and beliefs and are interacting in a shared situational context. These cultural conceptualizations enable members of a cultural group to share similar views of a given topic.

It is evident that when giving priority to some components of the source domain over others in the metaphorical structuring of a target concept, contextual and sociocultural considerations play a crucial role. A given conceptualization depends to a great extent on contextual and cultural elements. In fact, our conception of the target domain as expressed in a source-domain pairing is grounded in our knowledge and experience of how the reality expressed by the source domain is culturally and socially understood. In other words, metaphors are culturally loaded expressions whose interpretation depends on shared cultural knowledge. This is the reason why, for example, in the language of epitaphs or obituaries the religious euphemistic sense of the source domain in death-related metaphorical expressions like *go to Heaven* ('die') is understood instantly, given the marked tendency of the Christian faith to consider Heaven as a reward for those who have died. And, obviously enough, this is also the reason why speakers who have conflicting cultural or social values may not grasp the metaphorical meaning intended.[7]

1.3 A relevance-theoretic view of metaphor interpretation

It goes without saying that understanding an utterance implies more than simply recovering its semantic representation. Pragmatics aims at explaining the factors beyond the linguistic knowledge of the lexical unit that determine its use and interpretation, which is especially important when dealing with a sample of real language use in naturally occurring contexts, as is the case here. Within pragmatic theories, relevance theory (RT) provides a useful way to describe the differences between literal and non-literal interpretation, and, in doing so, explains how the receiver captures the meaning intended by the speaker.

As a reaction to Grice's (1975) work on the so-called cooperative principle and its related conversational maxims,[8] Wilson and Sperber developed a pragmatic account which reduces Grice's four conversational maxims to one: that of relevance.[9] These scholars proposed a relevance-theoretic account of communication based on one of Grice's basic assumptions: that a central feature of human communication is the expression and recognition of intentions (2004: 607). The key to inferential communication is the *principle of relevance*, which Wilson and Sperber formulated as follows: 'Every act of inferential communication creates a presumption of optimal relevance' (1990: 45). According to this principle, in communication an utterance is worth the addressee's attention and, at the same time, conveys a presumption of its own relevance. In this regard, the interpretation of metaphors is seen as a wholly inferential process which helps to explain how addressees construct the meaning intended by the speaker, that is, how they manage to bridge the gap between the lexically encoded meaning of the utterance and its intended (i.e. communicative) meaning that makes the metaphor relevant in its context. As Blakemore (2002: 64) notes:

> ... there is inevitably a gap between what the grammar delivers – the linguistically determined semantic representation – and the interpretation intended. And this gap is to be filled by pragmatically constrained inference.

From the relevance-theoretic perspective, communication is an act whereby the speaker makes his intentions accessible to the addressee, who is able to grasp the meaning intended on the basis of the evidence provided by the logical form of the utterance and contextual information. The utterance that the communicator produces is intended to attract an audience's attention and create predictable expectations of relevance which may help the audience to grasp the intended meaning. In this inferential model of communication the speaker shows the hearer his communicative intention and the hearer makes inferences and forms contextual assumptions in order to reach optimal relevance. In this regard, an utterance is *relevant* to an individual if it modifies his existing assumptions about the world – and does so as economically as possible – by yielding contextual effects which are worth the addressee's attention. From this standpoint, an utterance is *optimally relevant* if it meets two conditions: first, it achieves a wide range of contextual effects; second, it does so without any unjustifiable effort on the part of the hearer (Wilson and Sperber, 1990: 45).

In this process of pragmatic inferring, the recognition of the speaker's intentions is a key element insofar as for successful communication to take place, the addressee must be aware that the utterance produced by the speaker is deliberate and intentional, i.e. it pursues a particular communicative goal. After all, understanding cannot be achieved if the audience does not recognize the speaker's informative intention. In this respect, the process of making inferences from linguistic evidence is crucial in the recognition of the speaker's intended meaning. As Blakemore (2002: 60) argues, this inferential process 'integrates the output of the decoding process with contextual information in order to deliver a hypothesis about the speaker's communicative intention'.

In the initial version of RT, meaning detection entails looking for the so-called 'conversational implicatures', i.e. the additional meaning, not literally said but meant, which is necessary in order to make sense of the utterance. Following Sperber and Wilson (1986: 183), any assumption implicitly communicated is an *implicature*. In order to recover the meaning intended (i.e. deliberately implied) by the speaker, hearers must construct different appropriate hypotheses from the explicit content, i.e. proposition that is explicitly communicated (or *explicature*): first, they must identify the intended contextual assumptions, more or less accessible to the hearer (or *implicated premises*) and then, the intended contextual implications (or *implicated conclusions*). These stages, fully described in Wilson and Sperber (2004: 615), are *cognitive operations*[10] which addressees put into practice in order to grasp the intended meaning of utterances.

Different proposals have complemented and improved on the initial relevant-theoretic version by combining different aspects of RT and cognitive linguistics in an attempt to offer a common analytical frame capable of analysing the mechanisms that govern linguistic inference. One of the most influential contributions is that proposed by Ruiz de Mendoza Ibáñez and Pérez Hernández (2003: 32). They argue that figurative language does not really express a literal proposition which is used to derive relevant implicatures through the application of an inferential scheme based on implicit premises and implicated conclusions, as maintained in early relevant pragmatic accounts (see Clark, 2013); rather, metaphorical language leads to the generation of explicatures as a result of the creation of inferences from a basic scheme of meaning usually incomplete that provides an expression of figurative language. In the same vein, Carston (2010) argues that the communicative intention of the speaker is not implicitly, but *explicitly* communicated through the figurative language expression, and, therefore, to identify this explicature provides the utterance with its communicative relevance in the context in which it appears.

These proposals are coherent with the vision of metaphor and metonymy as *ad hoc* mechanisms that I adopt in the present book. From this viewpoint, the interpretation of metaphors is an active process of dynamic inferring motivated by the addressees' expectations of relevance and contextual considerations during which their inferential capabilities enable them to construct *ad hoc* concepts out of lexically encoded ones (Carston, 2002, 2010; Wilson and Carston, 2007). The construction of *ad hoc* concepts makes it possible for the hearer to bridge the gap between the concept encoded by the word and the actual concept communicated by the speaker. Therefore, *ad hoc* concepts are not linguistically given or necessarily stored in the lexicon, but pragmatically constructed in a given context as part of the comprehension process. As Carston (2002: 322–3) puts it:

> ... an *ad hoc* concept is accessed in a particular context by a spontaneous process of pragmatic inference, as distinct from a concept which is accessed by the process of lexical decoding, and so is context-invariant. [italics in original]

It is important to note that *ad hoc* concepts are not external to the proposition expressed by a speaker; rather, the process of *ad hoc* construction affects the explicit context of the utterance and thus contributes to the explicit level of communication. The *ad hoc* concept is not identical to the lexically encoded one: the former may be more specific or more general than the latter. As Carston (2010: 242) argues, the *ad hoc* concept may become 'a subset or a superset of the denotation of the linguistically encoded concept or it may be a combination, both extending the lexical denotation and excluding a part of it'. In this way, the pragmatic processes of *enrichment and loosening* of linguistically conceptual material (see Carston, 1997, 2002, 2010) lead to a modification of the lexically encoded concept represented in the source domain. The new pragmatically derived concept presents a different denotation, in which either conceptual constituents are added and then the concept is strengthened or the linguistically encoded meaning is relaxed (Wilson and Carston, 2007: 233). Romero and Soria (2012: 221) consider that these operations greatly depend on the speaker's communicative intention. This leads me on to the question of the rhetoric function of metaphors in communication that Steen (2011: 59) denominates *changing* in his three-dimensional model of metaphor (see 1.1.4). Indeed, as we will see in the course of the analysis, metaphors are deliberately used in communication with a conscious X-phemistic purpose whereby the communicator aims to change the perspective of the receiver with respect to the target domain being talked about.

The relevance-theoretic account of cognition has practical implications for a cognitively based account of metaphorical language. RT is a valuable framework to explain the inferential process of meaning detection that takes place in the case of figurative language, as metaphors tend to exhibit, by their very nature, a certain degree of indeterminacy which largely depends on the extent to which the metaphorical substitute is lexicalized with respect to its literal counterpart (see 2.3). In metaphorical conceptualization, the associative mapping between source and target domains explains why some metaphors can be understood more readily than some non-metaphorical expressions. In this sense, metaphor is a way to achieve optimal relevance insofar as metaphors tend to achieve contextual effects with no apparent effort on the part of the hearer. This demonstrates that some metaphors provide an easily accessible interpretation which is consistent with RT. Wilson and Sperber (1990: 52) put the point as follows: 'Since there is an accessible less-than-literal interpretation which is consistent with the principle of relevance, there is no need for the hearer to consider the literal interpretation at all.' Indeed, in some metaphorical items deriving from semi-lexicalized metaphors (see 2.3.2), there is no need for the hearer to consider the literal meaning, as it may be more time- and effort-consuming than the euphemistic metaphorical meaning intended (Wilson and Sperber, 1990: 52). In this sense, metaphor is a useful and economical way to achieve a range of effects which are, in the case of X-phemistic metaphors, deliberately communicated by the speaker.

The review of the standard cognitive approach to metaphor and the relevance-theoretic framework carried out in this section does not attempt to be exhaustive. For the sake of application to the subject matter of the present research, I have only focused on those principles, notions and redefinitions of the mainstream cognitive approach to metaphor and the relevance-theoretical implications of utterance interpretation that are especially pertinent for the analyses of the sex-based metaphors that I will present in later chapters.

2

The Cognitive Dimension of Euphemism and Dysphemism

2.1 Euphemism, dysphemism and metaphor

The force of taboo keeps language users from avoiding the forbidden concepts and compels them, depending on their intention, to mitigate the least acceptable traits of the topics being dealt with or, on the contrary, to intensify them. Put it simply, euphemism and its – roughly speaking – opposite, dysphemism, are two sides of the same coin in the ambivalent response to taboo subjects. Whereas through euphemism the taboo is stripped of its most explicit or offensive overtones, thus providing a way to introduce delicate or distasteful topics in polite conversation, dysphemism is the process whereby the most pejorative traits of the taboo are highlighted with an offensive aim to the addressee or to the concept itself.

Allan and Burridge (2006) define these antithetical responses to taboo by reference to concerns about *face* (i.e. one's public self-image). The notion of face was initially defined by Goffman (1955: 213) as 'the positive social value a person effectively claims for himself'. Brown and Levinson (1987: 13, 61) later redefined face as 'the public self-image that every member wants to claim for himself' and decomposed face into two coexisting dimensions or 'face wants': 'the desire to be un-impeded in one's actions (negative face) and the desire (in some respects) to be approved of (positive face)'. From this perspective, X-phemistic use is closely tied to *politeness* (i.e. concern for the feelings of the interlocutor(s) according to the norms of social behaviour) through the notion of face. More precisely, X-phemism affects the *positive* dimension of face, identified with the individual's desire to be positively regarded in social context.

Allan and Burridge place X-phemistic processes on a continuum based upon the degree of face affront caused by the X-phemistic verbal expression: from an overt damage to the hearer's face or that of some third party involved in the communicative act (dysphemism) to maintaining the hearer's face in social interaction (euphemism). In their words, 'dysphemism is a word or phrase with connotations that are offensive either about the denotatum and/or to people addressed or overhearing the utterance', whereas euphemism is an expression which tends to 'avoid possible loss of face by the speaker, or also the hearer or some third party' (2006: 32). In this regard, strictly speaking, dysphemism can be considered as offensive use of language which leads to some kind of face affront, while euphemism can be defined as the use of mild and polite-sounding language to soften the potential face affront both to the speaker (i.e. for self-presentational purposes) and hearer. However, as commented in the Introduction, the boundaries between both processes are rather fuzzy, and there are axiological subcategories under the label of X-phemism that arise in real discourse. In any case, X-phemistic processes are intrinsically linked to the conventions of politeness that govern a communicative act, and reflect the juxtaposition existing between linguistic and social dimensions.

From this viewpoint, euphemism can be explained in terms of mutual preservation of face: its main aim is to preserve the speaker's and addressee's images and, in this way, make conversation progress in a fluent and satisfactory way for the parties involved (Crespo-Fernández, 2005: 79). In Brown and Levinson's (1987: 61) words, 'everyone's face depends on everyone else's being maintained'.[1] Thus, euphemism is directly motivated by issues of tact, social respect and polite behaviour expected in communicative exchanges, in accordance with Leech's politeness principle, which implies considering to what extent the use of verbal expressions in communication is socially appropriate according to conventional norms of polite behaviour.[2] Dysphemism, however, is felt too harsh in polite communication, even hostile, which leads to an overt face-affront of the parties involved in the communicative act. Both euphemistic and dysphemistic references can be thus considered as linguistic politeness markers, faithful indicators of the way politeness concerns are manifested in communication.

As Casas Gómez (2012: 44) argues, when dealing with taboo topics in public, the conflicting emotions of human beings towards the taboo facilitate the existence of axiological categories which are halfway between euphemism and dysphemism: *quasi-euphemism* (including those items which are used positively to display friendship, solidarity, affection or intimacy despite their dysphemistic locution) and *quasi-dysphemism* (including those language expressions which, despite their socially acceptable disguise, are intentionally offensive). As mentioned in the Introduction, Allan and Burridge (2006: 33) also include orthophemism, which involves direct and literal language as an alternative to dispreferred expressions, i.e. linguistic taboos. Although both euphemisms and orthophemisms are typically polite and avoid possible loss of face, an orthophemism involves straight talking, whereas the corresponding euphemism is generally more figurative.[3] Different types of X-phemistic substitutes which perform diverse communicative functions are, in turn, included in the aforementioned axiological categories. Figure 2.1 (adapted from Allan and Burridge 2006: 34) shows how X-phemistic categories and types are related.

Orthophemism, euphemism, quasi-euphemism and quasi-dysphemism provide the language user with different types of politic (i.e. appropriate, non face-threatening) alternatives to dispreferred expressions in particular communicative contexts. The X-phemistic substitutes included in these axiological categories take their names from the functions they perform in discourse: *protective* (avoiding offence); *consolatory* (assisting to cope with the death of a loved one); *provocative* (attracting interest); *underhand* (deceiving and misrepresenting); *uplifting* (upgrading); *cohesive* (displaying in-group solidarity); *complimentary* (praising); *dirty* (sexually stimulating the partner); *ludic* (defusing the seriousness of taboo subjects); and *derogatory* (making a socially acceptable criticism).[4] Straight dysphemism is the only source of face-threatening expressions.

The cognitive view of metaphor outlined in the first chapter opens a new way to the analysis of euphemism and dysphemism, which are structured conceptually in many cases, and thus can be fruitfully studied along cognitive lines.

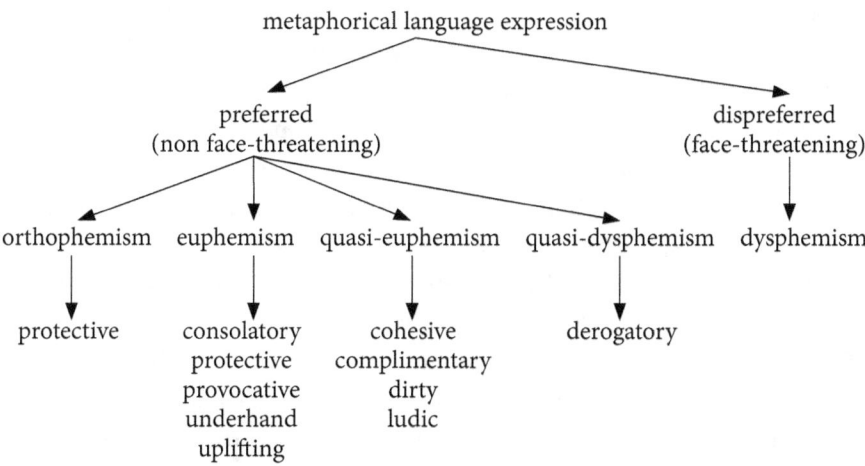

Figure 2.1 X-phemistic Categories and Types of Taboo Naming

Granted that language is metaphorical to the core, it comes as no surprise that out of the wide range of formal and semantic devices that give rise to both euphemistic and dysphemistic units (see Allan and Burridge, 1991; Warren, 1992; Crespo-Fernández, 2007), metaphor stands out as one of the most prolific ones in X-phemism formation; in fact, a great deal of X-phemistic units are the result of semantic change and extension.[5] Euphemistic and dysphemistic processes respond to the same linguistic mechanism which is shared by metaphors: that which permits to name an object with a name that does not literally denote it. Because of this, euphemisms and dysphemisms can be considered, as Chamizo Domínguez (2005: 9) claims, special cases of metaphors:

> If we assume that metaphor consists in giving the thing a name that belongs to something else ... it characteristically involves categorical falsity ... it is defined as carrying a structure from one conceptual domain ('a source') to another ('a target') ... and if we discover that all these characteristics also apply to euphemisms and dysphemisms, then euphemisms and dysphemisms should be regarded as metaphors or at least as a special case of metaphor.

It is in the transfer of semantic components between the source and target domains typical of cognitive association that conceptualization fulfils its X-phemistic function. The axiological value of a given word or expression greatly depends on the components of the source domain that are singled out and mapped onto the target domain for a particular communicative purpose. In fact, as commented in 1.1.1, the metaphorical utilization of the source domain is always *partial*; therefore, the interpretation of a target domain which a metaphor offers is necessarily partial and therefore subjective. This metaphorical utilization of source domains, whereby only certain aspects of the domain are actually mapped onto the target while the rest are disregarded, is important to understand how the X-phemistic value of metaphors projects in discourse. Lakoff and Turner (1989: 67) provide a good case in point. In the conventional metaphor DEATH IS SLEEP only those aspects of the source domain of sleep the speaker wants to highlight (physical rest, relaxation, inactivity, inability to perceive, horizontal position, etc.) are mapped onto death. This seems to prove that the choice for particular components of the source domain is not at random: they are used to highlight and give priority to those particular aspects of the target which are more likely to satisfy the speaker's communicative aim. Because of this, metaphors are readily accessible for X-phemistic reference.

This basic principle of the cognitive-linguistic approach to metaphor is pertinent for the study of the persuasive and evaluative function of X-phemistic processes in discourse. In this respect, metaphors are devices whereby events can be *construed*, i.e. viewed and represented, by the speaker in alternate and particular ways. In fact, language users conceive and portray a given concept in terms of a series of *construal operations* (Langacker, 1987)[6] which involve different kinds of perspective and subjectivity (Verhagen, 2007). Therefore, metaphors can be said to perform a distinctive cognitive role in discourse insofar as they provide a particular perspective of the concept being dealt with. In this sense, Kittay (1989: 13–14) formulated what she called the 'perspectival theory of metaphor' whereby metaphors 'provide a perspective from which to gain an understanding of that which is metaphorically portrayed'. This perspective that metaphors provide is especially suited for the study of euphemism and dysphemism, as X-phemistic naming necessarily involves making choices between different ways to deal with taboo concepts in communication.

Despite the close links between metaphors and the processes involved in managing taboo referents which derive from the partial nature of metaphorical mappings, the fact remains that, surprisingly enough, cognitive issues have been largely excluded from the study of euphemism and dysphemism, processes which have been analysed from different fields such as lexical semantics, sociolinguistics, rhetoric and pragmatics.[7] Few scholars, however, have considered euphemism and dysphemism from the standpoint of cognitive linguistics. One of them is Casas Gómez. He defines X-phemism as:

> ... the cognitive process of conceptualization of a forbidden reality, which, manifested in discourse through the use of linguistic mechanisms ... enables the speaker, in a certain 'context' or in a specific pragmatic situation, to attenuate, or, on the contrary, to reinforce a certain forbidden concept or reality. (2009: 738)

Casas Gómez introduces pragmatic considerations to account for the fact that both euphemism and dysphemism perform a communicative function and are thus intended to produce particular contextual effects.

Granted that metaphors and euphemism are cognitively connected and perform a pragmatic function, Lee (2011: 356) defines metaphorical euphemism as 'a euphemism that adopts metaphorical mapping of both source and target domains to express the notion of a forbidden domain as a result of conscious choices from pragmatic competence'. Lee's approach helps to explain the metaphorical value underlying a given euphemistic unit and can be useful to analyse how the conceptual association between the source and target domains serves a communicative function. Gradecack-Erdelijc and Milic (2011:

148) define both euphemism and dysphemism along a cognitive-pragmatic perspective as cognitive operations that emphasize certain elements in the target domain via the source domain with the 'clear intention of creating the following pragmatic effects: the hiding of less favorable elements in the target concept in euphemisms and the clear exposition of these in dysphemisms'. For his part, Herrero Ruiz (2009: 263) considers euphemism and dysphemism as 'conceptual mechanisms of meaning creation and derivation' that should be described in terms of the contextual effects that they produce. The contrast which derives from the cognitive operations of euphemism and dysphemism is understood in terms of the communicative functions (i.e. attenuation or offence) that these tropes perform in specific contexts of use. Metaphor is, from this perspective, a useful resource to scale down the emotional load of a particular taboo topic or, on the contrary, to strengthen it in real communicative use. In this respect, figurative language contributes to generate the additional meanings and contextual effects which are necessary for attenuation or offence in a particular communicative situation.

2.2 Neutralization, contrast and displacement in X-phemistic naming

The considerations stated so far lead me to claim that X-phemism goes beyond a matter of lexical choice between contextual synonyms or a mere lexical substitution strategy; rather, it is a contextually and culturally bound process which emerges as a linguistic manifestation of our cognitive system and fulfils a specific communicative intention in its context of use. In this process of conceptual makeup, metaphor effectively contributes to manage a taboo concept along the lines of euphemism and dysphemism in an axiological scale

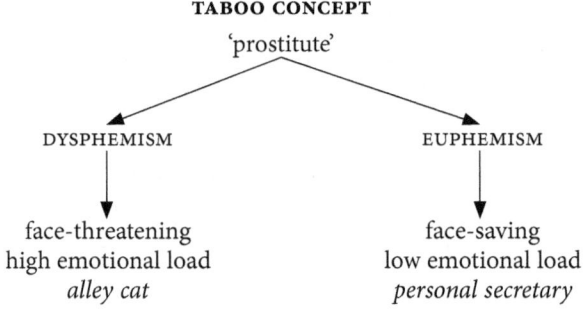

Figure 2.2 X-phemism, Face and Emotional Load

related to affective and emotional load and face concerns. In this sense, I agree with Herrero Ruiz's (2009) view of euphemism and dysphemism as cognitive models operating on a continuum from higher-level magnitudes (dysphemism) to lower-level magnitudes (euphemism) as shown in Figure 2.2 with reference to the designation of the taboo concept 'prostitute'.

By resorting to metaphorical expressions at the two extremes of the axiological scale like *personal secretary* and *alley cat*, the speaker establishes a sharp contrast between lexical alternatives to the taboo which are emotionally loaded. In this way, the speaker attempts to ameliorate the negative associations of the taboo referent (and thus avoids possible loss of face) in the first case, or strengthens its negative load in the second (which may lead to an overt face affront). Therefore, through dysphemism the language user intensifies the least acceptable aspects of a given concept in order to deliberately damage the hearer's face or that of some third party involved in the communicative act. Euphemism, however, acts as a linguistic safeguard whereby the speaker's and addressee's faces can be maintained.

For any X-phemistic item to perform its function in discourse, there is an important requirement that the metaphorical unit must adhere to: there must be a *contrast* between the literal and figurative meanings of the metaphor employed in the process of X-phemistic naming. Camp (2008: 14) describes this contrast in terms of the speaker's intention and the hearer's interpretation as the 'intuitively felt gap between literal and intended meaning, where the first provides the perspective for construing the second'. Obviously enough, the contrast between the literal and figurative meaning is radically different in the processes involved in the metaphorical manipulation of taboo referents. In the case of euphemism the contrast leads to a *neutralization* of the pejorative traits of the taboo referent: the euphemistic expression shares certain conceptual traits with the linguistic taboo, although it moves away from its literal meaning with the purpose of reaching the lexical neutralization of the taboo. Neutralization is a key concept in the analysis of euphemism, since it enables the adoption of new senses in lexical units by means of the temporal suspension of those conceptual traits considered inappropriate in social interaction (Casas Gómez, 2012: 43). However, when it comes to dysphemism, this contrast is motivated by an intensification of the least appropriate traits of the taboo topic being dealt with to such an extent that the dysphemistic metaphor strikes the reader as being less socially appropriate than any neutral or mild lexical alternative that may come to mind.

The notion of contrast is important in Herrero Ruiz's (2009: 263) approach to euphemism and dysphemism. According to this scholar, both processes are reasoning tools that can be described as Idealized Cognitive Models (see 1.2) which are constructed around the creation of contrasts. In his opinion, euphemism and dysphemism (along with other tropes like irony, paradox, oxymoron, overstatement and understatement)[8] involve the creation of two conceptual domains which are related through the cognitive operation of contrast. This operation is considered in terms of the communicative functions that euphemism and dysphemism perform and the contextual effects that the hearer may draw from them. In this vein, Herrero Ruiz (2009: 137) defines euphemism and dysphemism as 'meaning derivation processes whereby the hearer reinterprets the conceptual structure of an utterance or action ... to fit the requirements of that cognitive environment ... in order to produce certain contextual effects'. From this definition we can deduce two properties of these processes: first, there exists an intimate connection between human cognition, metaphorical language and euphemism and dysphemism; second, there is an interplay between cognitive and pragmatic issues that should not be overlooked if we try to offer a full picture of X-phemistic metaphorical language.

Closely related to the notion of contrast is that of *displacement*. McGlone, Beck and Pfiester (2006) claim that metaphor is a key strategy at the speaker's disposal to achieve displacement in euphemistic units. This displacement, which acts as a kind of 'camouflage' (see 2.3.2), permits to reduce the communicative discomfort associated with those topics which evoke negative affect. The displacement effect in euphemistic units is accomplished 'by avoiding direct, literal reference to an event (e.g. *he defecated, she died*) in favour of terms describing its consequences (*he relieved himself, she's no longer with us*), related events (*he moved his bowels, she took her last breath*), metaphors (*he heeded Nature's call, she jumped the last hurdle*), and other semantic associates of lower valence' (2006: 276). The displacement of the taboo meaning 'prostitute' (see Figure 2.2) that is accomplished by the literal meaning of the phrase *personal secretary* permits to avoid using a label which designates the activity of prostitution in an undeviating way. This euphemistic displacement derives from the juxtaposition of two radically different domains: the WORK domain provides a background to refer euphemistically to prostitution thanks to the notion of commercial activity that is implicit in this uplifting euphemism (see 3.1.1). However, displacement is not limited to euphemistic naming. When someone uses an expression belonging to the ANIMAL domain like *alley cat* to refer to a prostitute, the effect is clearly dysphemistic: the metaphor links the woman to filth, poverty and illness transmission (see 4.1.1.1). In this case, the displacement effect is achieved through the conflation of two different domains, but unlike euphemism, the domain used to target the taboo topic is used with an offensive aim in mind.

2.3 Metaphor types and X-phemism

In the process of manipulation of the taboo referent,[9] figurative language is at the user's disposal to model the taboo concept and present it without its most pejorative implications in the case of euphemism or, by contrast, intensifying those unacceptable conceptual traits with an offensive aim to the concept itself or to the audience, as happens with dysphemism. This metaphorical manipulation leads to different types of axiological substitutes for taboo concepts which, in turn, are characteristic of various types of X-phemistic categories differing in their emotional load, capacity for attenuation or offence and in their degree of association with the taboo.

The classification followed here is based on that proposed by Chamizo Domínguez and Sánchez-Benedito (2000). These scholars distinguish three types of euphemisms and dysphemisms according to their degree of *lexicalization*, i.e. the extent to which the tabooed conceptual traits have become associated with the euphemistic or dysphemistic metaphorical alternative: *lexicalized* (i.e. those in which the figurative meaning is regarded as the normal or literal meaning); *semi-lexicalized* (i.e. the metaphorical substitute is associated with the taboo because of its inclusion in a conceptual domain traditionally tied to the forbidden concept); and *creative* (i.e. the result of a novel association with the taboo, only accessible in its phraseological context). As metaphors are closely connected with euphemisms, Chamizo Domínguez (1998: 47–70) had already applied this distinction to metaphorical language and established a threefold classification of metaphors: lexicalized or dead; semi-lexicalized or conventional; and poetic or creative metaphors. In this way, he rejected the traditional dichotomy between *dead* (for all non-innovative kind of metaphor) and *alive* metaphors, in the line of Lakoff and other metaphor scholars who proposed different classifications according to the degree of activated metaphoricity in context.[10]

The different metaphor types motivated by the process of lexicalization of the taboo (lexicalized, semi-lexicalized and creative) give rise to their corresponding X-phemistic metaphorical substitutes (explicit, conventional and novel/artful) as shown in Figure 2.3 (adapted from Crespo-Fernández, 2011: 59).

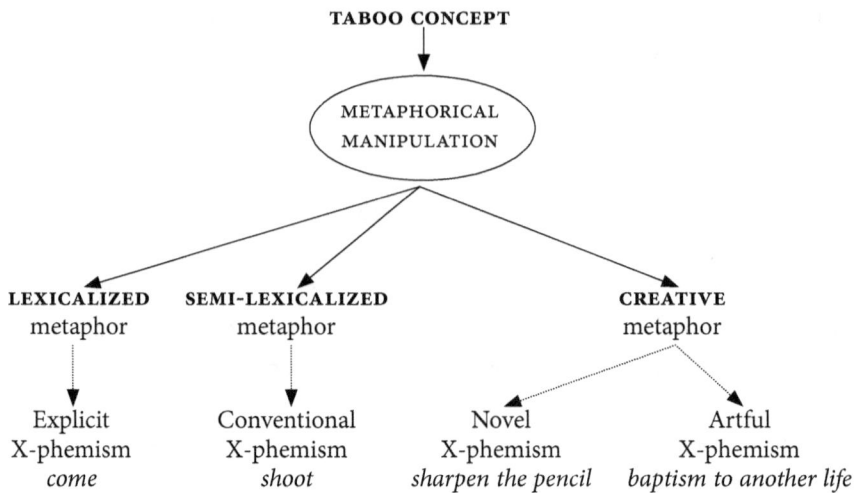

Figure 2.3 Metaphor Types and X-phemism

The effect of metaphorical language on sexual topics such as 'ejaculate' (*come* and *shoot*), 'getting prepared for sexual intercourse' (*sharpen the pencil*) and 'sexual pleasure' (*baptism to another life*) is the source of three types of X-phemistic substitutes, lexicalized in different degrees and included in different conceptual networks. In Figure 2.3 the taboo topics are verbalized through linguistic metaphors which show different degrees of ambiguity in relation with the taboo referents; of affective and emotional load; and of capacity for face-affront. In what follows I will discuss the different metaphor types, namely creative, semi-lexicalized and lexicalized, and their corresponding X-phemistic categories: novel/artful, conventional and explicit respectively.

2.3.1 Creative metaphors and novel and artful X-phemism

Metaphorical units motivated by creative or novel metaphors activate a novel meaning with respect to the sense generally accepted for the expression. This type of metaphors falls under the category of generic-level metaphors (see 1.1.2): they are not governed by pre-existing correspondences between the source and the target domain, and thus they do not have fixed lists of entities specified in the mapping.

Although creative metaphors are of little interest to research in language and cognition in that they do not reflect conceptual thought, they do offer an alternative way of comprehending reality which is worth analysing.[11] Unlike conventional metaphors through which language users make sense of the world, not all creative metaphors reflect conceptual metaphors; what is more, one could object to the label of 'conceptual' for the metaphorical schema that underlines novel metaphors. In this respect, Bartsch (cited in Forceville, 2006: 386) argues that 'a phenomenon deserves the name of "concept" only if it has a stable interpretation in a community and hence must by definition have been linguistically explicated'. The idea behind these words is that creative metaphors cannot have the status of conceptual as they focus on non-characteristic and non-conventional features. Uncommon as the source domain in creative metaphors may seem, these metaphors provide a particular understanding of the target concept, as hearers resort to contextual factors in making sense of them. In this regard, Kövecses (2008) calls metaphorical creativity 'context-induced' creativity insofar as creative metaphors are grounded in context. This scholar claims that the immediate linguistic context and the knowledge about the major entities that participate in the discourse (i.e. the speaker, the hearer and the topic) play a crucial role in the production and interpretation of non-conventional metaphors in discourse.

Creative metaphors are responsible for the lexical generation of novel X-phemistic metaphorical items. Given that these metaphors lack conventional connections between source and taboo target domains, the identification of the true referent behind the words and the speaker's X-phemistic intention is not at all obvious. According to Carston (as cited in Stöver, 2011: 68), creative metaphors involve a metarepresentational level at which the literal meaning is somehow retained but used to describe an alternative and imaginary world in which the speaker's intended meaning may be reached. Indeed, the meaning of artful and novel X-phemisms is only accessible in their phraseological and pragmatic context, which provides the frame for this imaginary world in which the X-phemistic capacity to refer figuratively to the taboo referent is activated. On many occasions they even have meaning only to those familiar in their context (hence Kövecses's label of 'context-induced'). This is why novel and artful metaphorical X-phemism allocates referents not found in a word's dictionary description in the majority of cases.

Novel X-phemisms are referred to as 'event-based' by Keyes (2010: 25–8) insofar as they 'enjoy the life expectancy of a fruit fly. Most die out with the memory of those around at their inception, if not sooner'. Novel X-phemistic metaphorical items arise every day in both private and public domains. Social and professional groups have their own X-phemistic expressions which are rather flippant and humorous in many cases. Take, for example, *sharpen the pencil* 'getting prepared for sexual intercourse', one of the X-phemistic labels posted in a blog in 2007 by the North American novelist David Terrenoire to refer to sexual issues taking vocabulary from the field of writing. This expression derives from an alternative way of comprehending the sexual taboo included in a conceptual metaphor which could be formulated as SEX IS WRITING. Other linguistic realizations of this metaphor posted in this blog are *simultaneous submissions* 'commit adultery' or *pound the old keyboard* 'masturbate'. These cases of ludic euphemistic expressions, as Burridge (2012: 71) notes, show to what extent 'the manipulation of language that speakers display is remarkably inventive at times'.

Creative metaphors also give rise to *artful* euphemistic units (Crespo-Fernández, 2007: 147–50). Artful euphemism is the modality of verbal mitigation in which the euphemistic disguise relies on ambiguous and connotative language. The same as happens with novel X-phemisms, artful X-phemistic units provide a fresh insight into the taboo, and their meaning is only accessible in their pragmatic context. However, in the case of artful X-phemism, the X-phemistic disguise is more elaborate and personal: the semantic disguise relies on a very personal and aesthetic value. A good case in point is the metaphor AN ORGASM IS A BAPTISM, extracted from D. H. Lawrence's novel *The Rainbow*:

> Their coming together now, after two years of married life … was the *baptism to another life*, it was complete confirmation. (p. 95)

Here the consideration of sexual pleasure does not respond to pre-existing metaphorical associations in the reader's cognitive system, but derives from Lawrence's personal view of sexuality and the particular associations that the novelist creates between both concepts, masking the physical aspects of coition and highlighting its spiritual side. This metaphor is innovative in that the word *baptism* is used unconventionally in the context of the quotation; indeed, to the best of my knowledge, the domain of BAPTISM is not mapped onto the target domain of SEX on other occasions. Novel and artful X-phemistic expressions like *sharpen the pencil* and *baptism to another life* reflect the importance of creative thinking in metaphorical naming (Deignan, 2005: 55).

2.3.2 Semi-lexicalized metaphors and conventional X-phemism

In conventional X-phemism the metaphorical reference to the taboo is widely accepted by the majority of language users. Most euphemistic and dysphemistic units deriving from semi-lexicalized metaphors are fixed in the lexicon and marked with their X-phemistic function in dictionaries. Conventional metaphors are potent and influential means of organizing experience and thought. They are alive in people's minds and active in communication.

Muller (2008: 179) argues that conventional metaphors become activated in discourse as long as they are perceived as having a literal meaning which provides a connection to its source domain counterpart. In fact, the X-phemistic unit that derives from a conventional metaphor maintains its literal sense, which coexists with the figurative one for euphemistic or dysphemistic reference; hence the link between the metaphorical item and its original source domain is maintained. In this regard, conventional metaphors provide a screen through which reality is presented from a particular angle with the deliberate purpose of leading to a particular response in the hearer; therefore, they are used with a persuasive aim in mind (see 2.4). As Steen (2011: 51) claims, deliberate metaphor-related words emerge from conventional metaphors rather than from novel ones: 'Deliberate metaphor seems to be a matter of revitalization of available linguistic forms and conceptual structures, not the creation of novel ones.' In this regard, semi-lexicalized metaphors are ordinarily used to structure and talk about reality, and they constitute the source of a considerable diversity of conventional X-phemistic language.

Let us see a case of conventional dysphemistic naming. A phrase like *shoot his load* to refer to the act of ejaculating offers an alternative way of comprehending reality by virtue of the conceptualization SEX IS WAR. Consider the posting that follows:

(1) For me the only reason to do oral on her after sex is to give her more orgasms once I have *shot my load* and can't use my penis any more without a rest which would cause her to "lose the moment". (TAM, 8 August 2012)

The phrase *shot his load* is included in a conceptualization which transfers different attributes from the source domain of WAR to the target domain of SEX. More precisely, it presents different sets of conceptual correspondences as a result of using the knowledge we have about war to talk about the taboo of sex: the lover is the enemy, to seduce the sexual partner is to overcome an enemy, the penis is a weapon, etc. The conceptual basis for WAR metaphors responds to an overall view of sex in terms of hostility, violence and dominance. Accordingly, the metaphorical substitutes that fall under this conceptual network tend to acquire dysphemistic overtones, as happens in posting (2) following. In a conventional dysphemistic expression like *shoot one's load* there are two meanings at play: the literal sense of the word, and the evocation of the taboo referent which is understood in terms of the conceptualization it belongs to.

Of course, not all semi-lexicalized metaphors generate euphemistic units with the same degree of conventionality, ambiguity and euphemistic capacity. Some X-phemistic substitutes that derive from semi-lexicalized metaphors are halfway between the categories of conventional and artful. Take the following example, excerpted from John Cleland's *Fanny Hill*, a novel first published in 1748, which can be considered a breeding ground for sex-related euphemism:

> The *die-away moment* was come upon him, which she gave signs of joining with, by the wild throwing of her hands about, closing her eyes, and giving a deep sob, in which she seemed to *expire in an agony of bliss*. (p. 31)

Here the taboo of reaching orgasm is conceptualized through a metaphor which equates orgasm with death.[12] This connection is not immediate because it is not based on pre-existing metaphorical associations which may form part of the reader's cognitive system (Lakoff, 1993: 210), as is the case of conventional sex-related metaphors like SEX IS WAR. The verb *die* is lexicalized with a sexual meaning in the third edition of the *Oxford English Dictionary* (2013) (*OED*3): 'To experience a sexual orgasm (most common as a poetic metaphor in the late 16th and 17th cent)'. The greater ambiguity of this substitute in the reference to the taboo concept than other conventional X-phemistic units derives from the fact that this metaphorical term was commonly employed as a poetic metaphor in literature to deal with sexual issues, and its sexual meaning has become obsolete in modern usage (Ayto, 2007: 80). In fact, no instance of the DEATH metaphor for orgasm has been detected in the corpus used for the present study.

Although conventional metaphorical substitutes are rather common labels for the taboo topics they are supposed to veil and some of them are deeply entrenched in the language, they do provide an effective euphemistic means to deal with certain taboo topics in communication. A phrase like *adult films* 'pornographic films' is considered as euphemistic on the grounds that it is actually used instead of a more direct or coarse expression. This phrase (although barely exempt from taboo) is deemed acceptable in polite discourse, and does not suppose a threat to the speaker's face. Therefore, the so-called 'associative contamination' hypothesis, according to which euphemisms become tainted by their associations with taboo topics through frequent use and become offensive themselves (Pinker, 2002; Burridge, 2004; Keyes, 2010), does not apply in all cases. As McGlone et al. (2006: 263) claim, conventionality in euphemistic naming may confer camouflage-like properties to euphemism which are based on the capacity of the euphemistic substitute of not calling undue attention to itself: 'Euphemism succeeds as a discourse strategy in the same manner camouflage succeeds in a military mission – by rendering its subject as inconspicuous as possible in the surrounding context.' In this way, this camouflage capacity of lexicalized euphemistic metaphors constitutes a safe way to refer to a distasteful topic within polite discourse.

2.3.3 Lexicalized metaphors and explicit X-phemism

Explicit X-phemistic units refer to the taboo referent they stand for in an undeviating way. These alternatives to the taboo are the product of lexicalized or dead metaphors, those which do not evoke a source domain counterpart. Following the Metaphor Identification Procedure developed by the Pragglejaz Group (2007), this type of lexical units are not taken to be metaphorical, as they are not perceived to have a more basic contemporary meaning in other contexts. Dead metaphors are 'opaque', as Muller (2008) notes, in contrast to transparent, conventional metaphors in which the connection between the linguistic form and the source domain provides a way to conceptualize the taboo topic in particular terms. Simply put, the metaphoricity of dead metaphors does not become activated in communication.

Explicit X-phemistic words, those coming from dead metaphors, reached the last stages in the process of lexicalization of metaphorical units, after which the lexical unit is deprived of its capacity to refer figuratively to the taboo due to its close association – not to say identification – with the sexual concept that it names. This phenomenon of taboo contamination leads to the gradual weakening of their euphemistic value, as commented earlier: the metaphorical units become tainted and thus require replacement in a kind of euphemistic 'treadmill' whereby 'bad connotations drive out good', in Burridge's (2004: 213) words. In fact, the taboo sense usually becomes more prominent and tends to leave out the literal sense of the word. As Allan and Burridge (1991: 23) argue, '[t]here is wealth of evidence that where a language expression is ambiguous between a taboo sense and a non-taboo sense, its meaning will often narrow to the taboo sense alone'. Take, for example, the word *cock* to refer to the sexual male organ. First used with the sense of 'penis' in the early seventeenth century (*OED3*), this word has picked up sexual connotations as a consequence of its frequent use in the reference to the penis over the years and is now considered as 'the current name among the people [for penis], but *pudoris causa*, not admissible in polite speech or literature' (*OED*3). Take the posting that follows:

(2) I would expect my wife to check with me if it was all right to go to some dude's apartment and grab his *cock*. I would say no. (MMSL, 19 October 2012)

The lexicalized metaphorical term *cock* does not offer an alternative way of comprehending reality. As nobody would think of a connection of *cock* with a male domestic fowl in the posting above, this word is unable to frame the taboo topic in a particular conceptual sphere. *Cock* does provide a way to refer to the tabooed body part in a colloquial register like that of (2), but not to reason about it or represent the taboo topic from a certain perspective, as happens in conceptual categorization. In the case of *cock* the sexual connotation has overlapped its literal meaning; therefore, it is inevitably linked to the sexual taboo it refers to. The same is true of many other sex-related words which have lost their once euphemistic or orthophemistic nature, such as *come* ('experience orgasm') or *bitch* 'lewd woman' (literally 'the female of the dog'), among many others.

The lexicalization of once orthophemistic or euphemistic metaphorical words with a taboo sense has considerably affected lexis: indeed, many homonyms of taboo terms have been abandoned as a consequence of their connection with the forbidden concept and the possible ambiguity between the taboo sense and the non-taboo sense. This has happened because ambiguity may arise when using certain words in communication and put the speaker in an embarrassing situation if the taboo sense is not intended. Although in British English *cock* persists with the meaning 'rooster', in American English, because of the taboo homonym meaning 'penis', this sense of *cock* started to disappear in the early nineteenth century and in Australian English is nowadays very rare (Allan and Burridge, 2006: 44–5). The lexicalization of this word has also affected words containing *cock*, like *weathervane* as an alternative to *weathercock* and *haystack* instead of *haycock* (Allan and Burridge, 1991: 105).

The conceptual categorization of taboos is greatly influenced by the degree of lexicalization of the linguistic substitute. As I demonstrated in a previous study (see Crespo-Fernández, 2008), using metaphors with a sex-related lexicalized meaning in discourse has an important consequence for one of the basic tenets of CMT – the principle of unidirectionality, according to which mapping in metaphor is always *unidirectional* in that only the source is projected onto the target domain (see 1.1.1). However, not always are metaphorical projections unidirectional. In words lexicalized with a sexual sense, the taboo sense will activate, either consciously or not, in the interpretation of such terms. Take the following joke in which *cock* is included:

> What's the most masculine animal in all the world?
> A rooster. He's all *cock* except his beak, and that's his pecker.

The taboo sense of *cock* leads to a sexual interpretation of a word belonging to the semantic field of animals; indeed, in this joke the sexual meaning of *cock* dominates the interpretation of the word. The ambiguity here arises from an intentional use[13] of the sex-related sense in *cock* for an intended humorous effect which derives from the polysemy of the term ('male chicken' versus 'penis'). In this regard, the source of humour here involves the combination of apparently disconnected domains or, as Nash (1985: 137) puts it, 'the happy confusion of a double vision'. This double vision is brought about by the very nature of metaphor, which creates a new and sometimes unexpected insight into the topic.

In the joke above the initial projection from the source domain of animals onto the taboo target domain is reversed. The use of *cock* here seems to demonstrate that the mapping of knowledge from the source domain onto the target domain can be somehow considered as *bidirectional*. A word lexicalized with a taboo sense may acquire connotations that, in some contexts, carry over to the non-metaphorical referents, which lends itself to humorous effects. From this it can be deduced that using metaphors with a lexicalized taboo meaning in discourse does not only involve a projection from the source domain onto the target domain, since the target domain may be also projected onto the source domain.[14]

2.4 The persuasive and evaluative function of X-phemistic metaphors

Metaphors are powerful vehicles of evaluation and persuasion.[15] The rhetorical and judgemental role of metaphorical language forms part of real-life communicative practices in a wide variety of contexts and settings, from mass communication to informal and colloquial verbal exchanges. Research on metaphors in discourse has emphasized the role of metaphors as effective devices to achieve an intended effect in different discourse types, such as advertising (Morris and Waldman, 2011), business media discourse (Koller, 2004) and, above all, political propaganda, a discourse type in which metaphors act as powerful rhetorical devices employed by politicians and orators in order to exert ideological control and make an audience believe something in an ostensive way (Musolff, 2004, 2010; Charteris-Black, 2004, 2005; Crespo-Fernández, 2013a). Although the persuasive function of metaphors is especially evident in the case of those texts which are carefully constructed with a persuasive aim in mind, like advertising or political speeches, persuasive and ideological metaphors are also used in other types of discourse practices of a more colloquial and spontaneous nature like online forums.

Steen's (2011) three-dimensional model of metaphor discussed in 1.1.4 is especially useful to deal with the rhetorical nature of X-phemistic metaphors. This scholar focuses on the communicative impact of metaphors and establishes a fundamental distinction between deliberate and non-deliberate use of metaphor in discourse. According to Steen, using metaphors deliberately in discourse involves using language with a persuasive purpose; that is, when people resort to X-phemistic metaphorical units and are aware that they are using a linguistic expression which derives from a given source-to-target mapping, their intention is basically to induce a change in the addressee's perspective on the target domain that is being communicated. From this standpoint, X-phemistic metaphors can be considered as effective vehicles of persuasion, as persuasive devices at the speaker's disposal to shape belief and induce a change on the audience.

Conventional metaphors suit the purpose of persuasion and ideological evaluation particularly well. These metaphors provide the source of much X-phemistic conceptual language used to talk about taboo topics. The metaphorical units arising from conventional metaphors depict reality from a certain angle which is deliberately used in communication with a particular persuasive function. This function is carried out through a change in perspective on the target domain that is provided by the choice of the source domain used to verbalize the abstract concept. That this is so can be gathered from Steen (2011: 51): 'Deliberate metaphor is an overt invitation on the part of the sender for the addressee to step outside the dominant target domain of the discourse and look at it from an alien source domain.' What sets this process in motion is the addressee's awareness of the fact that the source domain employed has a disruptive effect on the referential coherence of the conceptual structure of the target domain (Stöver, 2011: 76). Therefore, the choice of a source domain has a decisive influence on the emotional load attached to the metaphorical item and on the evaluative and persuasive function of the metaphor in question. Granted that a target concept can be expressed via different source domains (Kövecses, 2003: 79), the particular connotations of the domain used to refer to the target concept and its main meaning focus, in Kövecses's terminology, largely influence the X-phemistic force of the metaphorical substitute, and contribute to the ideological and evaluative function of the metaphor in discourse. Take, for example, the metaphor DEATH IS A REST. By euphemistically referring to a coffin as a *resting place*, the speaker is inviting the audience to view the topic being dealt with ('death') from a different perspective ('a peaceful rest'), which implicitly leads them to adopt a milder, even more trivial view of the target domain involved. This change in perspective is oriented towards causing a particular effect on the audience, namely to provide some sort of consolation to those left alive and help them accept the reality of the loss of a loved one: the deceased is not dead but sunk in a peaceful rest.

The same mechanism of contrast between domains operates in the case of dysphemistic metaphors. Metaphor is a potent source for dysphemistic reference; therefore, metaphorical dysphemism stands out as a powerful rhetorical strategy, especially in political discourse, in which it works as a technique of *delegitimization* (Chilton, 2004: 46) through which political rivals are presented negatively in an attempt to attract potential voters or get people to support a cause. An interesting case in point is Churchill's metaphorical dysphemism employed in his wartime speeches (Charteris-Black, 2005: 32–57; Crespo-Fernández, 2013a). The domains Churchill resorted to (MONSTERS, ANIMALS, CRIMINALS, etc.) were intended to make the audience change their perspective of Nazi Germans to those domains which best served Churchill's intention to attack the enemies of Britain. For example, through the dysphemistic conceptualization NAZI GERMANS ARE ANIMALS he invited the audience to consider Hitler in terms of vermin. In his speech *Preparation, Liberation and Assault* (30 December 1941), Churchill referred to Hitler as an adder and an asp:

> Their only guarantee is Hitler's good faith, which, as everyone knows, biteth like the adder and stingeth like the asp.

Here the contrast between both humans and animals has a clear persuasive and evaluative effect: it aims to convince British citizens that the foreign enemy of Britain is someone to be eliminated for the safety of the community. By using this metaphor, Churchill was trying to instil courage in the population in such difficult times for his fellow countrymen as those of a war against the powerful Nazi Germany.

Of course, the ideological function of metaphors also takes place in the case of sex-related language. The choice of particular source domains to talk about women as, for example, SMALL FURRY ANIMALS identifies the speaker as an individual who does not only overtly position himself as a heterosexual member of a 'macho-man' community, but also displays a misogynistic and dominant attitude over females (Coates, 2013). I will deal with the sexist dimension of metaphors in Chapter 4.

Evaluation and persuasion are also carried out through the entailments a metaphor gives rise to, as Deignan (2010) claims. In effect, metaphors generate sets of entailments which support the speaker's judgement about a particular version of events. Metaphorical entailments arise from the knowledge we have about the source domain (see 1.1.1) which is transferred to the target domain with a persuasive purpose. In Churchill's speech mentioned before, the VERMIN metaphor generates a series of entailments that suggest a particular ideological stance and greatly contribute to the speaker's dysphemistic and persuasive aim. These include that the enemy is inhuman, dangerous, harmful and untrustworthy, which ultimately justifies his annihilation (Crespo-Fernández, 2013a: 318).

Not only do the choice of the source domain and the use of metaphors to create entailments contribute to the rhetorical nature of metaphors. The partial nature of metaphorical mappings whereby some aspects of the source domain are highlighted whereas others are largely ignored plays a crucial role in the persuasive and evaluative functions of metaphors. Granted that, as Deignan (2005: 24) puts it, 'many, if not all, conceptual metaphors are reductions of a complex and abstract topic and thus inevitably distortions', the way in which mappings work contributes to the ideological function of metaphors. As metaphors present a partial interpretation of a situation, it is up to the speaker to choose those that best single out and emphasize certain aspects that are useful for talking judgementally and persuasively. This choice, following Deignan, contributes to a collective bias in understanding reality, and therefore supposes an effective persuasive and ideological device.

In summary, X-phemistic metaphors are likely to perform persuasive and evaluative functions in discourse. In fact, the way taboo concepts are managed usually responds to a persuasive or evaluative purpose, as we will see in the course of the analysis. As context-bound phenomena, the metaphors triggered by taboo subjects are not employed randomly; rather, the linguistic expressions that emerge from a given conceptualization are 'loaded' and used deliberately in discourse with a predominantly social function as a particular representation of reality.

2.5 Cognitive issues in the interpretation of X-phemistic metaphors

When dealing with X-phemism, the role of the receiver cannot be left aside. In the process of conceptual representation of abstract concepts the receiver is actively involved; conceptualization does not only play a significant role in the speaker's euphemistic or dysphemistic choice and serves the speaker's communicative purpose of being respectful or offensive, it also has an obvious effect in the dynamic process of understanding and interpreting linguistic metaphors. Indeed, as Indurkhya (1992: 111) argues, the human mind plays an active role in the process of finding similarities and associations between two entities: 'The world we see in our mind's eye is a world that is not "given" but is constructed by our cognitive apparatus.' In this sense, the meaning conveyed by a given conceptualization does not precede the metaphor; rather, it is produced by a combination between the deliberate use of the metaphor on the part of the speaker and the interpretative process on the part of a competent hearer, who is able to grasp the speaker's intended meaning. Hence, the process of finding similarities and detecting contrasts between entities and the subsequent assignment of the mitigating or pejorative traits to a term or expression is subject to the active and cooperative role on the part of the hearer to unravel the possible meanings of the utterance in accordance with the inferential process of meaning detection outlined in 1.3.[16] This process largely depends on the world knowledge the hearer possesses, i.e. his encyclopaedic knowledge, together with his expectations and the surrounding context.

In this process of metaphor interpretation the nature of the conceptual domains involved in the metaphorical association plays a central role. It is precisely thanks to the intrinsic uncertainty of metaphor with regard to the application of the word to a denotatum that metaphorical euphemism and dysphemism are able to suggest that there is a distasteful concept underneath the signifier (Chamizo Domínguez and Sánchez Benedito, 2000: 40–1), and, in this sense, may guide the hearer's interpretation and satisfy his expectations of relevance. For instance, the metaphorical phrase *departed his life* meaning 'died' is ambiguous, meaning something different in relation to journeys from what it means in relation to death. This implies that the literal meaning does not actually correspond with the meaning intended by the speaker in that context, which enables the receiver to opt for a plausible interpretation beyond the lexically decoded concept. So, in order to satisfy his expectations of relevance, the hearer must necessarily lean on contextual clues to identify the speaker's euphemistic intention.

On this view, I believe that not only is ambiguity the raw material of euphemism, as Chamizo Domínguez (2005: 10) claims. The ambiguity attached to metaphor also moves to dysphemism and compels the receiver to process at the metaphorical level and understand a metaphorical lexical unit like *cookie* with the figurative sense of 'promiscuous female', despite the apparent incongruity between both domains of experience, and establish a logical (dysphemistic, in this case) link between the domains of APPETIZING FOOD and SEX. Thus, both in euphemism and in dysphemism it is the intentional and deliberate ambiguity of metaphors that leads the receiver to explore beyond the literal meaning and arrive at the connotations hidden under the metaphorical disguise. By paying attention to the ambivalent nature of metaphors, the hearer will be in a position to recognize the X-phemistic force of the metaphorical unit and, by way of narrowing or broadening of the encoded meaning, arrive at the speaker's intended meaning of the utterance.

In the overall process of detection of the speaker's intended X-phemistic metaphorical meaning, there are other considerations that should be taken into account together with the inferential account of metaphor interpretation outlined above. The nature and particular connotations of a given conceptualization arising from the source-to-target mapping as well as the type of source domain used to target a taboo concept determine the perception of the metaphorical substitute, and, in this way, contribute to the process of disambiguation of metaphors. A good example is SEX IS WAR, a structural metaphor that constitutes the source of a remarkable diversity of sex-related vocabulary (Sánchez Benedito, 2004: 186–92). As a consequence of the conceptualization of sex in terms of violence – a tradition which dates back to Elizabethan literature (see Partridge, 1968: 23; Oncíns-Martínez, 2010) – our understanding of the metaphorical substitutes included in this mapping is inevitably shaped by pre-existing metaphorical associations deriving from the SEX-AS-VIOLENCE metaphor which form part of the hearer's cognitive system (Lakoff, 1993: 210). Because of this identification of sex with violence, the taboo target domain is easier to comprehend – although its nature is radically different from that of the source domain – and therefore it automatically activates the dysphemistic reference of the source domain in a given communicative context. Indeed, a dysphemistic interpretation of a metaphorical term phrase like *shoot one's load* in (1) seems reasonable and plausible.

The same as maintained by RT followers, the presence of a discourse context greatly affects metaphor interpretation. When focusing on the interpretation of X-phemistic units, we should bear in mind that a contextually consistent conceptualization significantly contributes to the understanding of euphemisms and dysphemisms. After all, as Allan and Burridge (1991: 28) argue, mitigation or offence ultimately depends on the context in which the word is used, and thus the euphemistic or dysphemistic quality of a word cannot be considered as an intrinsic quality of the word regardless of context. From this standpoint, Pfaff, Gibbs and Johnson provide evidence for the fact that the mitigating or offensive value of metaphors is easier to comprehend if there is a conceptual match between them and the context:

> A speaker should consider one X-phemism more appropriate than another in a certain context because he is conceptualizing that context metaphorically … Contexts can provide people with metaphorical concepts that influence the appropriateness or ease of interpretation of the X-phemism by cueing them to its metaphorical meaning. (1997: 61–2)

In effect, it seems that the mitigating and offensive nature of figurative language expressions belonging to a particular cognitive domain is easier to comprehend when the context is equally categorized in terms of the same domain. The following message illustrates the role of context in metaphor interpretation:

> (3) The difference between sex and food is the *full* spouse doesn't care if the *hungry* spouse *picks up a snack* downtown. So, does she want to be your exclusive *meal* or not? (TAM, 7 March 2013)

The conceptual basis of this posting is the conceptualization SEX IS EATING, a metaphor which organizes linguistic metaphors (*full*, *hungry*, *pick up a snack* and *meal*) into a coherent conceptual structure. The X-phemistic use of *pick up a snack* with the meaning 'have extramarital sexual intercourse' is easier to reach if the reader considers preceding other terms like *full*, *hungry* and *meal*, which all share a common sexual reference, namely 'sexually satisfied', 'in need of sex' and 'sexual partner' respectively. In fact, these metaphorical units belong to a conceptual equation that relates sex to eating – an association which favours their interpretation in a figurative sense within a conceptually consistent context. In this way, the conceptual nature of a given metaphorical term or expression is a relevant aid in the disambiguation of the X-phemistic effect of the lexical alternative. As a result, the conceptual structure of linguistic metaphors can effectively contribute to clarifying the intended meaning of metaphorical language.

Drawing on RT as a theoretical framework, there are three factors at play when it comes to the interpretation of metaphorical units, namely the linguistic form of the utterance, the context of use and the recognition of the speaker's intentionality. In the inferential process of moving from the encoded concept to the intended communicative meaning of the metaphorical utterance, the hearer plays an active role, as the world knowledge he possesses, together with his expectations and the surrounding context (including specific cultural constraints) play a vital role in the process of reaching the meaning originally intended by the speaker so that ostensive communication is successful. To this end, we should also consider the nature and particular connotations of the domains involved in the metaphorical conceptualization of taboo concepts. Source domains have a role to play in bridging the gap between the literal and figurative meaning and reaching the speaker's euphemistic or dysphemistic intention, as we will see in Chapters 3 and 4.

Part Two

Sex-Related Metaphors in Internet Forums

3

Euphemistic Metaphors

As I remarked in the Introduction, sex has traditionally been considered a powerful taboo and banned from the public domain. In fact, the way to deal with sexual issues is a faithful indicator of the degree of tolerance (or repression) of societies throughout history. In those periods characterized by strong moral and social censorship, like Victorian England, sex-related euphemism peaked in the English language. On some occasions, the taboo on sex proved to be more powerful than any verbal mitigation, and sexual concepts were even silenced in public discourse (Marsh, 1998: 215–30). The social interdictions surrounding sex are still alive in Western democratic societies in which the taboo of sex, especially in public discourse, is not an easy subject to discuss openly. Indeed, to resort to sexual matters without any kind of linguistic safeguard may lead to the breaking of a social convention and hence to a serious face-affront to both the speaker's and hearer's face.

The interdiction that surrounds sex is not only the consequence of public constraints or social impositions. Proscriptive practices are also self-imposed by speakers themselves on the basis of what they consider as distasteful or inappropriate in a given context. As Burridge (2010: 3) notes, ordinary people 'act as self-appointed censors and take it upon themselves to condemn those words and constructions that they feel do not measure up to the standards they perceive they should say'. It is then that language users resort to euphemism as the best way to refer to sex-related topics in public discourse. This is the reason why euphemism is not restricted to official or formal contexts; it abounds in informal and spontaneous communicative practices like those which take place in internet forums, as we will see throughout this chapter.

Of course, there are some categories within the domain of sex which are subject to stronger social and moral restrictions. The undeviating reference to certain sexual practices like, for example, anal sex, incest or bestiality is severely (even legally) sanctioned. The stigma of these taboo subjects proves to be more powerful than any euphemistic alternative, and not even the most indirect, vague or good-sounding euphemism is able to publicly refer to the taboo without a serious threat to the speaker's face. In cases like these, as Krajewsky and Schröder (2008: 595) point out, the only effective euphemism is silence, a 'culture-related' silence, inevitably connected with taboo, which, like other verbal mitigation devices, functions as omission strategy.[1]

One does not have to look at extreme, illicit or even illegal sexual practices. More common, socially accepted and 'standardized' sexual activities in Western democratic societies like non-procreative sex or extra-marital sexual intercourse are severely sanctioned by religion, which still plays a central role in the public censorship of sex, especially in Roman Catholic countries like Spain.[2] Although the censorship on taboo topics seems to be more relaxed in Anglo-Saxon societies (Allan and Burridge, 2006: 145), the stigma of sex in public life helps to explain the profusion of euphemism in English. As Ayto (2007: 67) notes, 'the Anglo-Saxon peoples, and particularly the British, are famous for their being embarrassed by sex, so it is hardly surprising that the English language contains more euphemisms for sexual activity than for any other topic'.

Given that, as commented in 2.1, metaphor stands out as a major device in structuring sexual euphemism conceptually, in this chapter we will see how source domains facilitate the mitigation of the taboo of sex and the possibility of using it safely in public discourse.

3.1 Euphemistic sex-related domains

As Kövecses (2003: 79) argues, a sex-related target concept can be expressed via different source domains. The type of source domain used and the particular components that are given priority in each case largely influence the euphemistic force of the metaphorical substitute employed and gives us a valuable insight into the way humans consider the sexual taboo, as we will see in what follows.

3.1.1 WORK

Let us start with the source domains that associate sex with WORK and with related subdomains like COMMERCE and BUSINESS. SEX IS WORK is a resemblance metaphor which is culturally, rather than experientially, motivated: it makes use of the shared knowledge of a given topic of those belonging to the same cultural group; in other words, this metaphor is grounded in the commonplace knowledge of the domain of WORK that people have. In fact, the metaphor which makes use of the WORK domain for euphemistic purposes is based upon the non-literal perception of some shared features between the source and target domains: both sex and work are serious activities which require time, effort and dedication as well as some degree of mastery and technique. In this sense, the use of terms like *job*, *business* or *work* introduces a contrast between the domains of SEX (which is presumably a pleasurable activity) and WORK insofar as work is, strictly speaking, opposed to pleasure. This contrast activates the euphemistic force of the terms included in this conceptualization, and offers the possibility to use them safely in public discourse. Despite this contrast, the literal meaning of work-related words provides the perspective for construing the speaker's euphemistic meaning – i.e. for pragmatically inferring the sexual intended meaning – which moves away from the literal meaning encoded by the verbal expression although, at the same time, it retains some of its semantic components in order to establish the connection between two apparently different domains.

A relevant source concept within this domain is BUSINESS. The generic term *business* has inspired different verbal usages among the classics in the canon of English sex-related euphemism. From its first euphemistic use meaning 'sexual intercourse' in the early seventeenth century (*OED*3), this word has undergone a process of semantic change: it has progressively broadened its meaning and is now a term with a wide denotation within the field of sex. *Business* is the result of a process of underspecification, i.e. the use of a general term which is required to be specified in its context of use to refer to a taboo subject and thus fulfil its euphemistic function (Allan, 2012: 12). Although *business* is a well-established lexical label to refer to prostitution as a type of commercial activity, as I will explain later, its generic nature introduces an element of intentional vagueness which facilitates the reference to sex-related topics. For example, in the two postings below *business* provides the euphemistic basis of the phrases *go into business* 'extramarital sexual relationship' in (4) and *get down to business* 'copulate' in (5):

(4) I am not one to jump on the "she's having an affair" bandwagon, but in this case, if she's not sleeping with this guy, it will really shock me. She's planning on *going into business* with him. (TAM, 14 September 2013)

(5) We do sideways 69 and it's good for sort of a pre-game warmup but that's about it. It serves its purpose for getting us excited and ready but then we *get down to business*. (TAM, 9 June 2013)

Because of its intrinsic ambiguity, the same as happens with *business*, the term *work* is also part of a wide range of euphemistic phrases, and may be used for almost anything that is the subject of a sexual taboo. In the following message the expression *did the work* refers euphemistically to anal sex:

> (6) We tried to have sex last night. The start was great but it ended sadly. He was too exhausted and I was afraid he would pass out if we did not stop. He *did the work* with my help in the first two positions and I *did all the work* in the last two positions … We stopped and neither of us had O. (TAM, 16 December 2013)

Work is also part of the euphemistic periphrasis *work of pleasure*, a good-sounding phrase used by a prostitute who participates in the board to refer to her occupation. Note how the protective function of euphemism projects in discourse:

> (7) I am and have been for many years a sex-worker. … I thought I was brilliant turning my "love for sex" into a money making machine. However, the reality is that I have now been so saturated in the *work of pleasure* that I am virtually numb. (SDF, 11 July 2013)

Job is another generic term which allows for the reference to different sexual topics in various phrases and compound nouns in which it is included. Take the following examples:

> (8) Leather suits every woman!! It's so sexy!! Give your boyfriend a *handjob* with them on. He'll love it. (FFF, 16 January 2011)

> (9) When giving oral sex, she won't *finish the job* due to her prior relationships where they would force it, plus she doesn't like the taste or consistency. (MMSL, 16 October 2012)

In these postings the metaphorical compound noun *handjob* ('masturbation')[3] and the verbal phrase *finish the job* ('make a man ejaculate'), however explicit they may seem in their contexts of use, exploit the source domain concept of JOB in order to euphemistically refer to sex-related issues which are subject to a high degree of interdiction. This is also the case of oral sex, a taboo topic that calls for verbal attenuation in public discourse. The word *job* fulfils a euphemistic function in the phrases *on the job* 'engaged in oral sex' (10) and *do a really good job* (11), one of the replies to a thread entitled "Dos and Don't during Cunnilingus":

> (10) I don't enjoy giving head unless the entire area is SUPER [in capitals in

the original] clean, I've been burnt before when he's come straight from the shower but has only washed his junk and whilst *on the job* gotten a noseful of unwashed crack. (MMSL, 16 December 2012)

(11) If I *do a really good job*, I usually have some "reminder" up my nose. (TAM, 16 September 2013)

To refer to oral sex in posting (12) below the participant in the forum takes a step further in the euphemistic disguise and hides the compound noun *blowjob* ('fellatio') behind the abbreviation *BJ* in which the initials substitute a word which might bring the taboo topic to mind in a more undeviating way. In this way, *BJ* effectively contributes to the concealing function of euphemism.

(12) I'm definitely not going to give him a *BJ* while he sits in his chair and plays madden over my head. (MMSL, 17 September 2012)

The use of conventional work-related expressions demonstrates that the way we understand sexual matters comes from the structure of our knowledge of the world of work (Lakoff and Turner, 1989: 62). From this general knowledge we may have, only some components of the source domain are transferred to the target domain and singled out for euphemistic purposes, as part of the hiding–highlighting property of metaphorical projections (see 2.1). As shown in the postings above, sexual topics which have traditionally been subject to moral and social censorship like oral sex and masturbation are conceived of as a form of service and obligation. This notion also applies to the consideration of sex within marriage, which is metaphorically referred to as a duty on the part of the spouse in euphemistic phrases like *marital rights* or *spousal intercourse* which conceive coition as an act of obligation each spouse has to avoid fornication (Coleman, 1999). This implies that sexual intercourse, more than a purely physical or affective need, is seen as an obligation which verges on the established right of married couples, in line with the notion of work as a respectable occupation which ranges over all the realizations of the WORK metaphor. Consider the use of *duty* and *spousal duty* in the following message:

(13) If I felt that I did not want him sexually do I have a *duty* to try to repair that? Can I even know to attempt repair of this if I dont see sex as more than a *spousal duty* to begin with? (MMSL, 8 September 2013)

The implication of using the WORK domain is that a sexual relationship is conceived as a serious activity carried out in a responsible way in which the participants involved are supposed to behave in a civilized manner, the same as workers do in the real world of labour. However, the dimension of the world of work whereby one gets paid for one's work is clearly disregarded. This hiding–highlighting property of metaphorical conceptualization, which involves a deliberate utilization of metaphors in discourse in line with the partiality of metaphorical structuring, provides the basis for the euphemistic reference to sex-related topics.

The partiality of metaphorical mappings allows for the euphemistic reference to prostitutes. The metaphor SEX IS WORK tells us how sex is being conceptualized in the world of labour through a set of mappings that characterize it, namely sex corresponds to the job, sexual intercourse corresponds to the work activity and lovers correspond to workers. This last correspondence ultimately gives way to the euphemistic metaphor A PROSTITUTE IS A WORKER. The conceptual basis of this metaphor lies in the fact that prostitution is perceived in strictly commercial terms, as any other job; for this reason, this metaphor gives rise to socially acceptable alternatives to refer to prostitutes such as *business woman, masseuse, model* or *working girl*, as recorded by Holder (2003). The underlying basis for this euphemistic strategy is that prostitutes are workers like any others; in this way, euphemism fulfils a relevant social function – that of dignifying a particular occupation, downgraded for a social or moral reason. Indeed, a common avoidance strategy to refer to prostitutes is to hide the linguistic taboo behind some other occupation not regarded in a negative light or subject to social stigma and condemnation. In these cases, according to Casas Gómez (2012: 53–4), mitigation combines with expressive enhancement in the creation of the so-called 'puffery' euphemistic uses, common in expressions implying a higher social status. In this respect, the aforementioned jobs used to refer to prostitutes are examples of the so-called 'uplifting' euphemism, based on the belief that prostitution is a respectable, even high-status job. An example of this type of euphemism is *masseuse*. This word refers to high-class prostitution, far from the dark side of street prostitution, usually associated with delinquency, drugs, venereal diseases, etc. Consider the posting below:

(14) So we are just sort of laying there I touch her a bit and she said that I should have been a *masseuse* or a gigolo you missed your calling. (MMSL, 5 December 2013)

The generic term *business* plays an important role in the euphemistic reference to prostitution and related activities, which are conceived of as different forms of commercial transactions. Its euphemistic capacity is based on the ambiguity characteristic of euphemism which acts as a means to disguise and somehow dignifies the real occupation we are talking about. Because of the indeterminacy of *business*, it is only the phraseological context that allows the reader to draw out the concealed implication of prostitution in the following message:

(15) The problems you speak of are not entirely unique to sex workers, but certainly are prevalent there. You've probably been *in the business* too long, and need to more on with your life. (SDF, 12 July 2013)

The phrases *sell sex* and *sell one's body* in the two postings below consider prostitution in terms of a commercial activity.[4] If prostitution is a commercial transaction involving an interaction between parties, an entailment that can be derived from this metaphor is that the man who makes use of prostitution is the costumer, i.e. 'the man who buys (or rents)', as in (17). This view of prostitution leads to a euphemistic conceptualization which has to do with man–woman relationships: HUMAN RELATIONSHIPS ARE BUSINESS TRANSACTIONS and MEN ARE CUSTOMERS (Kövecses, 2006b: 153–4).

(16) You want women to be free to *sell sex*, but want to prohibit men from *buying sex*? Do you honestly see a difference? (TAM, 17 September 2012)

(17) Don't advocate telling an adult woman she can't *sell her body*. The real offender in that equation is the man who *buys* (or *rents*) her. (TAM, 16 September 2012)

By using lexical alternatives to the taboo like *sell sex* and *sell one's body*, the posters in (16) and (17) do not have the intention of mitigating or hiding the taboo of prostitution whatsoever. Rather, their intention is that of criticizing the business of prostitution and those involved in it. To this end, they resort to socially acceptable lexical alternatives which, despite carrying a sense of disapproval and negative value judgement, serve the posters' critical purpose without any face affront. Here we find cases of what Grimes (1978: 22) first called 'derogatory euphemism'. This X-phemistic type – which belongs to the axiological category of *quasi-dysphemism* (see 2.1) – refers to those lexical alternatives to taboo concepts which are actually pejorative or condemnatory, although acceptable in polite discourse insofar as they avoid certain words considered too harsh or impolite.

Let us turn to (7) and (15). The noun phrase *sex worker*, lexicalized with a sexual sense, does not offer an alternative way of comprehending reality as a consequence of its continuous use with reference to prostitutes. Although the WORK metaphor tends to pass unnoticed in these postings, *sex worker* does provide an effective way to target euphemistically this touchy subject, especially in (15), a posting addressed to a prostitute who is participating in the forum. This seems to prove that, though lexicalized, *sex worker* is a socially acceptable, hence euphemistic, way to refer to prostitutes within the constraints imposed by sociocultural norms of polite talk which does not suppose any threat to the addressee's face. That this is so ultimately derives from the fact that, out of concern for those involved in this activity, this denomination presents prostitution as a respectable commercial activity. As a matter of fact, *sex worker* is used, according to *OED*3, 'with the intention of reducing negative connotations and of aligning the sex industry with conventional service industries'. In this regard, it can be considered as a case of PC language that merely provides a job description far from any moral judgement (Burridge, 1996, 1998: 64).

From the perspective that considers sex as work, prostitution as a business and a form of economic trade and prostitutes as workers like any others, sexual activity is seen in terms of an economic exchange as part of the broader generic-level metaphor for human relationships INTERACTIVE RELATIONSHIPS ARE HUMAN RELATIONSHIPS proposed by Kövecses (2003). This metaphor characterizes human relationships as interactive, as a shared experience between people – hence its euphemistic force to target the domain of SEX. This category of INTERACTIVE RELATIONSHIPS is a conflation of what Köveces calls the 'communication system' and the 'state' system:

> [S]tate system … includes states, relationships, and interactions. The metaphors for communication … indicate that communication is viewed as a form of interaction, and as such it fits the INTERACTIVE RELATIONSHIPS group naturally. (2003: 111–12)

This social and interactive component of the sexual activity constitutes the euphemistic basis of the once metaphorical term *intercourse*, now fully lexicalized as the word for 'coition'. *Intercourse* has become so much our everyday polite term to refer to copulation that we tend to forget its euphemistic nature and regard it as a purely orthophemistic term (Ayto, 2007: 76). The metaphoricity of this word does not become activated in discourse; indeed, *intercourse* is not perceived as having a literal counterpart, and therefore the connection between the word and its original source domain is not accessible to the average reader. In fact, nobody would think of a connection of a sexual relationship with a commercial activity or any other type of exchange between people other than the sexual one (Holder, 2003: 198). Despite this, *intercourse* functions as a protective lexical label: it retains its euphemistic capacity to refer to the taboo of coition in rather formal postings like that of (18) below, in which it is an appropriate alternative to give medical opinion and advice on a sexual problem, namely phimosis:

(18) A tight-foreskin can lead to a feeling oversensitivity and it can lead to problems during *intercourse*, as I've already implied. It's something much treatable, though. Go to your local doctor and tell him / her what the problem is. (SDF, 26 April 2011)

Another euphemistic word which derives from the view of sex as a type of commercial activity is *affair*. This word, highly ambiguous and therefore very effective for euphemistic purposes, has undergone a process of semantic change. Its origin with a sexual sense can be traced back to the second half of the sixteenth century, especially in fixed phrases like *affair of love*, first recorded in 1547 with the meaning 'sexual encounter' (*OED*3). The word then acquired the meaning 'extramarital sexual relationship' (whose first occurrence dates back to 1700) that presents in the message below:

(19) On that forum relationship section, a new "undercover" user unloads all this info about how she's having this *affair* and finally sex once after work, doesn't have any guilt but really wants to stay with the guy. (MMSL, 29 October 2013)

It is worth noting that in euphemistic terms which have their origin in the consideration of sex as a kind of commercial activity like *intercourse* and *affair* in (18) and (19) respectively, there is no imputation of payment. Rather, as Ayto (2007: 76) points out, these words are a semantic narrowing of the more general sense 'dealings' and thus the notion of payment is concealed for euphemistic purposes.

Despite the euphemistic nature of the source domain of WORK, as seen in the postings provided as examples in this section, Murphy (2001: 41) considers that this metaphor implicitly degrades the sexual act itself in that:

... men view their relationships with women through the lens of control, discipline, regulation and commodity. Men's reduction of their sexuality to work, business, and an economic exchange embraces their relations to women as part of the male economy.

From this viewpoint, the connection between SEX and WORK reduces sexual activity to an exchange devoid of intimacy and affection, and implicitly contributes to portraying women as inferior to men (see 4.3). This seems to demonstrate how the boundaries between euphemism and dysphemism are rather fuzzy and the difference is, in many cases, a matter of degree or perspective.

3.1.2 HEAT and FIRE

Such delicate topics as desire, sexual arousal and lust are commonly conceptualized in terms of heat and, to account for a higher intensity, fire.[5] The source domain of HEAT focuses on the physiological effects of lust and sexual excitement (namely increase in body temperature) to stand for lust and sexual excitement themselves. This metaphor has therefore a metonymic basis EFFECT FOR CAUSE whereby THE PHYSIOLOGICAL EFFECTS OF SEXUAL EXCITEMENT STAND FOR SEXUAL EXCITEMENT. It is thus closely connected with the metonymic principle THE PHYSIOLOGICAL EFFECTS OF AN EMOTION STAND FOR THE EMOTION (Kövecses, 1986: 12–13), as we tend to assume that sexual arousal is an emotion through which the individual experiences physiological effects.

Following Ruiz de Mendoza Ibáñez (2000), the HEAT metaphor is based on a 'source-in-target' metonymy insofar as the source domain is a subdomain of the target: heat derives from (and therefore is part of) sexual excitement. This type of metonymy is based on what this scholar has come to know as 'domain expansion': the increase in the amount of conceptual material which is relevant to infer the intended (in this case euphemistic) meaning is based on the point of access provided by the source domain, which determines the euphemistic nature of the concept represented in the source. Thanks to this domain expansion cognitive operation, we are conscious that there is more than heat involved when defining a woman as *hot*. This adjective gives us access to a more complex scene which includes (and euphemistically alludes to) passion, excitement and lust. In the same vein, Köveces (1988) argues that this metonymy derives from a basic emotion scenario for sexual passion: a cause (a sexual encounter) induces a person to have an emotion (sexual arousal), and the emotion causes the person to produce some physiological response (body heat). The underlying conceptual metaphor is BEING EXCITED IS EXPERIENCING HEAT, a reoriented version of the primary metaphor SEX IS HEAT, which is experientially grounded, i.e. grounded in our recurrent direct and daily life experience.[6] The emotion scenario for sexual passion in the HEAT metaphor is shown in Table 3.1 (adapted from Kövecses, 2003: 76).

Table 3.1 Emotion Scenario for Sexual Passion in the HEAT Metaphor

Source	Target
Causer of emotion	Sexual encounter
Emotion	Sexual excitement
Physical response to emotion	Body heat

There is a series of mappings that characterize the HEAT metaphor, namely: the object that is hot is the sexually excited person; the heat corresponds to lust; and the degree of heat corresponds to the degree of intensity of the lustful feeling (Kövecses, 1988). Put simply, lust and sexual excitement are associated with being hot, given that the increase of body temperature is one of the most characteristic physiological effects of sexual arousal. This metaphor is therefore motivated by the folk theory of the physiological effects of sex which considers that body heat increases as sexual desire and the intensity of the sexual encounter increase (Kövecses, 1986: 87–8).[7] In this respect, heat is the most characteristic perceived resemblance between the source and the target domains. It is precisely this connection between both domains that provides the euphemistic basis for this metaphor.

A common way to refer to a high body temperature as an indicator of sexual excitement is through the adjective *hot*. In (20) the state of sexual arousal which is attributed to the woman inevitably leads to considering that she is likely to get men excited. So it seems that the woman has the capacity of supplying heat derived from sexual excitement to other bodies:

(20) Was out to dinner with another lady I am dating. The 25 yo receptionist for one of my clients sees me and comes over and is talking to me and throws subconscious IOI's (hair twirling, etc.) Why is she standing there flirt with me? Because of pre-selection I am there with a *hot* woman, so she must come and flirt. (MMSL, 26 September 2013)

Similarly, in posting (21) below *hottest* alludes to the high degree of excitement that the thought of getting engaged in a sexual practice beyond the limits of what one would consider 'conventional' sex provokes in the poster. She resorts to the HEAT domain to describe a sexual practice known as 'frottage' (a technique which consists of deriving sexual pleasure by rubbing, especially one's genitals, against the body of another person) as extremely exciting, as one of her 'hottest masturbation fantasies':

(21) I can't believe that what you are doing on the Metro has been one of my *hottest* masturbation fantasies for ages. Many times I have imagined exactly what you describe, being in a crowded subway train with horny guys with a short little wispy skirt. (MMSL, 17 March 2011)

The word *torrid* is another realization of the HEAT metaphor used to reference intense sexual passion. In a heat scale consisting of various degrees of heat ranging from cold to hot, torrid is closer to the extreme of maximum heat, and therefore conveys a more passionate feeling than hot. In the following message this high degree of heat is transferred to an extramarital sexual relationship in order to euphemistically allude to the intensity of the sexual activity:

(22) Many men have concluded that their wives, who don't want sex with them, are simply asexual and wouldn't want sex with anyone. And many of them have been wrong. Many men on the Coping With Infidelity board had that belief until they caught their wife in a *torrid* affair with another man. (TAM, 20 November 2011)

Given that the most characteristic physiological effect of sexual excitement is heat, one of the logical entailments of the HEAT metaphor is that getting sexually excited is getting warmed up. The noun *warm-up* in (5) and its corresponding verb in (23) are used to refer to sexual arousal:

(23) If your partner is willing to have sex but not desiring it currently, *warm her up* in other ways first or initiate sex where you don't put too much focus on her and take pleasure in your own sexual response. (MMSL, 9 September 2012)

The notion of heat also features in the FIRE metaphor. This metaphor has the same conceptual basis as the HEAT metaphor: it points at the purely physical aspects of sexual desire and sexual encounters by focusing on the physiological effects they provoke. The use of the FIRE domain, however, makes sexual excitement more intense: sexual arousal is conceptualized as an emotion with the highest degree of intensity in a heat scale ranging from cold to hot (Kövecses, 1988: 48).[8] In fact, INTENSITY as the main meaning focus of FIRE as a source domain applies to the nature of sexual excitement. This notion of intensity characterizes the source domain of FIRE even more than that of HEAT. Despite the sexual intensity that FIRE evokes, this source concept allows people to talk about sexual excitement in a socially acceptable way. This happens in the message below in which the poster says that his body is 'on fire' as a consequence of having been 'watching porn for 12 hrs':

(24) I've been up watching porn for 12 hrs straight cause she's mad at me about her dog. I still haven't slept and my body is *on fire*. My muscles spasm from time to time, cracking my bones. (SDF, 16 June 2013)

Sexual excitement and desire are mapped onto fire at many different points (Deignan, 1997: 34), as evidenced in different realizations of this metaphor encountered in the corpus as a result of the entailments that the FIRE metaphor gives rise to. Sexual desire can start with a spark. In (25) sexual attraction is metaphorically conceived of as a spark which poses a threat to a well-established relationship in the same way as 'a spark that cannot be extinguished' threatens to cause a fire:

(25) A person has no business getting entangled with a person who is in a committed relationship. If there is *a spark that cannot be extinguished*, then the committed person needs to make their choice, and not carry on with anyone … until the other relationship is finished. (FFF, 18 January 2012)

In order to arouse sexual desire in the partner it will be necessary to 'light that fire':

(26) Nope, just a typical middle-aged post-baby hormonally ruined woman. Probably going to end up a typically divorced, alone … and although her new guy will *light her fire* for a while, she will return to her true self and resume her current behaviour. (FFF, 26 February 2013)

And if the once existing sexual desire has disappeared with the passing of time, the way to feel passionate and sexually attracted to the partner is by 'reigniting the fire':

(27) I am exhausted by all of this, everything is about him, what he wants, how he feels … i dont think he gives a toss about what he has put me through. how the hell do you come back from this? can that *fire* in my belly ever *be reignited*? (SDF, 6 December 2012)

Although some linguistic metaphors like *on fire* (24) and *light one's fire* (26) are lexicalized with a sexual sense, the fact remains that they actually provide a way to refer to this taboo topic in public. This does not mean, however, that by resorting to the FIRE metaphor the speaker aims to hide the topic of sexual excitement itself. By virtue of the nature of the source domain involved, this metaphor tends to emphasize the physiological response provoked by sexual arousal as the raw material for euphemistic naming. Therefore, these linguistic metaphors can be considered as cases of what Burridge (2012: 69–70) calls 'provocative' euphemism: they are designed not only to conceal; they are also intended to attract interest.

The emphasis of provocative euphemism partly derives from hyperbole. In fact, many of the surface realizations of the FIRE metaphor highlight the intensity of sexual excitement through hyperbole. Take, for example, *flame*, *burn* or *melt*. Despite the exaggerate view of reality that these words transmit, they are accepted as a means to introduce the taboo of sexual excitement in polite conversation. The way hyperbolic references to sexual passion emerge from the FIRE metaphor can be accurately described in cognitive terms if we accept Ruiz de Mendoza Ibáñez's (2011) claim that hyperbole is a cognitive mapping in which the source is a hypothetical domain containing an extreme case of a scalar concept or situation, and the target is a real-world situation that we want to talk about. In this regard, the hypothetical situation that emerges from the domain of FIRE has the effect of enhancing those attributes which are used to depict sexual arousal as an intense feeling; indeed, as mentioned before, the FIRE metaphor depicts sexual excitement as on top of the cold–hot scale. In this way, following Swartz (cited in Herrero Ruiz, 2009: 50), hyperbole supposes a way to structure reality through focusing on one aspect of the concept being dealt with and leaving others aside. This view is closely connected with the partial nature of metaphorical projections whereby only certain aspects of the source domain are used to represent the target domain.

Let us see how some surface realizations of the FIRE metaphor appear in the postings. *Flame* is a typical example of how to deal with sexual excitement in euphemistic terms. In (28) this word is used to talk about the poster's awakening of sexual desire:

(28) Age 15: somehow had it down that girls need to be "respected" which lead to my best friend snatching my *flame* because I did not make a move. (SDF, 28 November 2012)

The analogy between flame and sexual desire becomes evident if we look at the verbs that are collocated with *flame* in the reference to sexual passion. Flames can be *ignited* (when one becomes sexually excited), *subsided* (if sexual excitement disappears) or *reignited* (if sexual desire starts again after a period of inactivity). The verb *reignite*, which appeared with *fire* in (27), takes *flame* as its object in the following message:

(29) I hope that since there have not been any new posts on this thread by you that you and your husband are progressing nicely in your efforts to *reignite the flame* of intimacy in your marriage. (TAM, 16 May 2011)

The word *flame* also appears in *old flame*, an idiomatic phrase lexicalized with the meaning 'ex-sexual partner'. The metaphor which underlies this phrase is DESIRE IS FIRE: regardless of its idiomatic nature, *old flame* is conceptually motivated by the FIRE-AS-DESIRE metaphor, which confirms Kövecses's (2002: 236) assumption that the meaning of idioms is dependent on the metaphorical conceptual system. Accordingly, by virtue of this metaphor, the person referred to as *old flame* is seen as a source of sexual excitement in the past and (sometimes) a sexual temptation in the present. This is the case of the posting below, one of the replies of the thread 'Old love returns while in a bad marriage':

> (30) If the *old flame* really wants to give it a try he is capable of waiting for you to get your train wreck of a life back on track. (TAM, 12 September 2013)

The term *flame* also admits other collocations to refer to someone who played a role in the person's past sexual life, like *ex-flame, former flame* or *high-school flame*. In (31) the husband of the woman referred to resorts to the flame compound to express a strong sense of suspicion regarding the effect of one of her wife's former sexual partners on her present life:

> (31) I actually might agree with some of the folk about if we were only talking about *high-school flames* from ages past ... The one in particular who bugs me the most is the guy she dated a few months before we first got together. (MMSL, 30 May 2013)

The image of the potential danger that sex may involve is brought to mind in the compound *flame-throwing*. This metaphorical item draws on both the source domains of FIRE and WAR to convey a strong note of disapproval in (32). The poster associates the lustful attitude of a female participant in the forum with the devastating effect provoked by a flamethrower, i.e. a weapon that projects ignited incendiary fuel, thus combining two different domains which invoke destruction and devastation to introduce a sexual topic in the thread:

> (32) But when you insult a messenger of God's Word because of what he says to you from the Word of God, you are insulting the Word of God itself... I have no power to exact consequences on you for your ignorant *flame-throwing*... but there are some other *flames* you might want to be considering when you attack the Word of God. (SDF, 24 June 2013)

The image of a flamethrower clearly transmits here hyperbolic overtones: the source domain of FIRE coexists with that of WAR (more precisely with the source concept of WEAPON) to openly criticize a lustful and hence sinful (in the poster's opinion) sexual behaviour. By associating the effects of a flamethrower to a behaviour which is considered as an incitement to sex, the poster does not really attempt to avoid the taboo; rather, in his posting the WAR domain, commonly used for dysphemistic purposes (see 4.1.4), conflates with the FIRE domain. In such conflation, the woman being talked about is seen as the external stimulus that causes the emotion (sexual arousal) to come into existence. At a metaphorical level, it is the woman who provokes fire and destruction. Thus, the notion of the woman as a fire-making device, present in several myths from various cultures, is connected with patriarchal fears of female sexuality and considered as a threat to morality (Stanley, 1998: 19–20). The compound *flame-throwing* is a case of derogatory euphemism: the critical attitude of the poster is evident, although the word used for this purpose is polite enough to maintain his face. Here we can see again how politeness and face concerns determine lexical choice: the quasi-dysphemistic alternative reveals a condemnatory attitude on the part of the poster, and, at the same time, is a socially appropriate language expression according to conventional norms of social behaviour.

The religious influence in (32) is evident in the allusion to the flames of Hell ('other flames you might be worth considering') as a punishment for the sinful behaviour he is criticizing. By so doing, the poster automatically associates sex and lust with Hell through the powerful image of the flame, symbol of the destructive power of sin within Christian discourse.[9] Through the image of intense heat and consuming flames associated with Hell, the poster aims to warn the reader of the destiny that awaits those who do not keep away from lust. But he does so through euphemistic disguise; in fact, the poster's religious beliefs would not have allowed him to resort to direct words in reference to sex, not even to condemn a woman's lustful behaviour.

The noun *flame-throwing* illustrates the way in which conventional metaphors are *alive* in real communicative contexts. This linguistic metaphor derives from the associations of a well-established metaphor: SEX IS FIRE, a reoriented version of the primary metaphor SEX IS HEAT, grounded in common, physical and recurrent daily experience shared by all participants in the board. This seems to demonstrate that the linguistic realizations of conventional metaphors are somewhat unpredictable. In fact, a conventional metaphor like SEX IS FIRE gives rise to a non-conventional X-phemistic unit like *flame-throwing* in (32).

The intensity of sexual excitement is brought into focus by other heat-related words like *melt*, a hyperbolic metaphorical item which enhances the effects of heat through an exaggerated view of reality, obviously impossible in the real world. The image that this word brings to mind is from liquefying under heat: melting as the process whereby a solid changes to a liquid state by the application of heat. Through this powerful image sexual desire is seen as an emotion with the highest degree of intensity in the heat scale; in fact, melting has the capacity to modify the structure of an object because of its exposure to heat to the point that it eventually disintegrates. The word *melt*, Kövecses (1988: 86) argues, magnifies the intensity of love through the co-occurrence of the domains of HEAT and EFFECT: heat as cause leads to melting as effect. This supposes an extremely high degree of intensity which is applied to target euphemistically the taboo of sexual excitement. The word m*elt* thus provides the basis for a hyperbolic view of the effects of sexual passion onto human beings: the underlying notion is that sexual excitement can even consume your body due to the extremely high temperature. Take the posting below:

(33) He's telling you "How dare you stand up for yourself. I'm going to *turn up the heat until you melt!*" (TAM, 24 September 2013)

Here *melt* is seen as a logical consequence of the effect of heat. In order to excite the partner sexually to the point that she melts, he needs to 'turn up the heat', an action which metaphorically represents the act of sexually exciting someone. If heat stands for sexual excitement, the way to sexually arouse someone is by turning up the heat, as a logical entailment of the metaphor.

Within the FIRE metaphor, *ardent* is a case of what Lakoff (1987b) calls 'linguistically dead' metaphor. Etymologically derived from a word meaning 'burning',[10] the original, non-metaphorical sense of the word has dropped out of use in current English and is nowadays used as a realization of the metaphor EMOTIONS ARE TEMPERATURES (Deignan, 2005: 35). In the following message *ardent* links desire with sexual arousal:

(34) Being vulnerable as in expressing your *ardent* desire and need for sex may not be helpful, especially if he feels that you withheld sex for a long time. (TAM, 5 April 2011)

If sex is equated with heat and, going up the intensity scale, with fire by virtue of the HEAT metaphor, a logical entailment of the metaphor is that the cessation of sexual desire and arousal is conceptualized as cold. This leads to the metaphor LACK OF DESIRE IS COLD which operates in the message that follows:

(35) I'm writing this to say to all you guys that you can do this. You can go from a pretty *cold*, distant, and boring relationship to a very hot one if you both work at it. (MMSL, 6 July 2013)

As seen in the postings above, the domain of FIRE makes sexual desire especially intense, beyond the limit point on the intensity scale ranging from cold to hot. This intensity may even turn sexual desire into a threat for those who experience this feeling. In fact, among the negative entailments of this metaphor, we should consider the connotations of danger, devastation and destruction associated with fire. In this respect, as Deignan (1997: 34) notes, the FIRE metaphor 'highlights the notion of desire as a dangerous or even destructive force, which can spread rapidly in a way which is difficult to control'. Therefore, the effect of sexual desire may turn out to be harmful for those feeling it.

In summary, although highly conventionalized in English, HEAT and FIRE metaphors are powerful tools through which lust and sexual arousal are given special prominence and used to attract people's attention and interest. Take, for example, the lyrics of a rock-and-roll hit like *I'm On Fire*, made famous in the conservative North American society of 1964 by Jerry Lee Lewis. As a matter of fact, the domains of HEAT and FIRE do not, strictly speaking, hide the taboo of sexual excitement itself; rather, they are useful domains at the speaker's disposal to picture passion and sexual arousal as intense and lustful feelings without having to resort to explicit terms which may prove to be unpleasant in polite discourse. In this way, the HEAT and FIRE metaphors are the source of provocative euphemistic units, i.e. those which provide a socially acceptable alternative to talk about 'forbidden' topics in communication without any intention to hide them whatsoever, in a proof of the ambivalent nature of the sexual taboo.

3.1.3 GAMES and SPORTS

Sex is also depicted as a pleasurable activity for euphemistic purposes through the domains of GAMES and SPORTS. The imagery of the game favours an unbiased reinterpretation of a sexual encounter as a pleasurable and innocent pastime. The idea of a child playing games that this metaphor brings to mind determines the perception of the receiver, who is compelled to understand the sexual taboo from this particular perspective, leaving aside other unacceptable semantic traits of the referent.

The two basic ontological correspondences of the SEX-AS-A-GAME metaphor (the game corresponds to sexual activity, and those engaged in sexual intercourse are people playing) constitute the euphemistic basis of this metaphor. This resemblance metaphor coheres with the commonplace knowledge the language user possesses, which allows him or her to establish connections upon the non-literal perception of some shared features between the field of games and the realm of sex. However, not all components of the source domain are actually mapped onto the target. By virtue of the partial utilization of the source domain in metaphorical mappings, the GAME metaphor captures those aspects of the GAME domain that are more apt for euphemistic use, namely fun and innocence, which are activated in the comprehension of the target domain. On the one hand, the element of fun emphasizes the most playful elements of the sexual relationship; on the other hand, the consideration of sex in terms of a game relates sexual activity to an innocent pastime. After all, games are associated with childhood, a time when games are regarded as an innocent way to have fun. These components of the source domain are highlighted for euphemistic purposes in order to refer to a wide range of sex-related taboos, like children examining each other's genitals, even masturbating (*play doctor*), adultery (*play away*), casual copulation (*play around*), masturbation (*play with oneself*), sexual stimulation (*toy with someone*), etc.

The notion of playing features heavily in the expressions used to refer to sexual awakening in children. This is the case of *play doctor* in the following example:

(36) I think young teens/kids can consent to doing sexual stuff with each other, but not with adults. Like I once said to another poster, kids of almost all ages explore their sexuality, 6 or 7 year olds *play doctor* to explore each other's bodies, maybe with another kid they have a crush on, whatever. (SDF, 27 July 2011)

Here the imagery of game favours an unbiased reinterpretation of the delicate issue of children's initiation into sexuality as an innocent pastime. The phrase *play doctor* originates in the role play whereby children use the roles of doctor and patient for body – i.e. genital – examination.[11] Whether or not the role-playing doctor–patient is involved, this phrase refers to children's examining their own genitals. The consideration of fun and innocence attached to children's games provides the basis for the euphemistic reference to genital exploration.

Children's play at being husband and wife is evoked in the metaphorical phrase *play house*. The sexual overtones that this kind of game of initiation into sexuality implies provides the euphemistic basis to refer to the act of copulation:

(37) We have an otherwise healthy marriage ... we are good friends and *play house* together well. I don't try to initiate anymore as a "no" to me feels like a knife in my heart. (TAM, 8 December 2011)

The same euphemistic basis applies to talk about adult masturbation. Thanks to the positive connotations of the GAME domain, this practice is depicted as an innocent pastime in posting (38) below. In this way, the phrase *play with myself* allows the poster to talk about a taboo which has traditionally been subject to a strong interdiction: female masturbation; hence its protective function:

(38) I'm pretty adventurous in *bed-game* for all positions, have masturbated in front of him, etc. What he was asking me to do is not the way I *play with myself*. (MMSL, 17 September 2013)

In keeping with the vagueness principle as the raw material of euphemism, *play* is used to refer to a variety of sex-related activities. This verb singles out for euphemistic purposes the most playful, recreational and, to some extent, innocent elements of sexual intercourse; in this way, thanks to the metaphorical utilization of the source domain, all the aspects which link sexual activity with immorality are left aside. In (39) *play* provides an effective contrast between the connotations of the source and the 'twisted porn fantasys' mentioned in the posting. In addition, the indeterminacy of this verb contributes to avoid any explicit reference to unconventional sexual activities:

(39) I will never be able to satisfy him because i dont want to indulge in all of his sick twisted porn fantasys. Dont get me wrong im happy to *play* but will he ever be satisfied by normal intimate sex. (SDF, 6 December 2012)

The notion of playing also features in the euphemistic reference to sexual practices subject to a high degree of interdiction, like anal sex. The phrases *play around the anus* 'to stimulate someone's anus' in (45) and *butt play* 'anal sex' in (106) illustrate how the notion of playing paves the way to talk about a heavily tabooed area by adding an element of fun which tends to defuse the seriousness of the situation. Similarly, in the expression *play with one's backdoor* in (40) both GAME and CONTAINER (see 3.1.6) domains conflate to allude to this delicate topic in a humorous way:

(40) Wife of 18 years has started asking me to *play with her backdoor* while having sex. She only wants me to rub it and slight digit insertion. (TAM, 9 November 2013)

A high degree of ambiguity in euphemistic naming applies to compounds in which the noun *game* is included. For example, in (38) the compound *bed-game* alludes to a wide range of sexual activities without getting into particular details which might prove to be unpleasant for the reader; rather, the sexual practices are seen in terms of an innocent pastime. The displacement effect created by the euphemistic metaphor is again evident. It is also important to highlight the euphemistic function of *bed* in this compound. The bed is metonymically associated with sexual activity: the place where sex is usually performed stands for sex itself. *Bed* and *bedroom* are location metonymies for sex, euphemistically used with connotation of sexual intercourse (Ayto, 2007: 77). This is reflected in a considerable number of compounds like the already seen *bed-game*, *bedfellow* 'lover or mistress', or *bedwork* 'copulation', as recorded by Holder (2003).

Other compounds with the term *games* are used in euphemistic parlance to refer to some sort of erotic or pornographic activity. Take *adult games* in the posting that follows:

(41) There are *adult games* that are not appropriate for children out there. You know your kids the best and can help make the best decisions for (and with) them. (MMSL, 4 August 2013)

The metaphorical noun phrase *adult games* fulfils a euphemistic function by providing a lexical socially acceptable way to talk about a pornographic video game. By so doing, the adjective *adult* indirectly alludes to the sexual contents of the game referred to.[12]

Within this metaphor, compound nouns with *play* such as *loveplay* or *foreplay* are euphemistically used in polite discourse to refer to sexual stimulation as a prelude to penetration. This is the case of the following quotation:

(42) Before we have sex with my girlfriend during *foreplay* I tend to release significant amount of precum. Sometimes it drops on her and touches her and she thinks that is disgusting and gets on her mood a little. (FFF, 14 April 2012)

In some euphemistic alternatives included in this metaphor the displacement effect between the taboo and its lexical substitute is created through humour. Verbs like *roll* and verbal phrases like *have a roll* 'to copulate with', *roll over* 'to agree to extramarital copulation', or *get one's jollies* 'to get excited or to copulate with' – together with the already commented *play with one's backdoor* in (40) – seem to defuse the seriousness of sexual intercourse because of the playful element that underlies them. The expressions which refer to taboo topics in a humorous way – that Ayto (2007: 75) qualifies as *playful* – fall under the X-phemistic type that Burridge (2012: 71) refers to as 'ludic'. These expressions are included in the category of quasi-euphemism, as – we should not forget – 'pure' euphemism does not have a humorous objective. A good example appears in the posting below. The verb *roll* adds an element of fun to sexual intercourse, in accordance with the optimistic approach to sex that the poster seems to hold:

(43) It sounds like she was ready to *roll* in the morning-- maybe you can set the priority by initiating sex in the morning. If she is choosing not to have sex at night, tell her to crash so she can be ready in the morning. Again, playful and fun. ... Good luck! (MMSL, 12 July 2013)

A common phrase with this verb is *roll in the hay* 'casual sexual encounter'. Although this phrase has a bucolic origin making reference to the typical love scene in the hay, it does not imply, obviously enough, a sexual encounter in an agrarian setting in (44). Rather, it refers to casual copulation and transmits a view of sex far from any worries or engagements. The already commented BED metonymy for sex applies here, as *roll in the hay* derives from the metaphorical use of *hay* with the meaning 'bed':

> (44) No more marriage for me. But I'll take a *roll in the hay* and some good times. Then go back to your own place and take your toothbrush with you. (TAM, 4 April 2012)

In a metaphor which understands sex in terms of a game, it comes as no surprise that the word *toy* contributes to the playful element that characterizes this conceptualization. In the contexts of sexual encounters, *toy* refers to the object that is primarily used to facilitate sexual pleasure, such as a dildo or a vibrator. The word *toy* carries connotations of fun – not present in words like *plug*, *dildo* or *vibrator* – associated with a children's game, and tends to defuse the seriousness of certain situations in which these objects may be used. In this way, *toy* somewhat mitigates the taboo of female masturbation. In the following message, anal stimulation is conceptualized as a game in which the poster is advised to 'continue with the finger play' and 'play around the anus':

> (45) The problem with a *toy* is that you can not feel her reactions as well. You are more likely to push even though there is resistance. I would also continue with the *finger play*. I've noticed some women just like a lot of *play around the anus* and will naturally open up (actually push into you) when they are ready for digital penetration. (TAM, 9 November 2013)

In sex-related language, *toy* undergoes conversion from noun to verb in order to refer to the fact of getting someone sexually aroused, as happens in 'he toys with me in the car' (57). The use of the word *toy* in this posting does not necessarily mean that sexual excitement derives from using a dildo or a vibrator. There is a generalization of meaning at work: *toy* extends its reference to designate different concepts and appear in new contexts. This semantic change of the word, motivated by euphemistic reasons, makes it possible for *toy* to designate any kind of sexual practice preceding penetration.

Within the sphere of pleasurable and playful activities, sex is also conceptualized as a sport. This sporting imagery is invoked in a considerable number of terms which link sex to a competitive sport. In this metaphor, the same as happens in the SEX-AS-A-GAME metaphor previously mentioned, the element of fun characteristic of sports is transferred to the target domain and given special emphasis in order to talk about a taboo-laden topic. Take, for example, the euphemistic phrase *play away* ('commit adultery'). The partial nature of the source domain applies in euphemistic naming: the speaker singles out those components of the source domain which are more apt for presenting the taboo topic of extramarital sexual relationships in public; hence the components of aggression, hostility and confrontation which take place in professional sports are deliberately left out:

(46)   He might just have a poor little gal who can be steam rollered into him *playing away* which is not cool. If you don't like it, don't do it. (MMSL, 25 June 2013)

The sports vocabulary tends to support the view of the sexual partner as a powerful lover. The attributes of an athlete are transferred to sexual activity in order to represent the lover as the embodiment of athletic effort, physical power and determination to succeed. In this light, the sexual encounter is conceived of as a competition in which the lover is physically gifted, has been well trained and highly motivated to achieve his goals, which, at a figurative level, are equated with achieving and providing sexual pleasure. In turn, copulation is supposed to provide the male with good exercise; it is, after all, a physical activity (Holder, 2003: 15). In the message below, the view of the lover in terms of an athlete derives from the intake of pills to achieve erection:

(47)   It doesn't always work and sometimes won't at all. The misnomer is that you simply pop a pill and turn into a *sexual athlete* within 30 minutes. (TAM, 25 February 2011)

Another interesting term is *sexathon*, a nominal blend made up of the full lexical element *sex* and the splinter *-athon*, shortened from *marathon*. This word provides evidence for the lexical creativity of certain areas of human experience like sex. *Sexathon* designates a sexual intercourse which takes place in an extended amount of time. The imagery of sports is used to designate this concept thanks to the allusion to the footrace run on an open course of 42.2 kilometres. As a consequence of a process of semantic extension, the semantic components of the noun marathon are mapped onto sexual activity to refer to a sexual relationship characterized by great length and concentrated effort. Take the following example:

(48)   Two days ago I was on the receiving end of a 3 hour *sexathon* brought about by a huge blowup the previous day. (TAM, 20 November 2012)

In North American culture the vocabulary of baseball is a source of sexual euphemism. By virtue of the BASEBALL metaphor, sexual activities are described in terms of the bases in a baseball match. Here the sequence of 'running the bases' establishes, at a figuratively level, the degree of sexual intimacy achieved, from kissing to coition: *first base* 'mouth-to-mouth kissing'; *second base* 'manual stimulation of erogenous zones'; *third base* 'oral sex'; and *fourth base* (or *home run*) 'coition'. In this sequence of metaphors, the BASEBALL metaphor stands as a significant example of a cultural construct (Kövecses, 2006a: 69) rooted directly in American popular culture to talk about sex. Consider how this metaphor applies in the posting below to euphemistically refer to the first stages of sexual contact during adolescence:

(49) A lot of kids learn this stuff in high school. They're spending hours making out, a lot of deep kissing, *first base, second base,* etc. They spend time figuring out what works because they don't want to go all the way. They're not trying to reach the goal of the girl having an O, they're just having fun exploring each others' bodies. (MMSL, 23 August 2013)

Certain expressions use the imagery of sports to hide certain sexual practices which are especially subject to taboo. This is the case of the compound *water sports*, a lexical label which refers to a sadomasochist practice that consists of getting sexual pleasure by being urinated on.[13] This metaphorical compound appears in the following message, posted, significantly enough, in the subforum 'Paraphilias' of SDF:

(50) im a 22 male and for the last few years i have been acquiring lots of strange sexual aversions *watersports* lactation bestiality and rubbing against people in clubs sometimes. (SDF, 20 September 2012)

The use of *water sports* to refer to sadomasochist practices leads me to reflect on how euphemism works in the world of sadomasochism. The GAME metaphor plays a crucial role in the reference to practices in which pleasure is obtained from hurting or humiliating the sexual partner or from being hurt or humiliated during a consensual sexual encounter. Curiously enough, although sadomasochistic practices are violent and aggressive by definition, they are not conceptualized in terms of a violent act, but as a game.[14] From this it can be deduced that, if applied to sadomasochism, the domains of GAMES and SPORTS generate a stark contrast between the linguistic metaphor and its referent. Indeed, certain sadomasochist practices, however violent they may be, are seen in terms of a role play – a game in which the partners take particular roles and behave accordingly. As Murray and Murrel (1989: 6–7) write:

... sexual sadomasochism involves both 'wise practitioners' and 'willing victims' in a kind of role-playing activity that both people enter into for a mutual gratification of each other. It is an activity more suited to the theatre, in which players take on roles.

One of the most popular types of sadomasochistic practices derives from animal role playing: one of the sexual partners imitates animal behaviour, wears items like collars, bridles, saddles or leads (depending on the animal being imitated), and carries out tasks associated with animal behaviour. These practices are referred to with compounds in which the word *play* is included like *puppy play* in (51) and *pony play*[15] in (52):

(51) It is typically a male fetish. Out of all the fetishists on fetlife who list Transformation as a kink, or *puppy play*, 3/4ths are Male. I have no idea why, maybe it is similar to transvestitism. (SDF, 16 April 2013)

(52) I've searched, performed, viewed or participated in everything from CP, *pony play*, k9, rape, scat, ect ect. and when i saw it doesnt phase me its because some of it turns me on. other times its been no different than ironing a shirt. ... but, i did it, just to say i did or prove that i could. (SDF, 4 June 2013)

The metaphorical units in italics in the postings above do not only try to veil or mitigate the taboo concepts they stand for. It is evident that the poster in (52) does not use the compound *pony play* because of social or moral constraints. Cases like these demonstrate that sometimes it is very difficult to draw the line between euphemism and dysphemism; indeed, the lexical alternatives to taboo concepts can easily slide off into slang, as Epstein (1986: 59) notes. *Water sports*, *puppy play* and *pony play* are, in fact, slang lexical units from the field of sadomasochism and, as such, provide people who are involved or interested in these sexual practices a private code that reflects their particular sexual preferences. To this end, they resort to the game and sports imagery, which is common in the vocabulary of sadomasochism, as seen in some compounds in which the term *play* is included, namely *playmate* 'sadomasochist', *playroom* 'a room designed and equipped for sadomasochist scenes' and *playtoy* 'a device used in a sadomasochist scenario', as recorded by Murray and Murrel (1989). As Thorne (2005: 1) claims, slang 'derives much of its power from the fact that it is clandestine, forbidden or generally disapproved of'. Because of this, slang words from the world of sadomasochism are used to maintain group cohesiveness and group solidarity insofar as these words are commonly unknown to 'outsiders' and thus provide sadomasochists with a 'safe' (and obviously shared) lexical ground.

From the point of view of the relationship of slang words with the taboos they designate, rather than cases of euphemistic naming, the compounds with *sports* or *play* seen above belong to the category of *quasi-euphemism* in that they constitute alternatives to the taboo whose function is neither to mitigate or to save face (i.e. euphemism) nor to intensify the taboo with an offensive intention (i.e. dysphemism). These quasi-euphemistic names used by people who are involved in sadomasochistic practices are cases of 'cohesive' euphemistic units: they are a sign of social cohesion and in-group solidarity. Sadomasochism is a breeding ground for quasi-euphemistic labels and cohesive euphemism, the same as other more or less special or stigmatized activities like prostitution or delinquency which favour a vernacular use of language.

I will conclude this section by saying that sex is implicitly referred to as a social activity in all the occurrences of the GAME and SPORTS metaphor seen in this section. The social component of the sexual activity is highlighted for euphemistic purposes: sex is conceived of as something that people do consensually together, as an activity in which the participants are willing to play and follow certain rules of behaviour. From this viewpoint, the sexual intercourse can be considered as an acceptable model for social behaviour.

3.1.4 JOURNEYS

It is possible to avoid a direct reference to sexual topics by resorting to the SOURCE-PATH-GOAL image schema into which our everyday experience may be organized (Lakoff, 1987a: 275). According to this schema, a sexual encounter is understood as a process with a starting point, an end point and a time span. This, in turn, implies that the sexual relationship is seen in terms of a journey and the orgasm as its final stage, i.e. the end point of the journey. As Lakoff (1987a: 275) puts it, '[c]omplex events in general are also understood in terms of a SOURCE-PATH-GOAL schema; complex events have initial states (source), a sequence of intermediate stages (path) and a final stage (destination)'. In the JOURNEY metaphor this schema is used for euphemistic purposes: the source domain of JOURNEYS is employed to reason about the target domain of SEX in terms of a different domain of experience by virtue of the metaphor A SEXUAL ENCOUNTER IS A JOURNEY. The main meaning focus here is the idea of PROGRESS, of succeeding in reaching a goal in the figurative journey towards a destination. This metaphor therefore emphasizes the notions of progress and purpose. This central knowledge about the source plays a vital role in the way sexual relationships are conceived, as I will explain in what follows.

The SEX-AS-A-JOURNEY metaphor is a conventionalized specific-level metaphor in that it is specified in two ways: it presents both a fixed source and target domain and a fixed list of entities specified in the mapping. In fact, this schema transfers different attributes from the source domain of a JOURNEY to the target domain of SEX as a result of using the knowledge we have about journeys to talk about sex: first, the sexual encounter corresponds to the journey; second, the lovers are the travellers; and third, the final destination of the journey is reaching orgasm. These mappings of the JOURNEY metaphor underlie the posting below:

(53) I think men sometimes place too much emphasis on *reaching the destination* during sex, instead of *making the journey* pleasurable. The entire lovemaking and sex act is not about her reaching an orgasm. Its about both partners letting go, enjoying the sexual pleasure. (TAM, 17 November 2012)

The SOURCE-PATH-GOAL schema whereby sex is conceived of as a journey does not apply in the same way in all the linguistic metaphors detected in the sample. In the phrase *reaching the destination* in (53), the end point of the journey – that is, the ultimate goal of the sexual encounter – is highlighted. However, a phrase like *making the journey* in the same message refers to the act of being engaged in a sexual encounter. This different application of the SOURCE-PATH-GOAL image schema can be explained by the addition of profiling and a trajectory-landmark relation (Lakoff and Johnson, 1999: 33): either the destination can be highlighted, and thus identified as the landmark relative to which the motion takes place, or the motion itself can be taken as the landmark.[16] The profile-based distinctions that apply to the JOURNEY/DESTINATION metaphor can be analysed in reference to the domain of time (Verhagen, 2007: 50). The perspective from which the flow of time is viewed differs in the verbs that focus on the journey from those which emphasize the destination. In *making the journey* the process is represented as ongoing, in process, while the process that *reaching the destination* presents involves a change in the period of time being considered.

The euphemistic metaphor AN ORGASM IS THE END OF THE JOURNEY is based on a reoriented version of the primary metaphor PURPOSES ARE DESTINATIONS. As we move towards a destination in space we move towards a purpose in life. This primary metaphor arises from our experience of going to places we intend to reach and underlies any metaphor in which we talk about goal-oriented activities. As Lakoff and Turner (1989: 83–4) argue, this metaphor has a strong grounding in everyday experience. After all, the achievement of certain purposes usually requires going to a certain location. In this regard, reaching orgasm is metaphorically conceived as a purposeful activity through which one may reach a desired location. Despite the fact that this complex metaphor cannot be proven experientially, it is the product of combining primary metaphors together like PURPOSES ARE DESTINATIONS and ACTIONS ARE MOTIONS which are rooted in physical and sensory experience.

In the euphemistic reference to orgasm as reaching a desired location, *come* (and its variant *cum*) is equally applied to both males and females. This word, in constant use with a sexual sense since the seventeenth century (*OED*3), has lost its euphemistic capacity to refer to the taboo. However, *come* admits a non-dysphemistic use, as seen in posting (54) below – a significant example of the way the source concepts of JOURNEY and DESTINATION apply in real discourse. The poster here resorts to the image schema whereby the sexual climax is seen as the end point of a journey. If reaching orgasm is referred to as the act of 'coming', the person who is unable to experience climax is a 'no-comer'. Note how an orgasm as the final destination of the journey is euphemistically referred to by means of the vague word *there*.

(54) I've had a few muti-orgasmic women, and one that could (would) not *come* in front of anyone (only could *come* from masturbation). … With the *no-comer*, I was always thinking, "OK, this is the time she will *come*", and the muti-Os, it was, "Well she is almost *there*, I might as well give her #20". (FFF, 26 August 2013)

The underlying metaphor of orgasm as reaching a goal also applies in *completion*. This term conceptualizes sexual climax as the final stage of sexual activity, and connects this final stage to succeeding in reaching a goal. Consider the posting below:

(55) It sounds completely superficial to dwell on never getting oral to *completion*. But even that – we're talking about something you'd really enjoy. (MMSL, 7 April 2013)

Similarly, the euphemistic use of the JOURNEY metaphor in posting (56) below emphasizes the destination of the journey that the lover, figuratively speaking, embarks on. In this message, the abstract concept of orgasm, which does not really have a particular location, is associated with a place in space by virtue of the primary metaphor STATES ARE LOCATIONS (Lakoff and Johnson, 1980: 7). Indeed, the destination of the journey, which is left implicit in the linguistic realizations of the JOURNEY metaphor seen so far, becomes concrete: *finish line* ('get over to the finish line') and *paradise* ('get me to paradise'). The implications of these destinations of the journey are different, however. Whereas *finish line* implicitly transmits the idea of a reward and reaching a goal, in accordance with the use of the verb *finish* with the meaning 'achieve orgasm', the word *paradise* associates sexual climax with the ideal state for any Christian, which certainly includes hyperbole as part of the euphemistic material for the reference to orgasm.[17] Therefore, any skilful sexual partner can take you to Heaven through the sexual act.[18]

(56) Once he is aroused – but BEFORE [in capitals in the original] he *finishes* – you tell him: Baby I want you to do "oral", whatever it is that is for SURE [in capitals in the original] to get you over the *finish line* first. If he hesitates after you *get me to paradise* – I promise to bring you for a visit – and I will get you there whenever you want. (TAM, 9 January 2011)

Given that paradise is traditionally located up in the sky, an orgasm is euphemistically conceived as the climax of pleasure and happiness by virtue of the orientational metaphors HAPPY IS UP and GOOD IS UP (Lakoff and Johnson, 1980: 14–21). These metaphors are motivated by cultural and physical experiences associated with the upper vertical position: an erect posture of the body usually accompanies a happy emotional state.

In some cases, the final point of the destination is mentioned by means of a vague locative like the euphemistic *there*, as seen in (56) ('I will get you *there*'). The notion of getting 'there' as the end point of the journey with the meaning 'orgasm' also applies in the message below. The husband gets his wife *almost there* and then *walks away* and later *gets close* again, moving back and forth in that figurative journey by means of which the sexual encounter is euphemistically conceptualized:

(57) What my husband does is toys with me, *gets me almost there*, then *walks away*. He'll say we have to get dressed or we'll be late so we'll *finish* this later, then he toys with me in the car but not enough to *get close*, just enough to get my hopes up. (TAM, 27 August 2013)

I have also encountered a metaphorical label to refer to orgasm which has important implications at a cognitive level: *the edge*.

(58) If you want to please him in a sexual way and dont want to give oral or intercourse why not give him a nice sensual handjob ... I mean a nice slow teasing handjob pushing the right buttons that *takes you to the edge* a few times before climax, Its very intimate and I can tell you from

personal past experiences it the most intense orgasm both for girl and boy on this planet. (SDF, 13 September 2013)

By virtue of the JOURNEY metaphor 'the edge' represents, at a figurative level, the last stage of the journey before the traveller reaches his final destination, i.e. orgasm. The same cognitive basis applies in *edging*, a linguistic metaphor used for the designation of a practice which consists of stopping the sexual stimulation right before achieving orgasm. Consider the following message:

(59) It is great for myself to prolong the pleasure and delay the point of no return with *edging*, but not for my wife....she wants the climax without delay! (TAM, 28 August 2013)

The notion of 'edge' provides evidence for the existence of the image schema of sexual life and sexual relationships as a bounded region. The underlying ontological metaphor SEX IS A CONTAINER, which derives from the more general metaphor EMOTIONS ARE CONTAINERS, grounds the conceptualization of a sexual encounter as a bounded space which has an inside and an outside and is made of three parts, namely an exterior, an interior and a boundary (see 3.1.6 for details). This SPATIAL-CONTAINMENT schema leads to considering that sexual climax originates at the edge of the bounded space through which a sexual encounter is conceptualized, and happens beyond its boundary. Therefore, assuming that 'the edge' represents the last stage of sexual excitement, *get over the edge* alludes to sexual achievement in a rather subtle, hence euphemistic, way:

(60) I think that some women have a very difficult time reaching orgasm so that if you are that close and don't *get over the edge* it can be very frustrating. (TAM, 27 August 2013)

Not all metaphorical items within this metaphor focus on the final point of the journey to target euphemistically the topic of achieving orgasm. Another verb of motion, like *go* in the expression *go all the way*, does not refer to the act of achieving a sexual orgasm, but to the act of penetration during the sexual encounter. In the posting below, it is not the orgasm that is conceptualized as the final destination of the journey; rather, it is the act of penetration that is seen in terms of the journey. By conceptualizing penetration as the journey, the woman highlights the importance of penetrative sex:[19]

(61) We never go all the way! (advice needed). Whenever we make love (which isn't actually "making love" as we don't *go "all the way"*) we kiss, he might touch my boobs for a minute or two, then he touches me

"down there" within about 5 minutes (sometimes less than that) and I masturbate him at the same time. Whilst it's satisfying ... he rarely penetrates. (TAM, 22 May 2012)

Some metaphorical alternatives included in the JOURNEY metaphor focus on the journey itself, on the process of movement from one place to another along a path and leave the destination of the journey implicit, as seen in *make the journey pleasurable* (53). This is also the case of the verb *cruise (around)*, which refers to the act of walking about the streets in search of a casual sexual partner. Although commonly employed among male homosexuals, it is also used in heterosexual discourse:

(62) We *cruise around* looking for hookers, hitting strip clubs, and getting into bar fights. At least those are the good nights. (MMSL, 3 October 2012)

The world knowledge the language user possesses about a cruise provides the basis for the euphemistic reference to casual sexual encounters: first, a cruise is a pleasure journey; second, when we take cruises we stop at one port and then another, but rarely do we stop very long at any one. These characteristics of cruises are mapped onto the target domain of SEX to offer a view of casual sex as a pleasurable activity in which the voyage itself corresponds to the act of looking for sexual partners, and the ports where one stops correspond to the sexual partners. By looking at these entailments that this metaphor gives rise to, one can deduce that the metaphorical utilization of the source is partial: whereas the aspects mentioned are activated in the comprehension of the target domain, other components of the source domain are clearly disregarded. In the first place, although a cruise is a pleasurable way to travel, it involves going some place. This crucial aspect is ignored in the CRUISING metaphor, as its focus is on the journey, not the destination, which is left implicit. In the second place, there is therefore an element of passivity (see Turner, 1998: 35) in the source domain which is not mapped onto the target: cruising implies that the passengers can go nowhere by themselves, but where the ship takes them.

As seen in the postings used to illustrate the JOURNEY metaphor, there are two main versions of this metaphor at play: one emphasizes the journey itself and the other focuses on the destination. In the conceptual correspondences that the JOURNEY schema entails for both versions of the metaphor, the notion of the sexual encounter as movement from one place to another along a path plays a crucial role. This can be seen in the verbs of motion included in this metaphor encountered in the corpus, namely *come, go, walk, get to, get over* and *step out*. All these verbs map MOTION (as the euphemistic source domain) onto CHANGE (as the target domain) by virtue of the primary metaphor CHANGE IS MOTION, a metaphor which ranges over all the items that take JOURNEY as source domain.

3.1.5 ADVENTURES

The consideration of a sexual relationship in terms of an adventure implies that sex is conceived as an unusual and exciting experience, potentially hazardous and unpredictable, in which the lovers take part. From this perspective, sex is connected with the excitement commonly associated with living new experiences or with the taking of risks. That sex is an adventure can be gathered from Quillian (2009: 8):

> Every act of sex is an adventure. And not just in the clichéd, movie-romance sense, but in reality. One never knows what will happen between two people who love each other with all the passion, affection and occasional reptilian hatred that love involves.

One of the meanings of the metaphorical term *adventure* is 'extramarital sexual relationship'. In posting (63) below, looking for occasional sexual partners is considered a challenge, only at the reach of those who are willing to take risks. In this context, the term *adventure* fulfils a protective function that helps to maintain the poster's face: because of its vagueness in relation to the topic it stands for, *adventure* conceals the 'forbidden' or 'immoral' component of one-night stands:

> (63) I never included my wife's sexual health in my *adventures*! I could have given my wife a death sentence! Because I searched for fun! … It's terrible how we hurt the ones closest to us! (SDF, 27 April 2011)

In the same vein, the indeterminacy of the adjective *adventurous* contributes to its euphemistic effectiveness. Its concealing function avoids the undeviating reference to exciting sexual practices in the following message:

> (64) I never initiate sex … I'm too scared to try anything else as everytime I do, he loses his erection. It is frustrating for me as I like to initiate sex and I'm *adventurous*. I have spoken to him about it and he's said that my sex drive is higher than his. (SDF, 27 November 2013)

The commonplace knowledge of what an adventure involves provides the euphemistic basis for the reference to a wide range of sexual practices which are not within the limits of what could be considered conventional sex: threesomes, sadomasochism, homosexual relationships, swinging, etc. The ambiguity that characterizes the realizations of the ADVENTURE metaphor facilitates the euphemistic reference to unconventional sexual practices like frottage in (65). The entailments of the ADVENTURE metaphor are perfectly applicable to what rubbing one's body to strangers in a crowded area involves: a new, risky and unpredictable experience:

(65) Sometimes when my husband is at work ... I'll put on my white tennis skirt and wear it with a button-up halter top that I leave partially unbuttoned to show my lacy bra and cleavage ... Then I'll walk down the street to an underground metro station at rush hour and ride it. Worn in this manner, my tennis skirt is transformed into an incredibly sexy outfit. ... In the evening when my husband gets home and I'm still wearing that outfit, I tell him my *adventures*, which almost always lead to hot sex. (MMSL, 17 March 2011)

As seen in this posting, this metaphor is not restricted to occasional sexual encounters or unconventional sexual practices that are kept a secret. This metaphor also provides fertile ground for the euphemistic reference to those most daring or unusual sexual practices that may turn a physical relationship into an exciting experience in established couples.

The term *adventure* is commonly qualified by linguistic items from the target domain of SEX. When premodified by the adjectives *sexual* or *sexy*, the reader can deduce little from it. However, on some occasions the adjective used to linguistically qualify *adventure* makes the type of sexual component explicit, as is the case of *sadomasochistic* in the posting that follows:

(66) I got involved with a girl temporarily who also had a boyfriend other than I did. She took great pleasure in telling me about her *sadomasochistic adventures* with her boyfriend. I imagine this had a negative impact on my psyche. (SDF, 26 April 2012)

By virtue of the entailments that the metaphor SEX IS AN ADVENTURE gives rise to, a sexual encounter turns into a new experience with an uncertain outcome. The source domain of ADVENTURE adds an element of risk, fun and excitement, especially attractive for those lovers who are up for a challenge and willing to live new experiences. In this respect, the ADVENTURE metaphor coherently combines with the JOURNEY metaphor to portray a sexual experience as an exciting experience. After all, to set out on a journey also means engaging in new experiences and visiting new lands, which is likely to be a source of pleasure and enjoyment for the adventurous travellers who are willing to take risks. Both metaphors thus contribute to outlining a scenario in which the lovers are adventurers who engage in the challenge of raising their risk level and enjoying new experiences.

3.1.6 CONTAINERS

The CONTAINER metaphor is an ontological metaphor in which entities are seen as being made of three parts, namely an exterior, an interior and a boundary. The simple structure of a container is a powerful and pervasive element to reason about abstract entities insofar as it is closely related to our physical and bodily experience in the real world (Lakoff, 1987a: 267). However, the notion of a container used to conceptualize abstract concepts goes beyond this three-fold structure. It implies that expectations and inferences derived from our basic knowledge of containers are also mapped onto the target domain, namely what containers are used for, what boundaries are like, etc.

The SPATIAL-CONTAINMENT schema is euphemistically applied to different sexual topics, for example, anal sex. Given that we experience our physical bodies as containers of spatiality, our bodies are viewed as bounded and sealed spaces by virtue of the metaphor PEOPLE ARE CONTAINERS, a type of CONTAINER metaphor which maps the basic image schema of containers onto people (see Barcelona, 2003: 263). To refer to the anus as the *backdoor* in postings (40) and (67) below suggests that the container that conceptually represents our body can be penetrated from the exterior. However, the imagery of doors suggests that the boundaries of the container are kept intact: it is not a hostile invasion, but a welcome 'visit'. The view of the anus as a backdoor leads to a sexual reading of *backdoor activity* 'anal stimulation':

> (67) From what the OP said they indulge in some *backdoor activity* (fingers…) so it's not like she completely cut him off or is inflexible. I don't know how flexible she can be if him penetrating her there is painful for her. (TAM, 12 May 2012)

Similarly, the SPATIAL-CONTAINMENT schema provides the conceptual basis to refer to another tabooed part, the vagina, referred to as *a tuna cave* in (161). The world knowledge one possesses about caves (hollow, dark spaces with an entrance and an interior) provides the basis to consider the vagina in terms of a container of spatiality that provides access to the female body. The perceived similarity between a cave as a hollow and dark space and the vaginal cavity motivates the metaphorical reference to the female anatomy. The vagina is thus conceptualized as a container residing in the human body, with an interior which can be penetrated from the exterior since caves are not usually seen as sealed spaces. In this respect, Braun and Kitzinger (2001: 151) point out that terms belonging to the semantic category that they call 'space', i.e. form created by material absence, like *cave, tunnel* or *hole* 'implicitly constitute the female body as a landscape with attendant suggestions of exploration, colonization and ownership'.

The SPATIAL-CONTAINMENT schema coexists with the HEAT metaphor to conceptualize sexual intensity and passion in posting (68) below. This schema applies to the woman, who is depicted as a container for hot water, which is the force, in the form of liquid, that causes a pressure inside the container. The hot water inside the container is equated with sexual arousal at a metaphorical level by virtue of the metaphor LOVE IS A FLUID INSIDE A CONTAINER, a more specific version of THE EMOTIONS ARE FLUIDS IN A CONTAINER metaphor (Kövecses, 1986). In the advice given here on how to excite the sexual partner, the woman is represented as a pot in which water, i.e. the fluid that is associated with sexual excitement, must be heated by the sexual partner until it boils:

(68) At some point in there she is going to loyalty test if she wants to continue in the marriage. Just keep turning up the heat until she notices that the *pot* is full of boiling water. (MMSL, 16 August 2013)

The underlying conceptualization behind the pot as a metaphor for woman is THE SEXUALLY EXCITED PERSON IS A PRESSURIZED CONTAINER: a sexual stimulus or contact produces a force inside a person which causes that person to act and feel in a certain way. Sexual intensity is conceptualized as quantity, as amount of hot water which exerts a force on a container. As Kövecses (1986: 83) argues, 'the more fluid there is in a container the greater is the intensity of love'. Given that the change of location of entities takes place from inside to outside the container and not the other way round, as a logical consequence of the force exerted by the fluid inside the container, the boiling water will eventually come out of the pot. The spilling of boiling water represents sexual arousal as a very intense feeling.

In other occurrences of the POT metaphor the SPATIAL-CONTAINMENT schema applies in a different way. For example, in (69) *honey pot* refers to a vagina as a container for semen. In this way, *pot* transmits the notion of the vagina as receptacle for the penis and, by extension, for male sexual desire (Braun and Kitzinger, 2001: 151). The term *honey* here also has important implications at a cognitive level: it evokes the notion of the vagina as sweet and appetizing food by virtue of the metaphor WOMEN ARE SWEET (see 4.1.3).

(69) The single most important aspect of a woman, to a good deal of men, sits right between her legs. Sure, they like the rest. But without the *honey pot* they're out of there, you can bet your ass. (TAM, 29 January 2013)

The SPATIAL-CONTAINMENT schema can be also more generally applied to a sexual relationship. The view of sex and sexual encounters as a closed container leads me to consider that sexual activity implies a pressure from the interior of the container which may eventually perforate its boundary, a view which derives from the more general ontological metaphor EMOTIONS ARE FORCES. From this viewpoint, sexual excitement is the forceful substance in the container that provokes the explosion which perforates the boundaries of the region through which sex is conceptualized. Thus, the consideration of orgasm as an explosion in (70) and (71) derives from the PRESSURE metaphor, one of the FORCE metaphors proposed by Lakoff and Kövecses (1987) and Kövecses (1986 and 2005). In this regard, sexual arousal is conceptualized as a hot fluid in a closed container which is responsible for the pressure inside it. The EXPLOSION metaphor maps sexual passion onto the pressure provoked by the fluid, and reaching orgasm as the explosion of the container. This implies that sexual excitement itself is not open-ended: it has a limit point beyond which it cannot take up more heat and explodes. The conceptual analogy between anger and sexual excitement seems more than evident. In Kövecses's (1986: 17) words:

> The anger scale is not open-ended; it has a limit. Just as a hot fluid in a closed container can only take so much fluid before it explodes, so we conceptualize the anger scale as having a limit point. We can only bear so much anger before we explode, that is, lose control.

In accordance with the PRESSURE metaphor, the sexual partner is conceptualized in terms of the metaphor THE SEXUALLY EXCITED PERSON IS A PRESSURIZED CONTAINER, the same as happens in the representation of the woman as a pot in (68): a sexual contact produces a force inside a person which provokes a reaction in that person. Sexual excitement produces pressure on the container, which implies that the person engaged in the sexual encounter is not capable of any logical or rational judgement. Take the posting that follows:

(70) From my experience, my wife always has some sort of *explosion* of arousal during her orgasms ... easily detectable, from my standpoint, as I can feel her pulsate right afterwards. (TAM, 13 February 2013)

Here the explosion is depicted as a logical consequence of the intensity of the pressure that eventually perforates the boundaries of the container. The noun *explosion* acquires here hyperbolic overtones: it maps the effects of an explosion onto the physiological effects of orgasms (i.e. increase in muscle tension and rhythmic contractions in the sex organs) to describe sexual climax as a very intense experience, independent of the rational self. Similarly, *explosion* in (71) describes the experience of orgasm through prostate massage. In this case explosion is preceded by a definite article, which intensifies the connotative value of the noun:

(71) Absolute strong orgasms in my life are with finger up there ... such as getting a BJ [blow job] along with the prostate massage, it is quite *the explosion*. (TAM, 19 July 2012)

In the CONTAINER metaphor, the pressure of sexual passion leads to the symbolic representation of sexual climax as an uncontrollable force, ultimately responsible for the explosion, over which human beings have no control. This notion highlights a conception of sex as something for which a person is not responsible, the same as happens with the source domains which conceive sexual desire in terms of physical forces and insanity, as we will see later.

The CONTAINER schema is not only applied to sexual passion, it also provides the euphemistic basis for one of the most popular metaphors for homosexuality – that of the closet, a very powerful and evocative locative metaphor (Kushnick, 2012). The notion of closet derives from the idea of privacy (it implies something secret whose public exposure is a source of shame). In this metaphor, the parts that make up a container are used to talk about social issues and attitudes regarding homosexuality: the inside and the outside of the container conceptually represent the conventional and non-conventional society respectively. Here an image-schematic concept does not only structure our experience of space, it also structures a social and ideological concept by virtue of Lakoff's (1987a) spatialization of form hypothesis (see 1.1.1). Conventional society is thus seen in terms of a bounded and closed space (i.e. the inside of the container), which, applied to the homosexual community, implies pressure, oppression and difficulties to get out to the exterior (i.e. the outside of the container) and get sexually liberated. The underlying conceptualization can be postulated as follows: SOCIETY IS A CLOSET IN WHICH HOMOSEXUALS ARE LOCKED UP. Remaining in a closet means being locked away, even hidden from the outer world. In fact, a closet can only be open from outside and the interior is not accessible to public eye: it is behind doors. What is more, the 'closeted' person is defined by the condition of being inside a closet and living in a non-social space, in a kind of underworld. All these components of the CLOSET domain paint a picture of homosexuality in terms of isolation, sense of shame, loneliness, etc. as a consequence of the social rejection that the closet embodies (Rodríguez González, 2008a: 233).

The view of society in terms of a closet has inspired different verbal usages to euphemistically refer to homosexuality.[20] The expression *come/get out of the closet* is lexicalized with the meaning 'reveal one's condition of homosexual'. By contrast, *be in the closet* and *closeted* designate homosexuals who have opted for concealing their sexual orientation, whereas *semi-closeted* refers to those who have not totally revealed their sexual identity. The social rejection against homosexuals is clearly seen in the posting below, in which a male homosexual who has not revealed his sexual identity considers himself as being *closeted*:

(72) My parents think that people like me are abominations. So, for obvious reasons I'm *closeted*. I've only *come out* to my sisters and a couple of trans-friends. I'm terrified of my parents, especially my mom ... the disgusted way she talks about LGBT people. (SDF, 29 September 2013)

Although the CLOSET metaphor is socially accepted as a polite and non-offensive means to refer to homosexuality, the expression *come out of the closet* is also used in its abbreviated form *come out* in (72) or even *out*, which implies, as Ayto (2007: 108) suggests, an 'extra euphemistic effect'. These are cases of 'double euphemism' insofar as they are the result of two euphemistic processes: the first one achieved through a semantic resource (metaphor) and the second one through a formal device (shortening). Both processes contribute to the protective function of euphemism.

In accordance with the CLOSET metaphor, homosexuals who have revealed their sexual orientation are said 'to be out of the closet'. The note of joy that dominates the posting that follows is evident; after all, if being in the closet is equated with isolation and social rejection, being out of the closet is supposed to be a source of happiness:

(73) Oh, and welcome ... or should I say, glad you're *out of the closet*! I hope you can turn things around, but either way, YOU [in capitals in the original] are sitting pretty my friend, and you need to start knowing it and acting like it. (MMSL, 16 August 2013)

The use of abbreviated forms in the discourse of homosexuality as happens in (72) does not always respond to a euphemistic intention on the part of the speaker. A case in point which derives from the CLOSET metaphor is *out and proud*. This expression has become a trendy label to identify those who have revealed their sexual and gender identity without holding back and are proud of it. This expression, which undoubtedly deserves part of its success to its rhymed structure, is connected with the gay liberation movement and with the so-called 'Gay Pride', a movement through which gay activists try to claim their place in society. In spite of the euphemistic origin in the CLOSET metaphor, the effect of *out and proud* is not to mitigate or hide the sexual condition of homosexuals whatsoever. Rather, this expression is used by gays, lesbians, bisexuals and transgenders in their self-characterization. In this respect, the CLOSET metaphor is the origin of quasi-euphemistic labels used by people belonging to the GLBT community as a sign of cohesion within a group with the same sexual orientation or gender identity.

The CAGE metaphor – derived from Weber's (1958) analysis of the role of the individual in modern contemporary society – is another version of the CONTAINER metaphor with a stronger emotional impact than the CLOSET metaphor. Also based on the notion of an interior (i.e. conventional society), an exterior (i.e. non-conventional society) and boundaries, this metaphor is a more powerful tool for understanding sexual repression imposed by social norms. Through the CAGE metaphor, conventional society is considered as a bounded and closed space limited by bars (the idea that comes to mind is that of iron bars) which are equated with social boundaries at a metaphorical level. The image of the cage and the iron bars implies pressure, oppression and lack of freedom. This leads to a metaphor that can be postulated as SOCIETY IS A CAGE IN WHICH PEOPLE ARE LOCKED UP. Consider the following message:

> (74)   Many women are sexually repressed when they are younger due to parental upbringing, religious beliefs, what they have been taught, etc. I am soooo happy *to have come out of my cage* so to speak. (TAM, 3 November 2013)

For the poster of this message the moral and religious values of traditional society are conceived of as a cage which conceptually represents the force of sexual repression on women. As a logical entailment of the metaphor, the image of existence within a cage behind iron bars inevitably leads to consider society as a prison from which it is very difficult to escape.

3.1.7 PHYSICAL FORCES

By virtue of the PHYSICAL FORCE metaphor, sexual activity is portrayed as magnetism or electricity. These metaphors are grounded in the knowledge of the effect these forces may have on human beings, as for most people the effects of physical forces have no grounding in their direct experience. The notion of an external agent over which a person is not responsible provides the euphemistic basis for this conceptualization. In fact, the source domains of ELECTRICITY and MAGNETISM emphasize the fact that sex is something over which people have no control and no choice. Accordingly, the notion of passivity features heavily in the realizations of this metaphor. This ultimately implies that the person affected by the force is not even responsible for her behaviour, which may ultimately lead to justify certain reactions. As the PHYSICAL FORCE metaphors underlie the idea that the lover is a passive individual who falls prey to the intense force of lust, the main meaning foci of this metaphor are PASSIVITY and INTENSITY. The poster in (75) makes use of the domain of ELECTRICITY to conceptualize an orgasm:

> (75) For a long time I didnt realise what all the fuss was about, I much preferred a good hard F****** ... and go down on me, and I had one of the best orgasms of my life, *real fireworks electric shock* type stuff!! (FFF, 8 January 2013)

By describing an orgasm as an electric shock, the physiological effects of sexual climax are emphasized. Here the partial utilization of certain aspects of the source domain comes into play: the dangerous effects of the electric shock as a consequence of the exposure to electricity (burns, difficulties in breathing, heart failure, etc.) are disregarded, whereas the view of electricity as a strong source of energy that passes through the body is highlighted. The view of orgasm as an electric shock acquires hyperbolic overtones: to consider sexual climax in terms of a shock coming from an electrical source – and thus as a life-threatening experience – obviously implies an exaggerated reference to the effects of orgasm. The domain of ELECTRICITY does not only reference the achievement of orgasm, but also sexual attraction, represented in (76) as 'crackling sparks'. Also of note is the occurrence of the fire-related metaphor *ashes* in reference to lack of desire after a period of intense sexual activity:

> (76) I get what you are saying, there is a good chance my marriage is over and these are just the last few *crackling sparks* right before all that's left is *ashes*. (MMSL, 13 November 2013)

The consideration of sexual desire as an irresistible attraction is also conveyed by resorting to a powerful physical force: magnetism. The notion of magnetism as a physical phenomenon by which a material exerts an attractive force on another is transferred to target sexual attraction. For example, in posting (77) below, a woman's attraction is considered by her husband as a magnetic force with the power to fascinate men:

(77) Some women's smiles *attract* men like moths around a light bulb. My wife is one such woman. At one time she worked on check-outs. Her queue was generally three times longer than others … They all wanted to be in her presence, to see her smile and talk with her if just for a little while. It's charisma, appeal, allure, *magnetism* and sure many a man will think it's for him when in reality it is "just" who she is. (TAM, 14 December 2012)

The underlying notion here is that the sexual attraction that the woman exerts on men is an uncontrollable force that dominates them, who inevitably fall prey to her charms. This is linguistically realized by means of the verb *attract* and the noun *magnetism*. The woman has the power, through her physical presence, to attract men in the same way as certain materials attract others.[21]

In summary, this conceptualization is the source of euphemistic items that are halfway between the so-called protective and provocative types: they mitigate and, at the same time, highlight a particular aspect of the sexual topic being referred to. In fact, the PHYSICAL FORCE metaphors hyperbolically represent sexual desire as a material force that is impossible to dominate. In this regard, the person who feels sexually attracted is a victim to her own sexual desire, the same as happens with NATURAL PHENOMENA metaphors, as we will see in what follows.

3.1.8 NATURAL PHENOMENA

The metaphors that evoke natural phenomena base their euphemistic capacity on the association between sex and a wild and irrational nature. The same as happens with PHYSICAL FORCE metaphors, the notion of passivity features in NATURAL PHENOMENA metaphors: the lover is conceived as someone who obeys a strong force and cannot do anything against it (Kövecses, 1986: 90). There are two groups of metaphors that make use of natural phenomena as source domains: WATER and WEATHER metaphors.

WATER metaphors are employed in female representation of desire in American erotic fiction for women, in which they contribute to portray 'a world of watery passion that throbs through its characters' (Patthey-Chavez, Clare and Youmans, 1996: 81). One of the lexical materializations of this metaphor encountered in the sample is *wave*. This term, related to the image of an excessive flow of water, leads to the consideration of sexual pleasure as an external force, as an intense and overwhelming feeling over which the sexual partner has no control. Although the image of water that *wave* transmits in the two postings below is that of an irrational and chaotic event, the purpose and effect of this metaphorical item is far from being dysphemistic.[22] The imagery of a flow of water is used to euphemistically designate the achievement of orgasm (*ongoing wave*) in (78) and the sexual pleasure preceding orgasm (*waves of pleasure*) in (79):

(78) I guess because I'm a guy, its one and done, then a refractory period – but I just don't relate to how you can call an *ongoing wave* an orgasm, to me the receding sensation is equal part to the climax. (TAM, 23 July 2012)

(79) The last time she'd come so close to orgasm while giving another oral pleasure … she was shocked by her *waves of pleasure* that raced through her. (FFF, 10 October 2011)

The WAVE metaphor is not always realized in the same way. By virtue of the partial nature of metaphorical mappings, a particular element of the source domain of WAVES may be highlighted whereas the other(s) remain hidden. In (78) the concept is construed by the poster as ongoing, with no abrupt changes in the period of time in which it takes place. In fact, the phrase *ongoing wave of orgasm* evokes the body moving against the rhythmic movement of the sea and transmits an image of a quiet and peaceful flow of water capable of provoking sexual pleasure. However, in (79) the effect of *waves of pleasure* is more intense. Orgasm here is not brought about in a peaceful and gradual way, but as the consequence of a violent force capable of overwhelming the person who experiences it. The notion of uncontrolled water that comes to mind is more evident in posting (80) below, in which waves are rolling breakers that surfers ride. This message is highly significant of the way this version of the metaphor conceptualizes sexual encounters and orgasms:

(80) You know when you're in the ocean *riding waves*. The current is building and there's a good chance you can catch a good *wave* and ride it all the way to the sand. But it ends up being a *roller*. Still fun and still enjoyable and some women seem to only get *rollers*. Nothing bad about a roller. The trouble is they're so subtle. When I get *rollers* they are satisfying and enjoyable. But what I like best is to have a couple of *rollers* followed by a *super awesome crashing wave* that not only carries my all the way back to shore, but makes me fight to stay in one piece as I *ride it out*. That kind

of orgasm takes a lot of practice and my guess is that you and your girl will get there. (TAM, 13 February 2013)

Here the image of waves as uncontrolled water conceptualizes orgasm as an intense experience. The sequence of adjectives that qualify *water* (*super awesome crashing*) makes the effect of water especially intense and greatly contributes to the main meaning focus of the metaphor to conceptualize sexual climax: INTENSITY. In the hyperbolic description of an orgasm presented in (80) we observe the mappings that underlie this posting, namely, the sexual partner is a swimmer riding waves, the sexual activity corresponds to riding waves and the rollers are the sensations of sexual pleasure preceding orgasm.

The idea of sex and sexual desire as an irrational force seen in the case of *wave* is also noticeable in another metaphorical occurrence of this metaphor: *torrent* in the phrase *torrent of passion*. This is illustrated in the following message:

(81) The more you stand up to her, calmly, dispassionately, but resolutely, the more attractive you become to her on a primal level. If you continue with this, you can expect the dam to break and a *torrent of passion* will head your way from her like you have never experienced. (TAM, 18 September 2011)

The irrational and uncontrolled force of water is capable of breaking the dam, in a very powerful image that deliberately transmits the notion of sexual desire as a strong and intense feeling. Desire is, as Deignan (1997: 25) puts it, associated with an external force which seems to invade and possess the person who experiences the feeling and turn her into a 'passive experiencer of desire, overwhelmed by the force of a dominant partner'. Also of note is the co-ocurrence of the adjective *attractive* as a realization of the PHYSICAL FORCE metaphor (see 3.1.7). In the same vein, the adjective *torrented* emphasizes the notion of intensity and irrationality characteristic of extremely hard porn:

(82) I would pack a TB external drive full of *torrented* porn and edge for six or seven hours at a time in a dark hotel room. (MMSL, 8 March 2013)

Weather-related metaphors are also used to conceptualize sexual issues in particular terms. The WIND and STORM source concepts have a common experiential basis which transmits the idea of sex as a powerful, destructive and uncontrollable force. This combination is intended to highlight the intensity of the sexual attraction, its devastating power and the lack of control of those involved in it. The word *whirlwind* in the posting below portrays a relationship in which sex is an example of the destructive power found in nature:

(83) We only dated for 11 months before we married. It was a *whirlwind romance*. That is part of the problem, I suppose. Our relationship was very good at that point. (TAM, 18 November, 2011)

The image of a 'whirlwind romance' emphasizes the notion of sexual desire as a kind of invader, as an external and devastating force capable of provoking changes beyond the control of those involved in the relationship (Deignan, 1997: 25). This idea of desire as a potentially dangerous and malicious agent ranges over all the WEATHER metaphors seen in the sample consulted. For example, in (84) *storm* transmits the idea of a restless, even violent sexual passion longing to burst forth over which the person has no control. By transferring the attributes of a storm to the lover, the partner is depicted as someone sexually passionate and likely to arouse his wife:

(84) I have a pretty good history too. But my husband is just the perfect *storm* of being physically attractive, amply endowed and really talented with the way he touches me ... I've never had a better lover. (TAM, 14 June 2013)

The metaphors of natural phenomena describe sexual experiences and sexual passion as an intense, even destructive force for those involved. Hence the main meaning foci that characterize the way sexual issues are represented through these metaphors are INTENSITY and DESTRUCTIVENESS. These features of the source domain are mapped onto the target domain because they are the most basic and widely accepted knowledge about such strong natural forces as water and weather.

3.1.9 FIREWORKS

FIREWORKS is a source domain with hyperbolic overtones used in the conceptualization of orgasm.[23] The word *fireworks* first appeared with a sexual sense in the nineteenth century in the expression *draw his fireworks* 'to make a male ejaculate' (Sánchez Benedito, 2009). The exaggerated view of orgasm that the pyrotechnic image conveys is used by the psychological theorist Vivienne Cass (2004: 285) to explain to her readership how a woman feels during orgasm: 'How will this [an orgasm] feel? It may seem like tiny fireworks are exploding briefly inside you. Or it may feel as if a whole fireworks display is lighting up your body.' In Cass's words, an orgasm is depicted as an explosion that lights up the woman's body. In this sense, the intensity that this source domain transmits coexists with the domains of the PRESSURIZED CONTAINER and LIGHT insofar as fireworks emit an explosion that is accompanied by *bright lights*. In the posting below a woman describes the way she experiences her orgasms by means of the interrelation between these two domains:

(85)   When DH presses the right buttons, my head/feelings/attention just isnt there. The *fireworks* are in a whole different area and I like the *bright lights*. ... So maybe I cant tell because my head/body already *exploded*. ... All i know is that the inside nerve endings on the female anatomy are nothing compared to the outside ones, and those of many other places on a girl's body. (MMSL, 17 September 2013)

Here the imagery of fireworks compares sexual climax to an exploding array of light and colour. The explosion imagery is thus intended to show that experiencing an orgasm is an explosion of bright light, much as happens with fireworks in the night sky. Given its hyperbolic nature, this metaphor is the source of provocative euphemisms: *fireworks* and *bright lights* are inspiring and revealing ways to refer to an orgasm.

Similarly, both the domains of ELECTRICITY and FIREWORKS coexist in the description of sexual climax as 'one of the best orgasms of my life' in (75). The powerful image of a current of electricity passing through the body is increased in this posting by resorting to the noun phrase *real fireworks*, which leads to the consideration of an orgasm as an overwhelming and extremely intense feeling, in accordance with the hyperbolic overtones that characterizes this domain.

3.1.10 ILLNESS and INSANITY

The same as the domains of PHYSICAL FORCES and NATURAL PHENOMENA already commented, those of ILLNESS and INSANITY lead to the consideration of lust and desire as overwhelming feelings that lovers cannot control; what is more, the use of these source domains to target the topic of sexual arousal implicitly transmits the idea that lovers are ultimately victims of their own lust. Following Kövecses (1986: 88), the ILLNESS and INSANITY metaphors derive from one of the principles that we have in our folk model of love and, by extension, sex: 'There is a limit beyond which the physical effects of love impair normal functioning'. In fact, these metaphors are grounded in the world knowledge the language user possesses whereby excessive sexual desire, beyond the limits of rational behaviour, makes us physically and mentally unable to function normally.

There is metonymy involved in the LUST IS INSANITY metaphor: the links between the folk theories of the effects of lust and the effects of insanity provide the basis for the sex-related euphemistic metonymy INSANE BEHAVIOUR STANDS FOR INSANITY, which in turn leads to INSANE BEHAVIOUR STANDS FOR LUST. These are cases of the source-in-target metonymy type in which the source domain representing the effects of insanity is seen as a consequence of the matrix domain of LUST. In this way, it provides mental access to a more complex scene which includes passion and lust beyond limits thanks to the domain expansion cognitive operation that characterizes this type of metonymic associations (Ruiz de Mendoza Ibáñez, 2011). This metaphor therefore highlights the physiological and mental effects of insanity (lack of control, obsession, talking and behaving irrationally, etc.) to describe sexual arousal. In the following message the poster describes his sexual partner as 'crazed' in reference to his lover's state of uncontrolled sexual excitement, which stands in sharp contrast to his calm and rational behaviour during intercourse. Note the use of the colloquial expression *go nuts*, also included in the LUST IS INSANITY metaphor:

(86) Its me being the calm and rational one while the other is out of control and *crazed*. ... I'm playing the role of passive observer, even though I'm actually involved. By that I mean I like it because I get to just watch her *go nuts* without having to *go nuts* myself. (MMSL, 28 August 2013)

Similarly, in the posting below sexual attraction is described in terms of insanity through the adjective *insane*. The phrase *insane passion* provides a euphemistic way to refer to an addictive, even compulsive sexual behaviour which once led to significant conflict and distress for the partners involved:

(87) We both want the long term, so we are not as much about the *insane passion* we once had, and more about fixing what broke so the passion can naturally come back. (TAM, 3 November 2013)

By virtue of the INSANITY metaphor, the cause of insanity is the cause of lust, and a lustful person cannot behave normally, and has no reaction over her behaviour, as seen in (87). This leads to consider that the resultant actions of the EMOTION IS INSANITY metaphor are of application to the LUST IS INSANITY metaphor in order to describe the emotional effects of sexual arousal: the normal person becomes insane and the rational self becomes irrational. From this perspective, lust is seen as some kind of psychological force capable of affecting a person's behaviour and reactions. Table 3.2 (adapted from Kövecses, 2003: 74) shows how the INSANITY metaphor targets the concept of LUST as an emotion.

Table 3.2 Metaphorical Mapping of LUST as an Emotion

Metaphorical mapping	Force tendency	Resultant emotional effects
Source: Insanity	Intense psychological force	Normal person becomes insane Rationality becomes irrationality
Target: Lust	Sexual arousal	Normal person becomes sexually aroused

The mapping of insanity as an emotion implies that an emotional effect on a human being like sexual arousal may be considered in terms of the physiological and mental effects it provokes as a form of energy. That this is so can be gathered from Lakoff (1987a: 391): 'In the INSANITY metaphor, insanity is understood as a highly energized state, with insane behaviour as a form of energy output.' Such uncontrollable output of energy inevitably leads to loss of control, agitation and irrational behaviour. From this it can be deduced that the main meaning foci of the LUST IS INSANITY metaphor are INTENSITY and IRRATIONALITY. Therefore, it would be more precise to restate this metaphor as LUST IS AN INTENSE AND IRRATIONAL FEELING. In fact, the source domain of INSANITY is based on the commonplace knowledge we have about the effects of insanity pointed out before to highlight the intense and irrational feeling that lust provokes as a form of energy applied to the body. In (88) the intensity that this domain transmits is evidenced in the description of the lustful person as a 'sex maniac', a metaphorical label which depicts lust as an emotion with the highest degree of intensity capable of transforming people into individuals obsessed by sex, dominated by a powerful force they cannot control.

(88) My x wife seemed to share your view. She always acted like I was a *sex maniac* for wanting to make love frequently. However, I agree with those whole believe sex in a marriage is a normal, natural, great thing. (TAM, 14 June 2011)

Although in the postings provided as examples for this metaphor so far insanity is portrayed in adverse terms, certain realizations of this metaphor may admit a quasi-euphemistic use and acquire positive, even jocular overtones. For example, the compound adjective *sex-crazed* (89) and the adverb *madly* in the phrase *madly in lust* (90) refer to lustful women who are likely to lose control when involved in a sexual relationship. Here the physiological and mental effects of insanity, which are, strictly speaking, negative for the individual (going wild, behaving irrationality, etc.) are, however, considered as a way to make the sexual encounter more intense and exciting. In this way, the emotional state of being insane is not actually viewed as dangerous or harmful but as a source of pleasure for their sexual partners:

(89) I think this is a little like some of the threads here from the guys maping for a couple of weeks or months and expecting their wives to turn into *sex-crazed* wives that desire them. (MMSL, 6 August 2013)

(90) Husband couldn't be happier, but darn, peeing around till your 40's to have this kind of revelation is a bit ridiculous! Now I want to dress & act like an 18yr old seductive *madly in lust* girlfriend. (TAM, 3 November 2013)

Closely connected with the INSANITY metaphor, I have detected cases of the use of the domain of ILLNESS to conceptualize sexual desire.[24] In the adjective *sick* and the phrase *sick with lust* in (91) the source domain which represents the effects of illness is considered as a consequence of the domain of LUST. In this sense, it provides mental access to a more complex scene which includes lust thanks to the domain expansion cognitive operation characteristic of source-in-target metonymic associations. These materializations of the ILLNESS metaphor single out the fact of being sick to talk judgementally about sexual excitement and lust. In the posting below, the metaphor encodes the poster's disapproval towards a woman's lustful and selfish behaviour:

(91) Please tell me you aren't considering anything right now other than finding out how deep this rabbit hole goes. Otherwise you are just falling prey to a manipulator. She is *sick* John, *sick with lust* and selfishness. You won't get through to her unless you actively pursue tearing down her lies and deceptions and show her who she has really turned into. (TAM, 6 April 2013)

In the following example *fever of sensuality* constitutes a more elaborated realization of the ILLNESS metaphor for sexual desire:

(92) Last night I was awake till 4am with the *fever of sensuality* (high blood pressure). My Buddhist teacher said that the most skillful thing to do with sex is to let it go. (SDF, 28 June 2013)

Here, significantly enough, the ILLNESS metaphor combines with the HEAT metaphor to offer a portrait of the poster's sexual arousal. Fever, as a conflation of both metaphors, is seen as the most evident manifestation of a state of illness that affects the person who experiences the feeling of being sexually excited. This linguistic metaphor is a manifestation of the primary version SEX IS HEAT (see

3.1.2), which is experientially grounded, that is, based on our daily experience whereby one of the most characteristic effects of sexual excitement is an increase in body temperature. In the posting above, sexual desire is not merely equated with being hot; the increase in body temperature is hyperbolically conceived of as a feverish state in which heat negatively affects the human body. In this way, *fever* depicts sexual arousal as on one of the top levels of a cold–hot scale used to emphasize the intense and overwhelming feeling the person is experiencing. Despite the exaggerated view of reality that *fever* transmits, this term performs a clear euphemistic function, as the poster is able to refer to an intense, addictive and obsessive sexual excitement in a socially acceptable way. *Fever* therefore is a provocative euphemism: it provides a euphemistic and, at the same time, highly emotional alternative to the taboo of sexual excitement through the metonymic association THE PHYSIOLOGICAL EFFECTS OF SEXUAL EXCITEMENT STAND FOR SEXUAL EXCITEMENT, which operates in (92) as a combined realization of both ILLNESS and HEAT metaphors.

As seen in *fever*, many linguistic items included in the INSANITY metaphor do not really aim at hiding the topic of sexual arousal, but to emphasize lust and passion in a socially acceptable way. This is why linguistic metaphors like *sex maniac* in (88) or *sick with lust* in (91) are cases of provocative euphemism: they attract attention by highlighting the intensity and irrationality of lust, and at the same time function as socially acceptable alternatives to the sexual topic.

3.1.11 HEALTH

Despite the fact that the domain of HEALTH (and LACK OF HEALTH) is obviously related to the aforementioned domain of ILLNESS, the metaphor that takes HEALTH/LACK OF HEALTH as source domain deserves a separate analysis. It is true that both metaphors provide evidence of the connection between bodily experience and the realm of sex, and in both of them the body becomes especially salient, given that one is really aware of one's bodily existence when it starts malfunctioning and one gets ill (Boers, 1999: 49). However, the HEALTH metaphor does not focus on the physiological effects of sexual excitement, unlike the ILLNESS metaphor. Rather, it provides an evaluative view of sex and sexual desires, as happens with many occurrences of the DIRT metaphor (see 3.1.12). Given the evaluative power of the domain of HEALTH, it usually reveals more about the values of the person who uses it than about the reality being talked about.[25]

The HEALTH metaphor is experientially grounded: it makes use of our physical, embodied experience to understand the notion of morality. Lakoff

(2003: 97–8) offers a series of correlations between what he understands by morality (basically 'well-being') and ordinary experiences that lead to a series of primary metaphors for morality. In his view, the correlation 'It is better to be healthy than to be sick' provides the conceptual basis for the primary metaphors MORALITY IS HEALTH and IMMORALITY IS DISEASE, which, out of the metaphors that define morality proposed by Lakoff, are the ones that apply in the HEALTH/ LACK OF HEALTH metaphors detected in the corpus. In fact, the notion of disease is figuratively used to establish the moral status of certain sex-related practices, whereas the idea of health alludes to a moral sexual behaviour.

The adjective *unhealthy* is the materialization of the LACK OF HEALTH metaphor which carries a more evident value judgement. On account of its indeterminacy, unhealthy is used to euphemistically refer to a wide range of undesirable or potentially threatening sexual practices or behaviours which are not 'within the "normal" limits of conventional acceptability', as Deignan (1997) puts it.[26] For example, in (93) this adjective alludes to a sexual behaviour considered potentially dangerous both for the person who experiences it and for her partner. *Unhealthy* qualifies the phrase 'sex life' to avoid direct reference to a sexual behaviour that deviates from what is considered as 'normal' and conventional:

(93) Lay out your case in a reasonable manner and emphasise that your *unhealthy* sex life is placing undue strain on your marriage. (MMSL, 6 December 2012)

Similarly, in posting (94) below, *unhealthy* makes reference to certain pernicious sexual habits that one may acquire at an early age, too delicate to talk about openly, such as obsession with sex, addiction to pornography, excessive masturbation, etc.

(94) Of course, exposure to sex at an early age can also cause an *unhealthy* focus on sex. (FFF, 19 June 2013)

In the following example the taboo that *unhealthy* aims to veil is different. The euphemistic phrase 'unhealthy sexual attention' indirectly refers to some form of sexual molestation suffered by the poster during her childhood or adolescence:

(95) I was raised Catholic and it was implied that sex is something animals do so it makes you less human so "Uncivilized" and "Barbaric" and only "uncouth people" had sex, plus I received *unhealthy* sexual attention from men when I was too young and emotionally immature to handle it so my experiences reinforced the messages I had received from adults. (MMSL, 19 October 2013)

Here *unhealthy* provides a negative evaluation of desire and sexual practices considered, for some reason, immoral or potentially harmful. On account of the critical intention of the person who posts the message, *unhealthy* can be considered as a quasi-dysphemism.

Another occurrence of the LACK OF HEALTH metaphor that takes ILLNESS as source domain is the adjective *sick*. Unlike (91), in the following quotation *sick* is not metonymically applied to the effects of sexual excitement. It is used, in the same way as *pervy*, to criticize the immoral behaviour and attitude of the participants in the thread.

(96) Everyone knows it's you perverted scum that's posting the *pervy* remarks about Maddox, kind of telling when this site is the ONLY [in capitals in the original] site that has such remarks. You people are *sick*, *sick* in your minds. (FFF, 26 March 2013)

Let us consider now the adjective *healthy* as a materialization of the HEALTH metaphor. If immorality is equated with a sick and unhealthy sexual behaviour, as seen in the previous postings, being healthy is logically associated with having a moral sexual behaviour by virtue of the conceptualization MORALITY IS HEALTH. Consider how *healthy* describes a traditional and moral way (based on Christian dictates) to deal with sexual issues with children:

(97) Our church has many of the traditional views on sex, but they don't push it as being bad, more like it's not appropriate before marriage. And they are good at having the porn conversation with kids, which I do think is *healthy*. (MMSL, 18 November 2013)

In the following message *healthy* depicts a view of sex as within the limits of conventionality and moral norms in contrast to the 'clubs and anonymous staff' that the poster refers to:

(98) It is exactly like kicking booze ... and I imagine any other addiction but alcohol is the one I know best. Managed 1.5 yrs now sober. But I dont seem to be able to go more than a couple of weeks without acting out. Am not talking about normal *healthy* sex but clubs and anonymous stuff. (SDF, 7 December 2013)

Here the poster is clearly establishing a disparity between 'normal' and conventional sex, considered as 'healthy', and other sexual practices like prostitution and swinging, which are regarded as addictive and potentially harmful. Without a doubt, sexual practices like those alluded to in (98) could have been conceptualized on moral grounds by means of metaphorical adjectives of abjection included in the DIRT metaphor that I will discuss next.

3.1.12 DIRT

The metaphors that take DIRT as source domain perform different communicative functions. Although this domain carries, strictly speaking, negative connotations (Allan and Burridge, 2006: 41) and is usually employed to express negative value judgements of sexual behaviour, the fact remains that most of the materializations of the DIRT metaphor detected in the sample are not used with a dysphemistic purpose; otherwise said, they do not pose any threat to the poster's face. This is the reason why these metaphors are included in the present chapter, although, as I will explain in 4.1.1.4, the DIRT metaphor also admits a purely offensive use.

According to Lakoff (1987a), DIRT (or FILTH in his terminology) metaphors are grounded in our perceptual experience of the physical world and are central to our thinking. They are basic-level metaphors, or in Grady's terms, primary metaphors. The experiential grounding of DIRT metaphors is based on our common experiences with certain substances that stain our body, clothes, houses, etc. The proximity of the bodily organs of sexual desire and stimulation to the anus helps to understand the consideration of tabooed language related to these bodily organs as dirty (Turner, 1999). These metaphors are also grounded in our experience with objects or substances which are out of their right place. In this sense, Lizardo (2012: 370) argues that dirt is conceptualized as an entity which subverts an ideal arrangement of things in our world by virtue of the metaphor DIRT IS MATTER OUT OF PLACE, based on the hypothesis first proposed in the 1960s by the anthropologist Mary Douglas (see Horlacher, 2010: 8–9).

The same as DIRT metaphors, moral concepts are embodied in our physical and recurrent experience of the world. In fact, Lakoff and Johnson (1999: 309) claim that the notion of dirt serves as the experiential source for the notion of immorality: in the metaphor of moral purity, the body is seen as a source of impurity, which is equated with filth at a metaphorical level. In this respect, Lakoff (2003: 98) argues that the ordinary experience 'It is better to be clean than to be dirty' gives rise to the metaphor IMMORALITY IS FILTH which directly applies to DIRT metaphors. Accordingly, the main meaning focus of the DIRT metaphor is IMMORALITY. This notion of dirt (in contrast with morality, which stands for 'cleanliness') is used to establish the moral status of certain sex-related behaviours which are associated with different manifestations of dirt by virtue of the metaphor IMMORALITY IS FILTH or, in Lizardo's (2012) words, MORAL IMPURITY IS UNCLEANLINESS.

A common realization of this metaphor is *dirty*, a descriptive adjective qualifying a wide range of nouns. The most common is *talk* in the phrase *dirty talk* which refers to the use of sexually explicit tabooed words to sexually stimulate the partner during (or as a prelude to) coition (see Allan and Burridge, 1991: 149).

> (99) It's pretty common that *dirty talk* makes good girls uncomfortable. That *dirty* part either consciously or subconsciously bothers them. (MMSL, 27 November 2013)

Here the phrase *dirty talk* proves to be a safe way to indirectly refer to very sexually graphic language, highly obscene, including the so-called four-letter words. The adjective *dirty* is also used to qualify nouns like *conversations*, *messages*, *fantasies* or *secrets*, as seen in the forums, by adding sexual and sometimes obscene overtones to them. For example, *dirty* qualifies the phrase *night club* meaning 'brothel' in (100). In this posting, rather significantly, the DIRT metaphor coexists with *unhealthy*, a materialization of the LACK OF HEALTH METAPHOR which equates lack of morality with lack of health. The notion of immorality is thus reinforced by the combination of two metaphors that conceptually structure the sexual topic with a strong sense of disapproval:

> (100) I sometimes suffer from *unhealthy* sexual desires. I imagined that I am a singer at a *dirty* night club. The owner of the club assault me in return of letting me sing on stage. He touched my vagina and clitoris with his *dirty* fingers from behind. (SDF, 16 February 2012)

The use of *dirty* in *dirty fingers* is somehow ambiguous. The adjective here is halfway between the figurative sense of *dirty* 'immoral' and its literal sense 'not clean'. Probably in the poster's 'unhealthy' fantasy, both meanings overlap.

In (101) *dirty* is used to take a disapproving view of a liberal attitude to sex, deemed inappropriate by traditional and conservative standards, especially in females, who are supposed to have a more rigid sexual moral code than males:

> (101) Many women have been raised to be 'good girls' and that type of behaviour is *dirty* or unladylike. (TAM, 26 December 2013)

Similarly, *dirty* transmits a negative value judgement towards a particular attitude to sex based on moral grounds in posting (102) below, one of the replies in a thread entitled 'Male female male threesome'. A woman who has engaged into a non-conventional sexual practice is referred to as DIRTY with the underlying implication of 'immoral':

(102) I was turned off when I realised this woman was into this. It's just too *dirty*. (TAM, 31 December 2013)

Other realizations of the DIRT metaphor similarly used to make negative evaluations of sexual behaviours are *smutty* and the stronger *filthy*:

(103) Does she masturbate? If so, how often? Does she read *smutty* stories? Does she fully understand that you are thinking about ending this marriage? (TAM, 22 November 2013)

(104) It is possible that her mother is filled with hate for men and taught her that all men are *filthy* animals who only think of one thing. (MMSL, 23 November 2013)

Metaphorical items like *dirty*, *smutty* and *filthy* in the three postings above do not only perform a purely euphemistic or concealing function. These adjectives also categorize certain sexual behaviours like the participation of a woman in a threesome (102), pornography (103)[27] or a man's obsession with sex (104) in the moral domain by providing a view of sexual issues which is not approved of by the poster. Therefore, they belong to the category of quasi-dysphemisms.

These realizations of the DIRT domain demonstrate that the connotations of words are exploited for evaluative and ideological purposes; in fact, the adjectives included in this domain present negative connotations consistent with their literal meanings which are used with an evaluative aim in mind (Deignan, 2010: 363). In this sense, the DIRT metaphor proves to be a major source for the so-called derogatory euphemisms, i.e. those which carry a sense of disapproval or negative value judgement, and are used with a critical purpose. This type of quasi-dysphemistic references are widely considered as socially acceptable means of introducing a criticism in polite discourse in that they deliberately avoid certain words which could be considered too harsh or impolite, thus providing a 'safe ground' for the speaker's critical or offensive intention.

Before finishing the discussion on the metaphors of abjection, I must note that the metaphorical items included in the DIRT metaphor also admit a quasi-euphemistic use; that is, they are not always intended to talk judgementally about a particular sexual behaviour. Some occurrences of the DIRT metaphor are used to describe sexual practices that the poster evaluates in a positive way. This implies, as Deignan (1997: 37) argues, 'a covertly positive evaluation of sexual desire and erotic talk'. This is the case of the adjectives *dirty* and *smutty* qualifying *stories* in the following message:

(105) I think you should encourage your wife to fantasize ... Letting her know you'd like to know is different from asking her to tell you. How about you encourage her to read some *dirty smutty stories* as a jumping off point. (TAM, 12 February 2013)

However, some realizations of the HEALTH metaphor do not really imply a 'covert evaluation' of sexual practices that the poster approves of as part of the sexual excitement. Consider the posting that follows:

(106) She says I have unrealistic expectations created by porno. Don't other couples have *nasty* sex with oral, toys, butt play, *dirty* talk, etc.? I've never experienced any of those things ... I'm 36 and really want to *get nasty* before I get too old. (TAM, 22 December 2013)

Rather than providing a covert evaluation, the adjectives *dirty* in *dirty talk* and especially *nasty* in *nasty sex* and *get nasty*, overtly emphasize the view of sex that *nasty* and *dirty* imply: an attitude open to exciting experiences and new ways to enjoy sex to the full as part of the poster's sexual awakening.

3.1.13 FALLING

The FALLING metaphor is analysed in relation to love and sexual desire by Deignan (1997: 25). She argues that this conceptualization takes the form of a container in expressions like *fall in love* (understood as the beginning of sexual love) by virtue of the metaphor LOVE IS A CONTAINER. Although I have nothing to contend with this, I believe that in some realizations of the FALLING metaphor, like *fall for (someone)* 'be sexually attracted to someone', it is the metaphor SEX IS A CONTAINER that is at play. Take the following example:

(107) Why do many women *fall for* a man in uniform? Because a uniform, especially a man with a badge and a gun, is SO VERY ALPHA [in capitals in the original]. That's very attractive for a lot of women. (TAM, 30 September 2013)

Here sex is seen as a place you may fall into, driven by your sexual urges and by the sexual attraction of men in uniform, a source of sexual excitement for the woman who posts the message. The sense that *fall for* acquires in (107) has nothing to do with sentimental affection; rather, it is a purely physical attraction motivated by the idea of adventure and excitement that the man in uniform brings to the woman's mind. After all, uniforms (and related items like guns, badges or truncheons) are a fetish for many people; indeed, this kind of paraphernalia is used in sadomasochistic games as a means of sexual excitement. It is also worth noting that *fall for* presents negative connotations. As Rivano Fischer (2011: 26) claims, this verb transmits 'a sense of the inevitable', and suggests that sexual desire may become a dangerous and harmful force for the person who experiences the feeling. The analogy is the following: if when you fall you may be physically hurt, when you fall for someone you may be emotionally hurt. In this respect, this author considers that love and sex can be conceptualized as a trap, even as an accident.

Let us consider another realization of this metaphor: *(be) head over heels for*. Following Deignan (1997: 26), this expression highlights the upheaval and sense of chaos that for some people may suppose the experience of being sexually attracted to someone.[28] If we look at the orientational metaphors RATIONAL IS UP and CONTROL IS UP (Lakoff and Johnson, 1980: 14), we may deduce that the spatial orientation of this metaphorical expression transmits a total loss of irrationality and lack of control over one's feelings and behaviour. In this regard, *head over heels for* can be considered as a materialization of the metaphor DOWN IS BAD: feeling sexually attracted towards someone is equated with irrational behaviour at a metaphorical level. This irrational state seems more evidently expressed by *head over heels* than by *fall for*, as the 'down' component of *fall for* suggests that being out of control is a temporary event, whereas in *head over heels* the state of being 'down' is more permanent. This expression conceptualizes sexual attraction in the posting that follows:

> (108) Amazing sex life with a woman I was *head over heels* for. Then one day… bam. Our bouncing off the walls and not being able to keep our hands off each other sex became once-a-night duty sex. A lot of the passion and sensitivity just kind of disappeared. (MMSL, 28 November 2012)

In summary, the FALLING metaphors imply a loss of rational thought and control over one's emotions and reactions. These metaphors also suggest that those who get sexually excited become victims of lustful desire, and inevitably yield to the feeling as something that they cannot take control of. These notions of lack of control and irrationality underlie the conceptual structure of many of the metaphors used to talk about sexual desire seen in this chapter.

3.2 Reaching the intended euphemistic meaning

No cognitive approach to metaphor in discourse would be complete without considering the interpretative process which allows for the euphemistic force of metaphors. As seen in Chapter 2, according to the relevance-theoretic approach to metaphor interpretation, the meaning of a metaphorical item does not usually precede the metaphor. Rather, it derives, first, from a deliberate use of the metaphor on the part of the speaker; and second, from the hearer's capacity to grasp the sex-related intended meaning through the construction of *ad hoc* or pragmatically inferred concepts out of lexically encoded ones.

Conventional euphemisms (see 2.3.2) facilitate the interpretation of metaphorical words and expressions and the recognition of the poster's euphemistic meaning in the discussion boards. As Abrantes (2005: 88) argues, conventional euphemistic units are intentionally used to avoid the direct reference to a taboo topic and are perceived as such; that is, both the taboo referent and the speaker's concealing intention are decoded and recognized in discourse. According to Abrantes, the very fact of *concealing*[29] a taboo topic derives from what she calls a 'tacit agreement' between both discourse partners which enables the hearer to recognize the speaker's intended meaning. This tacit agreement between the participants in internet forums seems to govern the interpretation of the sex-related euphemistic metaphors in the postings seen in 3.1. The forum members tend to use conventional metaphorical items to deliberately introduce sexual topics in their online discussions. By resorting to conventional euphemistic metaphors, understanding is guaranteed by means of semantic collaboration, which results from a tacit cooperation between the parties involved in the communicative act whereby the reader will recognize the poster's euphemistic intention through pragmatic operations of *ad hoc* concept construction. The agreement that facilitates the interpretative process of conventional euphemism relies 'on the basis of a delicate compromise: hide it, but do not make it vanish' (Abrantes, 2005: 94). This kind of discourse complicity makes it possible to introduce the taboo topic in the forums, however unmentionable it may seem.

In the process of reaching the intended euphemistic meaning, ambiguity plays a crucial role. A euphemistic label keeps its attenuating force alive insofar as it suggests that there is a distasteful or inappropriate meaning underneath the literal meaning of the word. Chamizo Domínguez and Sánchez Benedito (2000: 40–1) argue that a metaphorical term acts as a euphemism because, in a given context, it is capable of generating an ambiguity which evokes a sexual topic behind the literal meaning of the utterance. For example, words like *wave* and *storm* through which sex is conceptualized as a natural force (see 3.1.8) can be understood both in terms of their literal meaning of weather-related phenomena and in terms of their sexual meanings; both senses are active and contribute to meaning in communication. Ambiguity, however, does not impede effective communication; rather, it is the intentional and deliberate ambiguity of linguistic metaphors that leads the participant in the forum to explore beyond the literal meaning and arrive at the connotations hidden under the metaphorical disguise. By paying attention to the ambivalent nature of metaphors, the forum member will be in a position to recognize the euphemistic force of the metaphorical unit and, by way of the pragmatic processes of narrowing or broadening of the lexically encoded meaning, arrive at the poster's intended meaning and satisfy his expectation of relevance.

RT explores the way languages users infer the speaker-intended meaning in a given context, as explained in 1.3. The forums' members are able to construct pragmatically derived concepts out of lexically encoded ones in sex-related euphemistic metaphors. By supplying contextual assumptions, and thanks to the world knowledge people possess, they are expected to easily capture the sexual meaning intended by the person who posts the message. In doing so, they succeed in getting adequate effects for no unjustifiable effort. The interpretation of metaphors is thus seen as an active process of dynamic inferring motivated by the addressee's expectation of relevance which leads to the construction of an *ad hoc* concept for the occasion necessary to bridge the gap between the literal and the metaphorical (intended) meaning. Consider the following online interaction:

> (109) P-1: I had a fling, of sorts, before the wife and this woman unlocked certain desires in me. First, she would watch her undress and then *play with herself.*
> P-2: That is HOT [in capitals in the original]. (TAM, 30 September 2013)

Here P-1[30] resorts to the GAME metaphor to refer to female masturbation. In the course of the inferential process of interpretation, P-2 uses the commonplace knowledge he has about games in order to move away from the literal meaning of *play with herself* to the intended meaning 'masturbate' (hence the displacement effect of euphemism commented in 2.2 comes into play). To this end, P-2 constructs a pragmatically inferred (or *ad hoc*) concept which presents a broader denotation than the encoded concept of the metaphorical phrase: 'playing with oneself' is not only a game, but a sexual activity in which there is an element of fun and innocence involved. By inferring these semantic components, the utterance becomes relevant in the context of (109).

As a consequence of the pragmatic adjustment of the concept PLAY WITH ONESELF, two related *ad hoc* concepts are generated: PLAY WITH ONESELF* and PLAY WITH ONESELF**: These pragmatically inferred concepts are not identical to the concept encoded by the metaphorical expression, although they share some of its inferential properties, e.g. sex as a playful and innocent pastime. Table 3.3 (adapted from Wilson and Sperber, 2004: 616) outlines the inferential process of euphemistic interpretation of *play with herself*.[31]

In the same posting the inclusion of the HEAT metaphor to conceptualize sexual excitement ('That is HOT') stands as evidence that P-2 has recognized P-1's euphemistic intention. By resorting to the metaphorical item *hot*, P-2 invites P-1 to construct the pragmatically inferred concepts HOT* and HOT** which share some of the inferential properties of the lexically encoded concept HOT (one of the effects of sexual excitement is that of heat). However, as a consequence of the pragmatic operation of loosening, the concept decoded presents a broader denotation: it does not only transmit heat, but also intensity (HOT*) and sexual arousal (HOT**). Thus, in the course of his inferential process

Table 3.3 Inferential Process of Euphemistic Interpretation: *Play with herself*

P-1 has said: 'First she would have watched her undress and then play with herself'		Embedding of the decoded logical form of P-1's utterance into a description of P-1's ostensive behaviour
P-1's utterance will be relevant to P-2		Expectation raised by recognition of P-1's ostensive behaviour and acceptance of the presumption of relevance in the context of the online interaction
P-2's utterance will achieve relevance by explaining his reaction to P-1's comment		Expectation raised by P-1's utterance. Such an explanation would be relevant to P-1
If she plays with herself, she must be having fun		First assumption to occur to P-2. Implication of P-1's utterance
'Playing with herself' is a playful sexual pastime	*ad hoc* concept PLAY WITH ONESELF*	Enrichment of the logical form of P-1's utterance plus background knowledge
'Playing with herself' is an innocent sexual pastime	*ad hoc* concept PLAY WITH ONESELF**	

of interpretation, P-2 uses cognitive operations that allow him to construct *ad hoc* concepts which reveal P-1's euphemistic intention, and construct a new and alternative concept for the occasion that satisfies P-1's expectations of relevance. P-2's utterance, in turn, invites his interlocutor to recover a set of explicatures for the concept HOT, and the whole process starts again.

The result of the interpretative process that takes place in (109) is that, despite its ambiguous nature, the sexual meaning of *play with herself* is immediately grasped by P-2, who contributes to the online discussion by agreeing on the sexual excitement that the situation described provokes, far from any misunderstanding as a consequence of using the domain of GAMES to conceptualize the taboo of masturbation. This phrase provides good evidence for the fact that there is no need for the hearer to consider the literal meaning of the utterance, as it may be more time- and effort-consuming than the euphemistic meaning intended in the context of the online discussion. The inferential process of meaning detection derived from *play with oneself* invites the hearer to reach the euphemistic meaning intended by the speaker ('masturbate') and thus contributes to the relevance of the utterance in its context of use. In this sense, metaphor is a useful and economical way to achieve a range of effects which are deliberately communicated by P-1.

The same process applies to one of the metaphorical realizations of the HEAT metaphor which highlights the intensity of the sexual excitement by intensifying the effects of heat: *melt*. Take the posting that follows:

> (110) P-1: I told her I was not taking no for an answer and started to passionately kiss her and then kiss her neck and nibble on her ears. She instantly *melted* ...
> P-2: That would make me *melt*... (TAM, 29 September 2013)

Obviously enough, P-2 does not take the adjective *melted* literally. He goes beyond the literal meaning of the word, which he associates with a particular instance of a well-established metaphor in the language whereby sex and sexual excitement are equated with heat and its effects. Thus, P-2 is able to create an *ad hoc* concept after having activated contextual information and encyclopaedic assumptions related to the physiological effects of sexual contact. The *ad hoc* concept MELT* is broader than the lexical meaning encoded by the concept MELT insofar as its denotation extends beyond the domain of HEAT to touch on the domain of SEX. In this way P-2 manages to reach the euphemistic meaning intended: sexual foreplay leads to sexual arousal on the partner, who eventually yields to her lover. The enrichment of the logical form of *melt* that is at play in the *ad hoc* concept construction in (110) establishes a contrast between the literal meaning of the verb and the taboo of sexual arousal. This contrast determines the mitigating capacity of the euphemistic item, and allows for an immediate recognition of the *ad hoc* concept MELT* intended by P-1. The characteristic displacement of euphemism explains how the metaphorical use of a term is justified even though this use, taken literally, may be false. Obviously enough, however *hot* 'sexually aroused' the woman referred to in the posting above may feel, she is not likely to disintegrate because of it. The hyperbolic reference involved in the use of *melt* is mitigated via a pragmatic operation of understatement on the part of the reader (Ruiz de Mendoza Ibáñez and Peña Cervel, 2005; Herrero Ruiz, 2009: 153–4) in order to make it reasonable and thus contextually relevant.

I will move on to the interpretation of those euphemistic labels which are not so easy to recognize. In posting (111) below, the metaphorical words *journey* and *explosion*, although not fully lexicalized with a sexual meaning, are not understood in their literal sense. Rather, these words acquire the euphemistic meanings 'sexual encounter' and 'orgasm' respectively intended by the participants in a thread in which a woman (P-1) asks for advice on how to improve her sexual life.

(111) P-1: I have spent the last 26 years of my marriage lying about having orgasms with a man who thinks sex is over once he has an orgasm. … Thoughts ideas?
P-2: read a while back that if a woman is capable of being aroused at all, she is capable of having an O. So remember that on your *journey*. It's old, but the book For Yourself was a help to me. Every other resource made it seem like the second you touched yourself you would *explode*. For some of us, it can take quite a bit of practice and experimentation.
P-1: … I will try the suggested ideas and appreciate them. (TAM, 2 September 2013)

The immediate recognition and interpretation of *journey* and *explosion* as cases of sexual euphemism results from the discourse cooperation between P-1 and P-2. P-1 recognizes, with little interpretative effort, the sexual meanings behind the apparently 'innocuous' words *journey* and *explode* by inferring the euphemistic, sex-related *ad hoc* concepts JOURNEY* and EXPLOSION* via a process of pragmatic adjustment of the lexically encoded concepts JOURNEY and EXPLOSION respectively; in fact, P-2 readily accepts the advice given by P-1 as a way to reach orgasm.

Let us see now the case of *flame-throwing*, a compound adjective derived from the noun *flamethrower*, a weapon used to project incendiary fuel (see 3.1.2). At first sight, this adjective, which belongs to the field of war, has nothing to do with the taboo of sex. However, in (32) *flame-throwing* is automatically associated with conventional metaphors used to talk about the sexual taboo: SEX IS HEAT and SEX IS WAR. The flame element makes it evident the allusion to the flames of Hell ('There are some other flames you might be worth considering') that the poster evokes, assuming that the reader shares this commonplace knowledge. Thus, the nature of the metaphor itself, together with the information provided by the context and the reader's encyclopaedic and cultural knowledge, contributes to the creation of the *ad hoc* concept FLAME-THROWING* which bridges the gap between the encoded meaning of the utterance ('a device which projects ignited incendiary fuel') and its intended meaning ('sexual provocation') so that ostensive communication takes place. By decoding *flame-throwing* in the context of the reader's encyclopaedic knowledge of fire, which involves religious images of heat, fire and Hell traditionally used in our culture, the participant in the thread is invited to derive a number of contextual implications created by the poster of the message. Thus, *flame-throwing* is to be interpreted by virtue of two metaphors: the primary metaphor which associates sexual excitement with heat as its main physiological effect; and also in terms of the WEAPON metaphor, which acts as the instrument to punish a lustful woman for inciting sexual intercourse.

When dealing with the interpretative process of conventional sex-related euphemistic units, it may be argued that many of the metaphorical items seen in this chapter, especially those of a hyperbolic nature, are semantically incomplete with regards to the state of affairs they describe. In other words, terms like *melt*, *explosion* or *flame-throwing* involve, according to Chamizo Domínguez (2005: 9), a certain degree of 'categorial falsity'. Otherwise said, euphemistic metaphors are, strictly speaking, forms of partial lying. This implies a violation of the Gricean maxim of Quality ('Do not say what you believe to be false. Do not say that for which you lack adequate evidence' [Grice, 1975: 46]). From this viewpoint, the use of linguistic metaphors might lead, strictly speaking, to false information. However, if we accept a relevant-theoretic approach to metaphor understanding, we should bear in mind that metaphors do not intend to transmit information that may be considered as true or false, but information that is contextually *relevant*. In fact, addresses try to make sense of metaphorical utterances without actually stopping to consider the degree of literality, truth or falsity of the utterance in question. In this sense, Carston (1997: 113) argues that the propositional form of metaphorical utterances constitutes, in itself, a literal and true interpretation of the thought the speaker tries to communicate; obviously enough, from this viewpoint, Grice's distinction true/false is totally irrelevant.

This is especially true in the case of the interpretative process that guides euphemistic hyperbolic utterances. Although hyperbole transmits an exaggerated view of reality which is impossible in the real world, hyperbolic expressions are not considered as deliberate lies. In this respect, Clark (cited in Herrero Ruiz, 2009: 50) claims that hyperbole depends on 'a kind of joint pretense in which speakers and addresses create a new layer of joint activity'. As part of this tacit agreement the reader somehow mitigates the exaggeration conveyed by the literal statement so as to make it reasonable and contextually relevant via a process of understatement. According to McCarthy and Carter (2004), the success of hyperbole depends precisely on the listener's acceptance of extreme formulations and the creation of impossible worlds, which are considered, at the same time, compatible with the state of affairs in reality thanks to the mitigation operation commented. In this way, the reader's cognitive operations during the interpretative process lead him to grasp the poster's intended euphemistic meaning of hyperbolic metaphors. For example, during the interpretative process of the term *explode* in (111) it is inferred that the woman's body is not going to explode, however intense the orgasm may be. In the same way, the woman alluded to in this posting is not likely to disintegrate because of the physiological heat provoked by sexual passion, however 'hot' she may become.

As metaphorical language does not mirror a state of affairs, the tacit agreement between discourse partners is an important factor when it comes to unravel the figurative meaning of the utterance beyond its apparent categorial falsity or its ambiguity. As Burkhardt (2010: 369) argues:

> ... the truth or falsity of a euphemistic proposition can only be judged from the point of view of shared knowledge of common consent with regard to the completeness of the relevant info. Euphemisms, therefore, can be true (or false) only against the background of a certain norm of expectation.

If we accept this position, euphemistic metaphors – be it hyperbolic or not – can never be considered as deliberate lies; rather, they are halfway between truth and falsity; or, to put it differently, their apparent falsity leads to the generation of an *ad hoc* concept which eventually invites the reader to capture the euphemistic sexual meaning intended and construct an alternative concept with a different (broader) denotation. Accordingly, the fact that any metaphorical utterance involves categorial falsity, and thus supposes a violation of the Gricean maxim of Quality, is irrelevant when it comes to the interpretation of euphemistic metaphors. On this inferential approach to metaphor interpretation, metaphorical units like *play with herself, melt, explode* or *flame-throwing* create an expectation of relevance which is satisfied by deriving alternative concepts that are communicative-relevant regardless of their truth or falsity. From this viewpoint, truth-conditions do not really play a role in a relevance-theoretic approach to metaphor interpretation. As Blakemore (2002: 77) claims:

> Linguistic semantics does not deliver truth-evaluable propositional representations, but rather schematic logical forms which are taken as input by pragmatic inferences constrained by the principle of relevance.

In summary, the sexual concepts underneath the lexically encoded concepts are pragmatically constructed in the reception process with very little processing effort on the part of the reader in spite of the indeterminacy of some euphemistic labels. Indeed, metaphorical understanding seems to be rather effortless in the corpus consulted: the forums' members seem to have no difficulty in grasping the intended (euphemistic) meaning of sex-related metaphorical utterances, which are, as one may suppose, meaningful for those taking part in an online forum devoted to sexual issues. In this situation, they immediately appreciate the metaphorical utterances as relevant contributions to the thread; after all, the fact that the participants in the online discussions are willing to cooperate, participate and, in many cases, help one another greatly favours the identification of the intended euphemistic meaning of metaphorical utterances.

4

Dysphemistic Metaphors

The language of sex is not limited to good-sounding expressions aimed at presenting sex-related topics according to the conventions of politeness expected in social communication, as seen in Chapter 3. The paradoxical nature of the taboo provokes conflicting emotions towards forbidden concepts: not only may speakers opt for presenting the taboo topic in a socially acceptable way, they may also decide to highlight its most pejorative traits with an offensive aim. Indeed, the sexual taboo generates a wide range of pejorative alternatives to sex-related topics, however unmentionable, obscene or insulting the verbal expressions may be. It is precisely on account of their potential for the expression of offence and disrespect that lexical units from the sphere of sex are chosen. In fact, the so-called 'dirty words' have a special fascination for us and exert a powerful effect on language use. According to McEnery (2006: 6), sex is a potent source for offence and negatively loaded language: It constitutes, as this scholar puts it, a chief 'object of offence', i.e. an aspect of reality identified as problematic.

Metaphorical language is a powerful resource to shape taboo concepts for dysphemistic use. According to Casas Gómez (1986: 86), metaphor is a 'dysphemistic engine' insofar as it emphasizes those features of the concept being dealt with that are most likely to cause offence. In fact, most metaphorical labels are not neutral in their evaluative stance; rather, they are ideologically charged. And sex provides the raw material for the offence transmitted through figurative language, as we will see in this chapter.

4.1 Dysphemistic sex-related domains

As happens with euphemism, the type of source domain used and the particular components that are given priority influence the dysphemistic value of the metaphor. In the following sections I will focus on the domains the forum members use to talk about sex disparagingly.

4.1.1 ANIMAL

The association of people with animals and with animal behaviour and instincts is a potent source of disrespect and offence. The ontological metaphor PEOPLE ARE ANIMALS puts in correspondence human and animal attributes which are mostly behavioural. This conceptualization is grounded on people's knowledge and perception of the natural world, which is figuratively employed to refer disparagingly to human beings. The ANIMAL metaphor is also grounded on ethnobiological taxonomies of animals which classify them according to five parameters: habitat, size, appearance, behaviour and relation of the animal to people (Wierzbicka, 1996). These parameters constitute key factors in the interpretation of the non-literal senses of animal vocabulary.

To explain how the ANIMAL metaphor is applied to humans, Kleparski (1990) coined the term *zoosemy* (subsequently developed by later works, most notably Kyeltyka and Kleparski, 2005), i.e. the phenomenon whereby certain animal categories (mammals, insects, amphibians) are used to characterize human qualities and behaviour. This phenomenon goes hand in hand with the process of semantic pejoration: when people are identified with animals, they are being degraded insofar as the ANIMAL domain tends to describe undesirable human characteristics and habits.

According to Kövecses (2002: 125), OBJECTIONABILITY and UNDESIRABILITY are the main meaning foci of the metaphors HUMAN BEHAVIOUR IS ANIMAL BEHAVIOUR and PEOPLE ARE ANIMALS. This implies that ANIMAL metaphors capture the most objectionable and undesirable characteristics of human beings, which makes them particularly effective for dysphemistic purposes. In fact, the association between animals and humans tends to carry negative evaluations: the ANIMAL domain generates undeviating terms of abuse that dehumanize and degrade people, especially women, and undermines their social and personal status; it reduces the sexual act to a purely animal activity devoid of any affection or tenderness; it depicts humans as devoid of any rational capacity and judgement; and it associates the sexual behaviour of humans with that of animals, as we will see in the postings provided as examples.

Especially useful to understand how the ANIMAL domain represents humans is the 'Great Chain of Being', a cultural model which locates the different entities in a hierarchy based on the attributes and behaviours of each one (from humans at the top, animals, plants, complex objects to physical things at the bottom). In Lakoff and Turner's (1989: 166–7) words:

> The Great Chain of Being is a cultural model that concerns kinds of beings and their properties and places them on a vertical scale with 'higher' beings and properties above 'lower' beings and properties ... The Great Chain is a scale of forms of being – human, plant, inanimate object – and consequently a scale of the properties that characterize forms of being – reason, instinctual behaviour, physical attributes and so on.

The Great Chain of Being has a tremendous explanatory power: it allows us to comprehend human character traits and behaviour in terms of non-human attributes; that is, it explains why we speak of higher forms of life (humans) in terms of lower forms of life or existence (animals, plants and objects). Following Kövecses (2002: 126), the Great Chain of Being is 'a hierarchy of things and corresponding concepts from a lower source to a higher target or from higher source to a lower target'. When humans are conceived of as animals, the conceptualization proceeds from a lower source domain (ANIMAL) to a higher target (HUMANS); hence its dysphemistic power.

The ANIMAL metaphor is a powerful dysphemistic means to conceptualize what the male heterosexual dominant ideology considers 'marginal' groups, namely male homosexuals and, above all, women. Some men, mostly male chauvinists, have an ideologically biased view of women and gays, which is reflected in the metaphorical terms they use to talk about them. Of course, the choice of the animal name applied to humans is not at random. Words from the animal kingdom such as *bunny, vixen* or *lioness* are ways to refer disparagingly to women and transmit sexist and discriminatory attitudes on account of some undesirable animal features which are used as the basis for the dysphemistic load of the metaphor. The type of discrimination involved and the pejorative force of the ANIMAL metaphor depend on two factors: first, on the animal used as source domain; and second, on the components of this domain that are given priority, as we will see in what follows.

4.1.1.1 SMALL FURRY ANIMALS

To consider women in terms of small furry animals like bunnies, kittens or pussycats has important implications at a cognitive level. First, this domain carries connotations of playfulness. However, the game is seen from the man's perspective, as an activity to be enjoyed only by men, whereas women are left aside from the enjoyment. Second, this metaphor implicitly transmits feelings of protection and superiority on the part of men, which ultimately leads to a view of women as sexual objects at men's disposal. Third, this metaphor is motivated on physical grounds: the small size of the animals used as source domain suggests that women are smaller and weaker than men and therefore easy to handle (López Rodríguez, 2009: 83). And fourth, the connection of women with furry animals also derives from the salience of pubic hair on female body (Allan, 2012: 29).

The pejorative attitude to women that this metaphor transmits is evidenced in the posting below, in which the term *bunny* depicts a view of the woman as a sexual object:

> (112) Keep your home, your assets, your friend wife, just find a nice young *bunny* for the side. Be perfectly clear with the wife that this is not your first choice, but you had no choice in the relationship being the way it is now, due to her inactions over time. (MMSL, 22 August 2013)

The link between *bunny* and sex is well established in the language. The sexual connotations of the rabbit have been exploited *ad nauseam* by its association with the icon of the world-famous North American men's magazine *Playboy* (later Playboy Enterprises, Inc.), which used a bunny as its logo and symbol of sexiness.[1] In an interview held in 1967 (cited in Levy, 2005) Hugh Hefner, the founder of *Playboy*, explained his choice of the rabbit as *Playboy*'s logo:

> The rabbit, the bunny, in America has a sexual meaning; and I chose it because it's a fresh animal, shy, vivacious, jumping – sexy. First it smells you then it escapes, then it comes back, and you feel like caressing it, playing with it. A girl resembles a bunny. Joyful, joking, … The *Playboy* girl has no lace, no underwear, she is naked, well-washed with soap and water, and she is happy.

From Hefner's opinion, it seems evident that the image of the woman that *bunny* brings to mind is that of a playful girl, ready to provide some enjoyment to men. The components of the source domain that are highlighted offer a stereotype of the woman as sexually attractive, amusing and readily available as entertainment.[2] The connection between the view of women that *bunny* transmits and *Playboy* appears explicitly in (113) through the compound *playboy bunny*, a label which alludes to the name of the waitresses at Playboy clubs, who used to be dressed as bunnies:

> (113) When I say I stopped, I mean I stopped all that. I am not punishing him, I just am not rewarding his lazy dump everything on SimpleGirl attitude.

Its not even uncommon for me to be lectured about not being the perfect *playboy bunny*/mom/housekeeper/nanny/cook. (MMSL, 17 September 2013)

Women are also considered in terms of small furry felines.³ The felidae family features metaphors touching on a wide range of sex-related attributes: sexual availability, promiscuity, attraction, etc. The type of offence carried out obviously depends on the felid used as source domain. For example, the notions of sexual attraction and availability are transmitted by the word *kitten*, which led Kövecses (2002: 151) to postulate the metaphor SEXUALLY ATTRACTIVE WOMEN ARE KITTENS. The nature and function of this metaphor are clearly dysphemistic: it singles out those components of the domain of SMALL FURRY ANIMALS seen so far (small size, availability, affection, etc.) to reduce women to the status of submissive and sexually available partners.⁴ In the following message, the adjective used to qualify *sex kitten* (*little*) contributes to the dysphemistic effect intended by the poster in that it portrays women as small, and thus easier to handle (see note 21, Chapter 4):

(114) I know that we all want our women to 'just get it' when it comes to pleasing a man and being a *little sex kitten*, but the truth is that many of them just don't. (MMSL, 29 August 2013)

As happens with other metaphorical labels, *kitten* is not always used with an offensive intention. In posting (115) below, this metaphor is employed with a quasi-euphemistic axiological value by a woman as a kind of 'in-group' solidarity. As in (114), this noun is qualified by a term belonging to the target domain (*sex*) which makes the link between the linguistic metaphor and its non-literal sense more explicit:

(115) This is your chance to give pleasure to your man. Think of this as one of the most passionate gifts you can give to him. So be enthusiastic about it! It's time you let that inner *sex kitten* out and play. Be powerful, strong and sexy. (FFF, 19 February 2011)

Despite the fact that the connotations of sexual availability and promiscuity that *kitten* conveys are overtly pejorative, they are employed by a woman to give some advice on how to improve another woman's sexual life in the posting above. The same quasi-euphemistic quality is to be found in the word *pussycat*. Although, strictly speaking, a term of abuse, its use as a term of endearment for women goes back to the mid-nineteenth century (*OED*3). In the following example *pussycat* appears to be used with affection:

(116) My husband calls me *pussycat*, when he's in a good mood that is. If he's in a bad mood he has been known to call me other things. (MMSL, 1 September 2012)

Let us consider a totally different case included in the FELIDAE metaphors for women: *alley cat*. Here the ANIMAL metaphor is based on the similarity between a stray cat that frequents alleys in search of food and a lustful and promiscuous woman in search of sex. The components of the source domain that are singled out for dysphemistic purposes hint at the idea of illicit sex and create an image of the woman as morally disgusting, far from the connotations of availability or sexual appeal that other metaphorical terms from the family of felines carry. Whereas, for example, a kitten brings to mind a small, graceful and affectionate animal, the image of a homeless, mixed-breed cat links the woman to filth, poverty, illness transmission or stealing food. However, the characteristics that link cats to pets (small size, affection, loyalty, company) are not exploited in the encoding of the metaphor. This pejorative label appears in the message below, posted in a thread in which the thread starter complains that his wife has had an extramarital relationship:

(117) Your wife may have the morals of an *alley cat*, but she is no fool. You will have to keep your temper under control. Don't even try to be some sort of tough guy, because if you touch her or insult her in public or in front of witnesses, she will crucify you in court. (TAM, 31 August 2012)

Here, the unfaithful behaviour of this woman is portrayed in disgusting terms by associating her with an alley cat. Such disgust is linked to moral decay which, in turn, suggests that the woman in (117) acts out of carnal lust.[5] In this case the filthiness of an alley cat is understood at a metaphorical level as 'dirty' behaviour. Thus the metaphor IMMORALITY IS FILTH (Lakoff, 2003: 98) applies here with a dysphemistic purpose, contrary to the cases seen in 3.1.12 in which DIRT metaphors are intended as derogatory euphemisms. Following Galera Masegosa (2010: 26), what we have in here is a case of a single-source metaphorical complex, in which the metaphors PEOPLE ARE ANIMALS and IMMORALITY IS FILTH interact in the semantic derogation of the woman in question.

It is important to note that some specific mappings of the metaphor HUMANS ARE ANIMALS like WOMEN ARE BIRDS and WOMEN ARE SMALL FURRY ANIMALS implicitly reduce women to their sexual organs, which contributes to portraying a picture of women as no more than desirable sexual objects. This view derives from the similarity that is established between birds or small furry animals and the sexual female organ: hairy, soft, small, etc. (Kövecses, 2006b: 157). Therefore, this type of realizations of the BIRD and FURRY ANIMAL metaphors presents a metonymic basis (PART FOR WHOLE): a part of the body (vagina) stands for the woman. The metonymic allusion to a woman through her genitals is evidenced in *pussycat* (116) and *pussy*, a term used since the eighteenth century to refer to women as sexual objects (Rodríguez González, 2008a: 224). These are cases of source-in-target metonymy: *pussy* and *pussycat* provide a mental access to women in an offensive way by virtue of the cognitive operation of domain expansion which enables the conceptual association between both entities (Ruiz de Mendoza Ibáñez, 2011). In the posting below, this metonymic association is used for insulting purposes:

(118) Does this work to build attraction in the reverse? Depends on the tone. Sly and sexy? Very cool. Disgusted like 'I know, you tell me all the time, you pathetic *pussy*' this would not be very cool. (MMSL, 11 October 2012).

Apart from the similarity between a furry animal like a pussy and a vagina based on visual grounds, López Rodríguez (2009: 84) maintains that this association is also motivated by the image of the baby animal playing with a ball of wool, which, according to this scholar, hints at the idea of playfulness. This image reinforces the notion of the woman as a sexual plaything at man's disposal.

The concept of female genitalia is also designated by the name of a furry semi-aquatic rodent, a beaver. *Beaver* is part of several compounds like *beaver cleaver* 'vaginal penetration' or *split beaver* 'a woman showing her genitals', among others recorded by Sánchez Benedito (2009). The taboo quality of *beaver* as applied to female genitals is observable in the following posting, in which this word was felt to be too harsh for a woman who overheard a joke between two men:

(119) Men can't make jokes because it upsets women. Years ago at work, a woman – in another office – overheard a conversation a guy and I were having about Canadian money and debating whether one of their coins had the queen on it or a beaver. I said, 'Maybe it's the queen's *beaver*'. The woman was listening in on a private conversation and I had to apologize. (MMSL, 23 May 2013)

Beaver also designates a lustful woman in the rhyme compound *eager beaver*. A PART FOR WHOLE metonymy is at work here: the woman is seen in terms of her sexual organs, as happens in *pussy* and *pussycat*. By using this metonymic allusion, quite dysphemistic in intention, a lustful woman is implicitly reduced to her sexual organs, and thus to a sexual object:

(120) Wife has never been an *eager beaver* in the bed. Its always me that has to beg. I guess I am getting tired of begging. (TAM, 1 April 2013)

It is precisely due to their consideration as 'dirty', that certain words lexicalized with a sexual meaning may be employed to sexually stimulate the partner, in a verbal practice known as 'dirty talk' (see 3.1.12). This practice is the source of what I call 'dirty' X-phemistic units. Consider the posting that follows:

(121) My wife would laugh if I called her 'wench'. She's not good at dirty talk so I keep directing her.
me: 'Tell me that *pussy* belongs to me'.
wife: 'This *pussy* belong to you'. (MMSL, 8 October 2013)

A tabooed-body part term like *pussy*, lexicalized with the meaning 'vagina', is widely recognized as an obscene word, inappropriate in polite conversation and likely to provoke discomfort. In (121), however, *pussy* goes beyond the designation of female genitals and fulfils a quasi-euphemistic function as part of the seductive talk that paves the way for coition.

4.1.1.2 BIRDS

Much of what has been said about the metaphor WOMEN ARE SMALL FURRY ANIMALS applies to the term *chick*, one of the realizations of the metaphor WOMEN ARE BIRDS. The view of the woman as a sexual object at man's disposal that *chick* transmits responds to three main motivations: first, on account of the small size of birds, this metaphor conveys the idea that women are smaller and weaker than men; second, in relation to age, *chick* denotes that the woman is young and likely to be sexually desirable; and third, chicks and chickens constitute a source of nourishment (López Rodríguez, 2009: 83), which connects this metaphor with the domains of FOOD and EATING that I will explain later.

The sexist attitude that *chick* conveys is evident in the posting below. The fact that this pejorative label is employed by the poster to talk about his own wife (whom he describes as 'a hot chick') makes this linguistic metaphor especially offensive, and reflects the poster's sexist attitude which, in this case, stands close to misogyny:

(122) I need more sex and this isn't gonna cut for the rest of my life. I married a *hot chick* because I wanted to have a lot of sex. (MMSL, 10 October 2012)

Although *chick* is, according to middle-class politeness conventions, a derogatory label to refer to women, it is not always used with an offensive intention. In (123) *chick* fulfils a quasi-euphemistic function: despite its sexist overtones, it appears to display affection:

(123) My *chick* loved me, and I gave her the good stuff, but after that I was done and had sht to do. … love and sex are major players in a marriage, you gatta have boundries and responsiblity for each others! (TAM, 10 October 2013)

Let us consider the term *cock*. This word does not really activate a metaphorical meaning; that is, it is not perceived as having a source domain or literal counterpart. *Cock* is fully lexicalized with the meaning 'penis' in current English, or, more precisely, 'the erect penis'. Although *cock* can be considered a dead metaphor for penis (see 2.3.3), its use in reference to the male member (first recorded in 1618 according to OED3) has important implications at a cognitive level. A cock is, literally, the generic term for 'adult male chicken', and, as such, included in the class of domestic fowl within the category of birds. The reference to the penis in *cock* derives from several sources. Apart from the root sense of 'domestic fowl', the COCK metaphor for penis is intimately connected with a pipe or spout serving as a channel for passing liquids through in the shape of a cock's nest. In this respect, as Murphy (2001: 20–1) argues, the penis is represented as a mechanical device engineered to pour liquids: '[T]he use of the word as a synonym for penis emphasizes a screwing mechanism that characterizes the penis as an insentient tool.' From this viewpoint, *cock* can be included in the MACHINE conceptual equation (see 4.1.6).

Cock brings to mind the image of the proud cock who dominates in the henhouse. In this regard, as Allan (2012: 21) maintains, the cock, as a dominant male, evokes 'the very essence of manhood': it suggests an image of the male member with the attributes of an arrogant cock transferred to it. As Thorne (2005: 102) notes, *cock* also alludes to the image of the brave fighting rooster. Thus, the male member is seen as an instrument of (sexual) dominance over the defenceless and weak hens which, by analogy, are equated with women. In this sense, the (erect) penis is attributed the characteristics of a brave and powerful fighter cock, which brings an image of force and violence to mind; accordingly, the COCK metaphor also touches on the domain of WAR and VIOLENCE (see 4.1.4). This metaphor appears in the posting below:

(124) A few days later during our sexy time she told me that if she could have pulled my *cock* out in the parking lot (after the way I was helping her

out), then she would have blown me right there. (MMSL, 5 October 2013)

An interesting development of the word *cock* is the compound *cocksucker* (literally 'a fellator'), which Hughes (2006: 88) considers 'the most powerful word in terms of its obscenity and insult impact'. Although not exclusively, this homophobic label aims at disparaging homosexuals and, by doing so, imposes the dominant ideology of male heterosexuality. According to López Rodríguez (2009: 79), dysphemism aimed at belittling marginal groups is motivated by the dichotomy between 'the self' and 'the other', the former represented by the male heterosexual and the latter by homosexuals. Note how the pejorative nature of the word *cocksucker* is so taken for granted that its public use is restricted to 'male to male shit talking', as P-2 puts it:

(125) P-1: After the movie, wife and I got talking about the term *cock-sucker* (and all the different forms and variations), and it seems to me … very negative … So maybe we are hurting ourselves by using such terms in a negative stance.
P-2: Agreed that *cocksucker* seems to be most aptly applied in male to male shit talking, generally to denegrate each other as the less alpha. (MMSL, 1 February 2013)

As a tabooed-body part term, *cock* may also perform a quasi-euphemistic function. Consider the posting below:

(126) My wife tries to act all cute and innocent about it but when I hold her down and say something like, "shut your mouth and take my *cock*" … she starts dripping hard. (MMSL, 10 October 2013)

Here *cock* – the same as *pussy* in (121) – is used as a dirty X-phemism in order to sexually stimulate the partner as a prelude to coition, in a clear example of the so-called 'dirty talk'.

4.1.1.3 WILD ANIMALS

Using a wild and predatory animal as source domain is very different from employing small and harmless animals like kittens or bunnies as the raw material for dysphemism. In fact, to associate a woman with a wild animal implies that females are not considered as playthings under man's control; rather, they are seen as dangerous creatures likely to kill their prey and feed on it.

Let us start with *fox* and its corresponding adjective *foxy*. In posting (127) below *foxy* represents a woman who is sexually appealing, flirtatious and capable of provoking sexual arousal. The notion of sexual attractiveness implicit in *foxy* derives from the folk knowledge people have about foxes: the fox is traditionally portrayed as a beautiful and elegant creature whose pelt is a very valuable and quality fur (Palmatier, 1995: 155).

>(127) My wife is a really hot, *foxy* woman with a very sexual appearance and looks. (MMSL, 7 September 2102)

By using this metaphor not only is sexual attractiveness emphasized. The adjective *foxy* also depicts women as cunning and crafty, attributes traditionally associated with foxes. Here there is an element of challenge involved: the attractive woman is not merely seen as an innocent animal subject to man's control. She is not easy to tame or catch, you need to be an experienced 'hunter', as she may tease you, turn you in and run away. The main meaning foci of this metaphor (SEXUAL ATTRACTIVENESS and SLYNESS) confer sexual appeal to the woman and make seduction a challenging and exciting experience.

The case of *vixen* is similar in cognitive terms, although there are some significant differences. Both fox and vixen carry connotations of cunning and sexually alluring women, but the vixen is even more tricky than her male counterpart. In the following message, these attributes of the female fox are mapped onto the sexual behaviour of a woman, who is depicted as an animal that, although not easy to chase, may be tamed by the man for a sexual purpose:

>(128) Build the attraction in her and I would not at all be surprised if you don't have a little *vixen* on your hands. (MMSL, 12 August 2013)

However, in the posting below, *vixen* has different connotations. The term alludes to a woman's sexual promiscuity and lustful behaviour during intercourse. Note the contrast that is established between *vixen* and *prude*:

>(129) Definitely not a prude, not sure what qualifies someone as a *vixen* either. I guess I am a little bit more a middle of the road kinda girl. Open to being sexual as long as it remains the 2 of us (no others) and prefer to skip on the anal. (TAM, 3 April 2013)

The attributes of the vixen are transferred here to target a woman who is active in bed and likely to take the initiative, not like a small bird or chick at man's mercy. This implication of the VIXEN metaphor stands in close relation with the metaphorical meanings the word *zorra* 'vixen' has in Spanish: 'prostitute' and 'sexually promiscuous woman'. However, in contrast to what happens in English, *zorra* does not imply attractiveness, sensual appeal or craftiness (Fernández Fontecha and Jiménez Catalán, 2003: 776–8). This stands as proof that the same metaphor to refer to women may have different implications in different languages and cultures, which confirms that metaphors are culturally loaded and employed in different ways in different cultural and social contexts.[6]

In the three postings above, both foxes and vixens are personified as sexually appealing, cunning, even malicious. These attributes support the stereotype of the 'femme fatale', the sexy woman who uses her sensuality to trick men into lust. In this respect, Hines (1999: 11) considers that the PREDATORY ANIMAL metaphor is a special case of what she calls the 'FEMME FATALE' metaphor insofar as in the WOMEN-AS-PREDATORS metaphor both the notions of the animal as dangerous (in the sense of life-threatening) and tricky conflate.

The stereotype of the femme fatale is more directly conveyed by other names belonging to this domain like *vamp*, end-clipped from *vampire*. The use of *vamp* derives from the folk belief whereby vampirism is associated with promiscuous sexuality, a view of vampirism exploited in *Bram Stoker's Dracula*, a film directed by Francis Ford Coppola in 1992. Furthermore, the fact that vampires are associated with the night triggers the connection between vampires and illicit sexual encounters. *Vamp* appears in the posting that follows:

(130) You seem to have little or no respect for yourself; why else would you bother to think whether or not you are prettier than some cheating dirty *vamp*; Love yourself first. (TAM, 3 January 2013)

Vamps are usually portrayed as seductive and lusty females who exploit men by use of their sexual charms. In (131) *vamp* is grammatically converted to a verb meaning 'sexually seduce' with the underlying implication that the man falls prey to the woman, who has attained power over him through sexual attraction. Indeed, we can deduce from the following message that the man has naïvely fallen into a sexual trap laid by a cunning woman, who used her sexual experience and appeal to lure him in:

(131) They would say she *vamped* him. She used her sexual wiles to ensnare him. Poor sweet. Brad never had a chance. (FFF, 9 October 2011)

When big predator mammals are used to metaphorically represent women the danger of the act of predation itself becomes especially salient. Take the term *cougar*. The image of a wild feline is transferred here to the human to refer to a mature and sexually active woman who is involved in a relationship with a younger man. In (132) this noun undergoes a process of grammatical conversion to an adjective in order to express, not behaviour, but a characteristic associated with the noun it qualifies:

(132) This is how the *cougar* phenomenon exists. In absolute terms, they are less attractive than their younger counterparts. But in relative terms, they are hotter because they make themselves sexually available. (MMSL, 18 October 2013)

The main implication of the COUGAR metaphor is that the woman, the same as a voracious predator in search of food, acts out of carnal lust. The predatory aspect of wild animals is thus transferred onto the representation of a mature woman who preys on younger men. Furthermore, the fact that a cougar is a big cat is associated with the mature age of the woman (note the difference between a cougar and the immaturity and small size that kittens bring to mind). Indeed, in *cougar* the salient features of the source domain used for the dysphemistic reference to women have much to do with the big size and strength of cougars, despite the fact that the image presented by a big and strong cat is not very feminine; after all, attractiveness is not part of the reference of the metaphor.[7]

As seen so far, the ANIMAL metaphor is the source of derogatory images for describing women. However, the WILD ANIMAL domain is also applied to the sexual behaviour of men. When this happens, the axiological value of the ANIMAL metaphor is radically different, which stands as proof of the sexist bias of metaphorical naming in accordance with the heterosexual male dominant ideology. I will consider first the pair *lion/lioness*. Take the metaphorical noun phrase *starving lioness* in the following message:

(133) A monogamist without a man, or with the wrong man, is a *starving lioness*. She is on the prowl, and is incredibly dangerous. (MMSL, 12 February 2013)

Here the description of the woman as a *starving lioness* emphasizes the negative stereotypes associated with being a 'monogamist', i.e. single and independent women, in traditional societies. By using the image of a lioness in search of food, the woman is considered as a dangerous and voracious animal, as a threat to the man, who may become the victim of the aggressive and fierce behaviour of a hungry lioness who preys on men. In this sense, the metaphorical use of *lioness* can be considered as an instance of the OPPONENT metaphor, which focuses on the danger to others, in close connection with the metaphor PASSIONS ARE BEAST INSIDE A PERSON (Lakoff, 1987a: 392). This conceptualization singles out for dysphemistic purposes that part of human beings that is a wild animal, usually hidden and kept in private as part of the civilized behaviour it is expected from people as social beings.

In the same posting the view of the 'man-eater' (i.e. women as sexually active, dominant and dangerous) that *starving lioness* transmits threatens man's hegemonic masculinity and involves a challenge to the conventional sexual role of females in society (cf. Cameron and Kulick, 2006). Different realizations of this WILD ANIMAL metaphor (*lioness*, *tigress* or *cougar*) evoke the powerful figure of the devouring woman, which in the Western culture has been thought to pose a serious threat to her sexual partner. That this is so can be gathered from Bordo (1993: 116–17):

> [F]emale hunger as sexuality is represented by Western culture in misogynist images permeated with terror and loathing ... The sexual act, when initiated and desired by a woman, is imagined in itself an act of eating, of incorporation and destruction of the object of desire.

The implications are totally different if we use the male counterpart, lion, to refer to men. In (134) *lion* provides the basis for describing the man as sexually active and powerful. This word is loaded with favourable associations which capture supposedly positive characteristics of males like courage or ferocity, hence its inclusion in the axiological category of quasi-euphemism. Of course, no offence is meant: when applied to males, the word appears to be intended as a praising X-phemism which tends to reinforce the macho stereotypes of manliness and dominance over women:

> (134) Now that I am able to ask for my needs to be met (that's right, sex) I can ask for or talk about anything without fear. I feel like a *lion* that used to be a mouse. No fear, just say what I want. (MMSL, 24 September 2013)

The same is true of other linguistic metaphors from the domain of WILD ANIMALS used to praise the virility and dominant behaviour of men. Take the case of *wolf*. Although traditionally associated with fear, destructiveness and greed, when applied to male sexual behaviour it turns, paradoxically enough, into a compliment:

> (135) If she wants to provoke the *wolf*, she's going to get the teeth. Which she likes when in the proper frame – so I want to encourage teasing from that frame, and not from an "I'm messing with your head" frame. (MMSL, 23 August 2013).

The greed and ravenous appetite of the wolf operates at a different level when talking about sex: the otherwise negative attributes serve to reinforce the stereotype of the sexually active male: in fact, *wolf* clearly carries positive connotations in (135). The wolf behaviour is used to allude to the lustful attitude of the man ('she's going to get the teeth') by virtue of the metaphor A WOLF IS A LUSTFUL PERSON.[8] The analogy between wolves and men is clear: in the same way that wolves have a ravenous appetite for meat, 'the human wolf has a ravenous appetite for members of the opposite sex', as Palmatier (1995: 418) notes. This metaphor also appears in association with the folk image of Little Red Riding Hood as a way to establish a contrast between the lust of the man and the innocence of his sexual partner:

(136) My wife says that's my "*wolf* look." Like I'm about to eat little red riding hood. (MMSL, 31 August 2013)

What we have from (134) to (136) is a mapping from animal behaviour (lions and wolves as fierce and aggressive when chasing and killing their prey) to corresponding human behaviour (men as fierce and aggressive when engaged in a sexual encounter).[9] Although lions or wolves are dangerous and threatening animals, usually with an ill reputation, the words are loaded with favourable associations to praise men's sexual performance. As López Rodríguez (2009: 82) argues, the positive import attached to lions and wolves reflect the high rank these animals have within the animal kingdom and points to different relevant parameters in the encoding of the LION and WOLF metaphors when applied to males: the physical appearance of lions and wolves (i.e. big size), their living conditions (i.e. not subject to man's control) and their behaviour (i.e. ferocious and aggressive).

Another animal-based word which deserves attention is *horny*. This adjective, lexicalized with the meaning 'sexually excited, lecherous' (*OED*3), is metaphorical in origin: it alludes to the maleness of the horn characteristic of strong and powerful mammals like bulls or rhinoceros to represent virility. Furthermore, a visual metaphor reinforces this sexual allusion: the shape of the horn clearly resembles that of the penis in erection (McDonald, 1996: 70). The allusion to an erect penis in *horny* is used to refer to male sexual excitation in postings (21) and (188). Despite its association with the penis, *horny* also applies to women:

(137) I am having this feeling down there, with my clit it keeps throbbing and pulsating. Im getting the extreme erg to have sex and feel incredibly *horny* when it happens. Is it normal? (FFF, 16 July 2013)

Before finishing this section, it is worth emphasizing that men are not always represented in a positive light through the WILD ANIMAL metaphor. Consider the use of *predator* in the posting below:

(138) Boy scout leader is a skilled *predator*. Access to other men's wives is probably a big part of why he volunteers. (MMSL, 30 March 2013)

Here a man is depicted as a ravenous wild animal in search of food, but, unlike the realizations of the WILD ANIMAL metaphor used to talk about men seen so far, the word *predator* is not used to reinforce masculine stereotypes like maleness or virility. In (138) *predator* is an overtly pejorative word for a man who preys on women in an illicit way.[10]

In summary, the PEOPLE-ARE-WILD ANIMALS metaphor captures the most salient features of the domain of WILD ANIMALS (ferocity, strength, dominance, independence, etc.), which are generally used as a praise in the case of the sexual behaviour of males and as a threat to man's hegemony and self-assurance in the case of women. Let us move on now to a dysphemistic domain which is closely connected with the animal kingdom: that which employs hunting and riding imagery as a way to refer to sex-related topics.

4.1.2 HUNTING and RIDING

In accordance with the metaphor that associates humans, especially women, with animals, men are conceived of as hunters whose aim is to capture the woman, who is ultimately seen as the prey. By virtue of the metaphor SEX IS HUNTING, the woman is metaphorically viewed as a predatory animal (obviously enough, farmyard animals or pets are not likely to be hunted). In this metaphor different elements conflate: first, the notion of the woman as a sexually alluring creature; second, the man as the hunter; third, sexual desire as hunger; and fourth, the woman as edible and appetizing food to eat. As Hines (1999: 16) puts it, 'women-considered-sexually are described not just as animals, but specifically as those which are hunted or possessed, conflating not just sex and appetite, but quite explicitly, control'.

Although the salient features of the WILD ANIMAL metaphor may vary depending on the animal used as source domain – cunning and trickery (in the case of fox and vixen) and dangerous, strong and fierce (cougar, lioness and tigress) – the characteristic that all the animals included in this domain share is the difficulty to be chased and the danger involved in it. As the woman is not depicted as a defenceless animal at man's mercy, there is an element of challenge involved which clearly supposes an element of added excitement for men. The conceptual correspondences of the HUNTING metaphor are observable in posting (139). The sexual conquest is conceptualized as a hunt through a set of mappings that characterize it: namely, the man corresponds to the hunter, the woman is equated with the prey, and the sexual approach on the part of the man corresponds to the steps leading to the capture before finally copulating or, figuratively speaking, 'enjoying the prey':

> (139) When you first started dating you made her feel wanted. You acted more aggressively to get your needs met. You *pursued, chased down, hunted for, captured* and enjoyed your *prey*. You kept her off balance and made her feel passion. (TAM, 23 July 2012)

The HUNTING metaphor echoes images of violence, oppression and hostility. This is especially evident in (140). The poster metaphorically describes himself as a hunter who preys on the woman, who is represented through two contradictory metaphors. The first one is *piece of meat*, a realization of the metaphor WOMEN ARE FOOD (see 4.1.3) whereby the woman is reduced to food ready to be cooked and eaten. The second one is *wild prey*, an instantiation of the WILD ANIMAL metaphor which portrays the woman as a menacing animal whose chase is challenging for the hunter. The adjective *wild* brings to mind the notion of the woman as a dangerous animal, which ultimately justifies its chase and capture:

> (140) Dude, act like a caveman. I have this look I give my wife that she feels like *a piece of meat*. I stare her down, and don't say shit. Shortly thereafter I *attack* her like she's some *wild prey*. (MMSL, 4 October 2013)

Note how the verb employed (*attack*) directly connects the HUNTING to the WAR/VIOLENCE domains. Indeed, both domains conflate to offer a portrait of sex that goes back to primitive societies (as a matter of fact, the poster describes himself as a 'caveman'). The verb *attack* invokes the notion of non-consensual sex; rather than an act of seduction, it represents sexual assault – a violent action on the part of the man in which the woman, represented as a prey, is threatened and coerced.

In the following message the man who plays the role of the hunter is metaphorically reinterpreted as a *sexually charged lion*, in accordance with the view whereby a lustful man is an aggressive creature prowling for female meat. Here we can see some of the entailments the HUNTING metaphor gives rise to. If the act of seducing and eventually copulating with a woman is conceptually equated with the act of hunting, the chase is the seduction, and the poster's sexual adventures are 'his hunting days':

(141) I also think its the *chase* that gives us the thrill! When we are single, we are on the prowl, like a sexually charged lion ... having sex with as many different women as possible. Its our basic animalistic instinct. Then we get married and suddenly we realise (sub-consciously) that this lady is the only person we are going to have sex with for the rest of our lives. Our *hunting* days are over! (TAM, 13 August 2012)

The view of sex metaphorically depicted in the three postings above ultimately serves to establish male dominance and authority, however cunning, dangerous or threatening sexually alluring women may turn out to be, and ultimately justifies an aggressive behaviour on account of the male 'basic animalistic instinct', as explicitly mentioned in (141).

The fact that foxes are traditionally used in fox-hunting should not be overlooked. To portray the woman as a fox brings to mind the image of fox-hunting as an activity in which the domains of HUNTING and SPORTS conflate. This domain conflation ultimately serves to justify the violence exerted in chasing and killing an animal on the grounds that it follows the rules of a traditional, legal and well reputed pastime of ruling classes. Following Baker (cited in López Rodríguez, 2009: 91), '[t]he fox is an animal that men chase, and hunt, and kill for sport. If women are conceived of as foxes, then they are conceived of as prey that is fun to hunt.' The image of fox-hunting, therefore, contributes to reinforce dichotomies that help to understand how the domain of WILD ANIMALS conceptually works (hunter versus prey; active versus passive; dominant versus dominated; agent versus victim, etc.). By so doing, this image plays a part in the expression of gender roles and in the unequal power relations between men and women.

Let us move on to another metaphor which is also closely connected with the ANIMAL metaphor for humans. Given that horses can be ridden by people, the image of mounting or getting upon a coital partner leads to the conceptualization TO COPULATE IS HORSE-RIDING or, more generally speaking, SEX IS RIDING, as postulated by Chamizo Domínguez and Sánchez Benedito (2000). In posting (142) below, 'mount your sleeping wife' suggests that the woman involved in the sexual relationship is the horse, while his partner is the rider who 'mounts' her by staying in the male-above sexual position.

(142) If you want more sex, might I suggest you not *mount* your sleeping wife in the middle of the night. I can't imagine many less sexy things for a woman. (TAM, 1 June 2011)

The equine imagery constitutes a good source domain for the expression of disrespect towards women, who are depicted as less than human, and confers on the man a position of control and dominance over the female sexual partner. In fact, the woman adopts a passive role whereas the man is the agent that performs the action of mounting. In this way, the dichotomy active/passive applies to target dysphemistically the act of coition. The verb *straddle* also refers to copulation through the riding imagery:

(143) My wife has moved away from giving them when I'm on my back–for the most part. The typical way is her on her back, with a couple of pillows under her head while I *straddle* her. (MMSL, 23 October 2103)

The category of equidae does not only apply to women as animals to be straddled or ridden. Men can also be portrayed in the role of horses ridden by their female sexual partners. In (144) the roles are reversed: it is the woman who sits astride the man when copulating and takes the initiative in the sexual encounter:

(144) Once she *mounted* me, bit my chest super hard, and *rode* me with vengeance in her face. When we were done, she rolled off and was sweet again. (MMSL, 15 November 2012)

Of particular interest here are the violent overtones that the RIDING metaphor transmits. The man reports how his sexual partner *mounted* and *rode* him wildly, as if the sexual act had the capacity of turning 'sweet' people (as the poster says the woman is) into violent and irrational beings.

Whether applied to males or females, the equine imagery is dysphemistic in two senses: first, it is offensive towards the dignity of the sexual partner, who is depicted as a horse, as an animal at the rider's mercy; and second, it portrays coition as a purely basic animal activity deprived of any rational control, intimacy or affection.

4.1.3 FOOD AND EATING

The FOOD/EATING domain constitutes a common source for naming sexual organs and sex-related actions. Allan and Burridge (2006: 190) argue that the close association between the alimentary and the sexual can be explained on the basis that 'food is often the prelude to sex … Eating and love-making go together.' As these authors note, the condition of euphoria that both activities bring on, together with the range of bodily sensations that both sex and eating involve (sight, touch, taste and smell), gives food its sexy and erotic reputation.

Furthermore, some foods are believed to have sexually stimulating effects (e.g. oysters, figs, chocolate, etc.). These links between eating and sex have an obvious influence at the linguistic level; indeed, the FOOD/EATING metaphor for sex is pervasive in our ordinary language and throughout the history of English slang (see Hines, 1996, 2000; Allan and Burridge, 2006: 194–7; Kövecses, 2006b: 155–6).

The association between sex and eating leads to the conventional metaphors LUST IS HUNGER (Lakoff, 1987a) and SEXUAL DESIRE IS HUNGER (Kövecses, 1998: 30). These conceptualizations structure lust and desire in terms of hunger, and, in this way, feeling hungry and eating are used to express sexual desire. This is reflected in adjectives like *starved* (145) and *hungry* (146). These terms may be qualified by items which belong to the target domain, like *sex* or *sexually*, as an indication that these adjectives are not to be interpreted at a literal level.[11] This is the case of *sex-starved* in the message below:

(145) Nancy, who went by Nancy Dow at the time, starred in the soft-core porn flick The Ice House as a *sex-starved* housewife. The film, which also starred porn legend John Holmes, did not make Nancy a star. (FFF, 19 July 2011)

Following Kövecses (2002: 93–4), the adjective *starved* is a typical realization of the metaphor LOVE IS A NUTRIENT in which the source domain utilizes only some aspects of the concept and leaves others aside, by virtue of the hiding-highlighting property of metaphorical projections. In *sex-starved* only the desire for food and the negative consequences of a lack of nourishment are activated in the comprehension of the target. The activation of these aspects allows the poster to refer to the housewife's unsatisfied need for sex by upgrading her desire through a metaphor with hyperbolic overtones. In this way, as Kövecses (2002: 94) argues, 'the nutrient metaphor for love utilizes chiefly the "hunger/thirst" and the corresponding "desire-effect" aspect of the concept of nutrient'. And, obviously enough, what Kövecses says about love in this metaphor can be said, *mutatis mutandi*, about sex.

Of course, items from the target domain do not always qualify words from the source domain, which does not imply that non-qualified words from the FOOD/EATING domain are to be interpreted literally, contrary to Deignan's findings in relation to *starve* (see note 11, Chapter 4). The poster of the following message resorts to words belonging to the FOOD/EATING domain to comment on his need for sexual relationships. The activation of the second order meaning in *hungry, chicken-pot* and *banquet* favours a sex-related interpretation ('in need for sex', 'superficial sexual encounter' and 'full and exciting sexual relationship' respectively) without any premodification:

(146) If you've been *hungry* for such a long time, even a *chicken-pot pie* will seem like a *banquet*. (MMSL, 5 October 2013)

The domain of FOOD and EATING also generates dysphemistic alternatives to the topic of oral sex. The activities of eating and performing cunnilingus or fellatio share a crucial component: both involve taking into the body by the mouth. It is thus the oral component which allows for the structure of the taboo of oral sex in terms of eating. In the two postings below, cunnilingus is metaphorically represented as the act of *eating pussy* and fellatio as *eating cock*:

(147) I would rather *eat pussy* than food. It's not fattering, it makes your wife/girlfriend/someone else's wife VERY [in capitals in the original] happy. (FFF, 27 May 2011)

(148) My reply would have been: "me too but its the emotional connection and affection i miss the most ..." For some humor i might add " ... Tomorrow night is all you can *eat cock* night on the couch! how awesome is that? (MMSL, 9 August 2012)

In posting (149) below the verb *devour* presents the conventionalized meaning 'sexually possess' and invokes the figure of the 'woman-eater'. This realization of the EATING metaphor combines with the ANIMAL metaphor: it links the sexual encounter to a purely animal activity, that of devouring. This word presents hyperbolic overtones in the reference to the act of eating: it brings to mind the image of a predator eating up its prey voraciously and greedily. Indeed, this verb implies that the man acts aggressively and irrationally, guided by basic, purely animal instincts when engaged in the sexual encounter:

(149) Try this, look her up and down and then in the eyes like you're going to *devour* her. Then say "woman, come here and kiss me". (MMSL, 6 September 2013)

The verb *devour* here relates the man's sexual behaviour to animal behaviour when eating. Despite the fact that this verb uses the ANIMAL domain to talk about a human being, the effect that the poster tries to achieve is far from being offensive. It highlights supposedly positive characteristics of males like braveness and ferocity which, when applied to sexual encounters, reflect and legitimize the macho stereotypes of virility and dominance over the woman, who is ultimately seen as the prey. The same positive view of man as a sexual predator appears in other praising X-phemistic realizations of the WILD ANIMAL metaphor: *lion* (134) and *wolf* (135) and (136).[12]

As part of the food imagery, hunger represents sexual desire by virtue of the metaphor THE OBJECT OF LUST IS HUNGER (Lakoff 1987a). This metaphor considers the sexual object in terms of food or, more precisely, as Kövecses (2006b: 156) points out, appetizing food. Edibility appears to be a relevant factor in the encoding of metaphors used to designate the sexual partner as desirable.[13] The conceptualization of women as appetizing food combines with other food-related metaphors for sex such as WOMEN ARE DESSERTS (Hines, 1996, 2000) and WOMEN ARE MEAT (Kövecses, 2006b). The former is particularly relevant in the encoding of sexual metaphors. Following Hines (1996: 190), this metaphor is the result of the conjunction of the metaphor PEOPLE ARE OBJECTS, the stereotype 'women are sweet' and the metaphor ACHIEVING A DESIRE OBJECT IS GETTING SOMETHING TO EAT. In fact, metaphorical realizations of the metaphor WOMEN ARE DESSERTS like *cookie* and *cheesecake* depict women as sweet objects to be eaten, a view rooted in cultural stereotypes whereby women have a natural tendency to be sweet (or, at least, sweeter than men).

> (150) I was going to start a new thread specific to FO's as it relates to hormone health, bit figured his thread is watched by some pretty smart *cookies*. (MMSL, 26 September 2013)

The compound *cheesecake* also echoes the notion of sweet and attractive women. According to Holder (2003: 62), *cheesecake* is not merely a realization of the APPETIZING FOOD metaphor. It also derives from the smile-inducing 'cheese' demanded by photographers, which brings to mind a picture of an erotic, compliant and smiling woman, ready to please men:

> (151) Looked up a kick ass lady that does pin-up *cheesecake* style photos, dropped a wad of cash, and booked an appointment for my wife. (MMSL, 26 September 2013)

The metaphors which conceive of women as desserts tend to reduce females to the status of objects of lust. As part of the Great Chain of Being metaphor PEOPLE ARE OBJECTS, women are degraded insofar as they are considered in terms of lower order of beings: as desserts, they can be bought, sold, sliced, shared and, of course, eaten. Hines (2000: 146) is aware of the dysphemistic power of the DESSERT metaphor when applied to women:

> It is unremarkable that the WOMAN AS DESSERT metaphor reduces women to the status of (sex) objects, with the attendant implications of powerlessness,

inanimacy and procurability ... What is surprising is the degree to which the metaphor is extended: Women here are not just objects, but *sweet* (that is, compliant, smiling), and not just desserts, but *pieces* or *slices* [in italics in the original].

From Hines's words it can be deduced that the terms which depict women as desserts carry connotations of promiscuity as well as sexual attraction because of two reasons: first, because women are portrayed as a way to satisfy men's sexual appetite; second, because some of the terms included in this metaphor (like *piece of cake*) target women as a separate portion, as a dessert to be cut, even shared, and therefore totally at men's disposal. Indeed, by conceptualizing women in the guise of appetizing food, the male dominant role over his sexual partner is reinforced. This is the case of the posting below in which the woman, referred to as a *sweetie-pie*, is seen as a passive and submissive sexual partner:

(152) She was just too much of a *sweetie-pie* for me. Scared of her own shadow ... I took the dominant role, so that obviously wasn't going to work for me forever. (MMSL, 27 September 2013)

That the WOMAN-AS-DESSERT metaphor portrays females as promiscuous is especially evident in the case of *tart*. This word has undergone a process of semantic derogation: from a term of endearment applied to 'a young woman for whom some affection is felt' in the mid-nineteenth century to 'a female or immoral character; a prostitute' by the end of the century (*OED*3). Today *tart* is strongly derogatory; in fact, both the meanings of 'licentious woman' and 'prostitute' coexist in its denotation, as happens in the following description of the 'ideal' woman:

(153) I prefer a chef in the kitchen, a lady in the living room and a *tart* in the bedroom. (TAM, 16 July 2011)

The consideration of a tart as a prostitute, as Hines (2000: 154) argues, corresponds to the conflation between the metaphors A WOMAN IS A PROSTITUTE and A WOMAN IS A DESSERT: the customer pays for both, and both can be 'consumed' immediately if the customer decides to do so. From this perspective, a prostitute is seen as a commodity whose main role is to serve as an object or product consumed by men. As commodities, prostitutes provide men a service, that of male sexual gratification. This view of prostitutes in terms of commodities is dysphemistic in essence. As Murphy (2001: 40) notes, this metaphor 'transforms labor into a commodity that alienates the worker from his humanity in such a way that men's relations to women assume a sense of urgency and estrangement'.

Apart from the implication of commoditization in connection to prostitution, *tart* singles out the components of sexual availability and promiscuity to portray the woman as licentious and immoral. To these semantic features of the word, another one should be added: a tart is a dessert that is usually decorated and dressed in a flamboyant manner. Here again the analogy with promiscuous women and prostitutes is evident, as these women usually apply make up to improve their appearance and seduce men. In fact, both target concepts are closely connected in the metaphorical use of *tart* in posting (154) below, in which this word has undergone a conversion from noun to verb with the meanings of 'behave in a promiscuous way' and 'act out like a prostitute':

(154) What was it like before, when you were 27–28 and he was 37? And really, you're not an old crone. You need to *tart* yourself just to get his interest. (TAM, 15 June 2011)

The same as happens in some realizations of the ANIMAL metaphor, *tart* also admits a quasi-euphemistic use. Consider how the word is used in the following example:

(155) You are one righteous *tart* for your hubby! I love it! If only more wives were as adventurous as you. (TAM, 10 May 2011)

Although *tart* is an undeviating term of abuse in reference to women, it is not employed here with an offensive intention; rather, the poster deliberately uses the pejorative connotations that the word carries as a compliment for the woman's attitude towards sex. Again, it is the context that establishes the axiological value of the linguistic metaphor.

The fact that many of the metaphorical realizations of the DESSERT metaphor for women are desserts which have been baked, and therefore heated, like *cheesecake* or *tart*, is also significant in cognitive terms. From this viewpoint, this metaphor conflates with the SEX IS HEAT metaphor, which, as seen in 3.1.2, is a conventionalized way to deal with sexual arousal and lust. This cross-domain structural coherence reinforces the view of women as sexual objects to be eaten by alluding to their capacity to sexually arouse men (Hines, 1996, 2000).

The FOOD and EATING metaphor has also inspired different verbal usages whereby tabooed body parts are seen in terms of different types of fruits. There are fruit terms for both male and female genitalia like *cherry* 'hymen' (by extension 'virginity'), *cherry-pie* 'vagina', *melons* 'breasts', *strawberries* 'nipples', *chestnuts* 'testicles', etc. Take the posting below excerpted from a thread entitled

'Virgin at 25'. Although the message is not intended to be offensive whatsoever, the dysphemistic reference to the fact of losing virginity seems evident:

(156) Make it special sweetheart. You've held on to it for long enough, no need rush into something you'll regret later. And please don't *pop your cherry* in a one night stand. (FFF, 27 July 2011)

Here *pop your cherry* refers to the rupture of the hymen during the first intercourse of a female virgin. The use of *cherry* does not only derive from the conception of women's virginity as a sweet fruit that men can take and eat, it is also motivated by the red colour of blood when hymen breaks (*OED*3). In this way, the red colour of cherries disparagingly alludes to a woman's first sexual intercourse. Here *cherry* is, following Allan (2009: 631–3), a colour-based metaphor within the subclass of appearance-based metaphors insofar as the red colour is associated with a visually perceivable characteristic of the denotatum, i.e. blood. The connection with menstrual blood increases the pejorative value of this expression. In fact, the taboo of menstruation is a type of what Allan (1990: 170) calls 'pollution taboo', i.e. 'the pollution of women's unique physiological processes at certain times', and corresponds to the 'revolting bodily effluvia theory' whereby female genitalia are derogated because of their secretions and close associations with urination and excretion.

Woman's virginity is also alluded to in *cherry-picker*. This compound describes the stereotype of a womanizer in search for female virgins – and, by extension, girls – to have sexual intercourse with. It is significant to mention that this male stereotype acts out of carnal lust, looking for cherries to pick in the same way as voracious predators hunger for female meat. The already commented allusion to menstrual blood in *cherry* increases the dysphemistic value of the compound.

(157) I think your husband is a *cherry picker*, they are common around here. (MMSL, 6 September 2012)

In spite of the fact that the FOOD metaphor is exempt from the violent overtones that the domain of WILD ANIMALS presents when applied to men (see 4.1.1.3), the underlying notion of both metaphors is similar: the man as an experienced, active and dominant agent who plays a leading role in the sexual conquest, whereas the woman, either depicted as a prey or as fruit, is the passive element at man's mercy. Metaphor thus plays an important role in expressing gender roles, as shown by Patthey-Chavez et al. (1996) in a corpus of 16 erotic romances written for women in which metaphors portray females as passive and males as active, which contributes to reaffirm unequal power relations.

Although not a dessert as such, the notion of sweetness in connection with sexual promiscuity and availability constitutes the dysphemistic basis of *sugar baby*, i.e. a young female who is provided with money or other benefits by an older man (or *sugar daddy*) in exchange for companionship and sexual favours. Here *sugar* carries connotations of sweetness, compliance and availability, in accordance with the DESSERT metaphor for women.

(158) I talked inappropriately, sent explicit photos to guys I've never met (usually always guys from the internet for the anonymity), went to dating/sex sites to make relationships with guys ... and even worse I've sold my body for sex as a *sugar baby*. (SDF, 27 March 2013)

The domain of DESSERTS has an additional dysphemistic component which is worth mentioning. The image of desserts has the capacity to belittle women insofar as it equates them 'with not just edible objects but with peripheral food items', as Hines (2000: 147–8) argues. At a metaphorical level, importance is understood by virtue of the metaphors IMPORTANT IS CENTRAL and LESS IMPORTANT IS PERIPHERAL (Lakoff and Turner, 1989: 148). The fact that desserts are not the central part of a meal leads to trivialize and degrade women, who are considered as non-essential, simply as a pastime for men. The way this metaphor belittles women and minimizes their role in a sexual relationship does not only apply when the domain of DESSERTS is involved in the metaphorical structuring of the target. In the following message, the female partner is no more important than the coffee the man drinks. After all, coffee is as peripheral and optional in a menu as desserts may be; hence the metaphor LESS IMPORTANT IS PERIPHERAL also applies here:

(159) I like my *coffee* like I like my women. Ground up to a uniform consistency and steeped in near-boiling water for exactly four minutes. (MMSL, 10 September 2013)

The view of women as food is also present in their association with meat. One of the occurrences of the MEAT metaphor for women is the metonymic expression *piece of meat*, which appeared in connection with the hunting imagery in (140) and is used to offer a degrading picture of the woman as a purely sexual object in the posting below:

(160) One problem I see with his fantasy is that it is basically using a third person as nothing more than a sex toy, and it puts you in the position of being just *a piece of meat* as well performing for your husband. So he wants to get off on two *pieces of meat* performing for him. (TAM, 27 November 2011)

This view of women as meat involves further elaboration. It leads to the metaphor WOMEN ARE WHITE MEAT TO EAT, proposed by Kövecses (2006b: 156). Within this conceptualization not only is land meat included. Fish, usually classed as white meat by nutritionists, is part of the realizations of this metaphor, and tuna, as a type of white fish, belongs to this subclass. In (161) the word *tuna* is metaphorically applied to female genitalia, disparagingly represented as a *nasty tuna cave*, a phrase which also realizes the CONTAINER metaphor for vagina, as explained in 3.1.6.

(161) Yeah I heard a pair of strippers catting away at each other one night, and one called the other a *nasty tuna cave*. (FFF, 9 December 2012)

In the two examples above a metonymic process (PART FOR WHOLE) is at work: 'a piece of meat' in (160) and a part of the body (vagina) in (161) stand for the woman. This source-in-target metonymy suggests availability, compliance and promiscuity. As seen in different realizations of the SMALL FURRY ANIMAL metaphor like *pussycat* (116), *pussy* (118) and *eager beaver* (120), this type of metonymic naming is intrinsically dysphemistic in that it reduces humans to the status of sexual objects. In addition, the adjective *nasty* in (161) contributes to the pejorative overtones of the fishy metaphor in order to offer a description of the vagina as something disgusting which is transferred to the woman and used for insulting purposes. In addition, the supposedly similarity between the odour of the vulva and that of fish (Sánchez Benedito, 2009: 166) highlights the disgusting image of female genitalia as something smelly, and thus makes the pejorative force of the insult stronger. Indeed, the role of the sense of smell plays a role in the metaphorical structure of the FISH metaphor for female genitalia. As Allan and Burridge (2006: 195) note, words from the sphere of fish and seafood 'play on the slipperiness of vaginal secretions and the fishy aromas evoked by a woman's intimate body parts'. In this sense, it is not surprising that Braun and Kitzinger (2001: 151) consider fishy metaphors for female genitalia as metaphors of abjection, which is partly connected with the pollution taboo discussed in 3.1.12.

4.1.4 WAR AND VIOLENCE

The metaphors SEX IS WAR and SEX IS VIOLENCE transfer different attributes from the source domains of WAR, VIOLENCE and related subdomains, like WEAPONRY, onto the target domain of SEX. The WAR metaphor presents different sets of ontological correspondences as a result of using the knowledge we have about war to talk about sex: the man is a warrior, to seduce the sexual partner is to overcome an enemy, the sexual encounter is a battle, the penis is a weapon, to ejaculate is to shoot, etc. The conceptual basis for WAR/VIOLENCE metaphors responds to an overall view of sex in terms of hostility, violence and dominance (Beneke, 1982). Accordingly, the main meaning foci of this metaphor are HOSTILITY and VIOLENCE, which leads to the reinterpretation of the WAR metaphor as SEX IS A VIOLENT AND HOSTILE ACTIVITY. Therefore, the metaphorical substitutes that fall under this cognitive equation tend to acquire dysphemistic overtones, as we will see in the postings provided as examples.

The WAR domain is a way to assert male dominance in sexual encounters through violence. According to Murphy (2001: 76):

> In war men experience the violent, aggressive, and death-defying occurrences for which they have prepared for most of their adolescent and adult life. That is, war epitomizes the socially constructed masculine world.

As Deignan (2010: 361–2) argues, the choice of a particular source domain is a mechanism for framing ideology and evaluations through metaphors. In this regard, the choice of this domain responds to a view of sexual relationships in accordance with hegemonic masculinity that includes the typical heterosexual and dominant male. The entailments that the WAR domain creates favour an aggressive view of sex in which males are the dominant party. In the same way as the hunter preys upon his prey (see 4.1.2), the warrior aims at annihilating his enemy through violence; in fact, war engenders acts of violence whose aim is conquest and destruction. As these components of the WAR domain are transferred onto the target domain of SEX, the metaphors included in this conceptualization bring to mind violent imagery. In the posting below, a sexual encounter is equated with a battle:

> (162) A needy man, who is never satisfied, is a big turn off to women ... Until you come to the realization of how destructive this addiction is, or hit bottom, you may not be ready for *battle*. (SDF, 14 June 2013)

As part of the same warfare imagery, the consideration of the lover in terms of a warrior appears in the following message. *Warrior* brings to mind the notion of invasion and warfare; in this way, the sexual act is portrayed as an essentially aggressive and violent action:

> (163) As some of you may know, I am the weekend *warrior*. Great sex on weekends, not much during the week. (MMSL, 15 November 2011)

The shooting imagery is a powerful dysphemistic means to target the male member. The WEAPON metaphor invokes the penis in erection and emphasizes its leading, even threatening, role in the sexual encounter. By virtue of this metaphor, in (164) the penis of a transsexual woman is described as a *big gun* and, as such, capable of posing a threat and killing. This stands as proof that the connection between a weapon and the penis, which can be traced back to the Anglo-Saxon period (Hughes, 2006: 85), is still in current use.

(164) The highlight of the last two days has definitely been dealing with two high profile if not actively better put flamboyant/brazen/outrageous women ... even though one of them threatened to kill me with her *big gun*. In the end, that's OK with me, craziness like having to wear heels comes with the job. (FFF, 6 October 2011).

A logical entailment that can be derived from the PENIS-IS-A-WEAPON metaphor is that shooting is ejaculating. In fact, the actions of 'shooting' and 'firing' are figuratively used to refer to the act of ejaculating in the sample consulted. The posting below is a good case in point: the phrase *shooting one's load* provides evidence for the co-occurrence of two correlated metaphors within the domain of WAR: TO SHOOT IS TO EJACULATE and SPERM IS AMMUNITION:

(165) Find it impossible to orgasm during sex. So, instead after hubby has *shot his load* inside me I masturbate myself with him assisting in stimulating me. (FFF, 10 September 2013)

By the same logic, if the physical act of ejaculating is metaphorically referred to as shooting or firing, the penis is conceptualized as a weapon specifically designed to shoot and, as such, as a potentially dangerous object. By virtue of this analogy, the man needs to recharge his weapon after having shot once, in a clear allusion to the refractory period, i.e. the recovery phase after sexual climax during which it is physiologically impossible to have additional orgasms. This military imagery applies in the following message:

(166) Women tend to be much softener, gentelner and less intense and demanding than guys but there are exceptions on both sides. The biggest permanent difference is that after each "act" guys have to stop and *recharge* where as we can just keep going. (FFF, 2 February 2011)

The same conceptual basis which represents the penis as a gun is responsible for the phrases *fire blanks* or *shoot blanks*, used to denote male incapacity for procreation. *Shooting blanks* evokes the image of the cartridge containing gunpowder but no bullet. The view of sperm as ammunition in *load* commented before also applies here:

(167) I'm *shooting blanks*, but it was my choice. Do not do this unless you are 100% sure that you NEVER want another child with ANY woman [in capitals in the original]. (TAM, 16 October 2012)

Apart from *gun*, other terms belonging to the weaponry imagery are used to conceptualize the penis. One of them is the praising X-phemistic word *missile*. This term is a realization of the WEAPON metaphor for the erect penis which involves hyperbolic overtones, given the weight, dimensions and destructive power of a missile. In the following example the penis is conceived of as a 'love missile F1-11'[14] that must be tested to avoid an undesired pregnancy:

(168) Just get checked, boys, test that *love missile F1-11*. Had a buddy that didn't and proceeded to rack up 5 kids. Had two sets of vas on both sides. After the fifth and second vasectomy, accused his wife of cheating. (MMSL, 15 October 2013)

It is also interesting to look at some derivative words from the noun *weapon* encountered in the sample. The verb *weaponize* conceptualizes the sexual encounter as a potential weapon, that is, as menacing and hostile for the sexual partner. In (169) *weaponize* combines with a verb from the domain of WAR and VIOLENCE, *attack*, to criticize the sexual behaviour of women:

(169) Well actually women are known to *weaponize* and also *attack* you when you're helpless (asleep). (MMSL, 15 October 2013)

Although certain words used to talk about sexual activities do not belong to the field of war, they do carry connotations of violence and hostility. Take, for example, *bang*, a dysphemistic alternative to 'sexual intercourse' which echoes the image of hitting the partner's genitals.[15] In the following message the negative connotations that *bang* carries provides the basis for the dysphemistic reference to an extra-marital sexual relationship:

(170) I would almost bet my life your wife is *banging* someone else. Swinging, vacations without you, texting, girl road trips are all red flags. (MMSL, 21 October 2013)

Similar connotations of violence are transmitted by the verb *beat* in the phrase *beat one's meat* in reference to male masturbation. As happens with *eat cock* in (148), the domain of VIOLENCE interacts with the FOOD domain in the dysphemistic allusion to the sexual taboo:

(171) Hahaha are you serious about the masturbating?
Yes. Possible outcomes are:
1. The sight and sounds of you *beating your meat* triggers her "responsive desire" and you both have sex. (MMSL, 28 April 2013)

The WAR and VIOLENCE metaphors seen in the postings above carry connotations of non-consensual sexual relationships. Terms of warfare (*gun*, *attack* or *shoot*) as well as verbs of weaker violence (*bang* or *beat*) evoke hostile imagery. The violent and aggressive behaviour these words suggest is specifically applied to reaching one's (usually the male's) sexual objective. This implies that women are generally conceptualized – whether consciously or not – as the targets of the male sexual attack, which helps to explain why some men may endorse certain conceptual schemas that most women reject.[16] In this vein, the WAR and VIOLENCE metaphor tends to implicitly justify and, to some extent, legitimize violent sexual behaviour. This component of violence should by no means be underestimated: it ultimately reinforces male dominance and superiority over women. In this vein, Coleman (1999: 147–8) claims that the violent vocabulary used to deal with sex implies hatred: 'If hatred is suggested by violent terms then it may be hatred of sex and of sexuality as much as of the partner.' Thus, the hostility transmitted by WAR and VIOLENCE metaphors bears witness to a particularly aggressive attitude of men towards sex as a whole.

4.1.5 PLAYTHINGS

The notion of the sexual partner as a plaything that is implicit in some of the realizations of the SMALL FURRY ANIMAL metaphor like *kitten* or *pussy* (see 4.1.1.1) constitutes the conceptual basis of the metaphor LOVERS ARE PLAYTHINGS, which derives from a view of sex in terms of a game. However, the game here is not the source of euphemistic naming, as in 3.1.3. It generates dysphemistic labels of a sexist nature that undermine and degrade women. The reason why the GAME metaphor for sex generates terms of abuse to refer, mostly – although not exclusively – to women is because the game is seen from the man's perspective, as an activity to be enjoyed by males. This 'playful' view of sexual relationships leaves the woman aside from the enjoyment by conceptualizing her merely as a plaything at man's service, available for his sexual gratification and deprived of the control of her own sexuality. These salient features of this metaphor provide the dysphemistic basis to refer to sexual partners. The main meaning focus of this metaphor is thus SEXUAL AVAILABILITY, which leads to a reinterpretation of this metaphor as LOVERS ARE SEXUALLY AVAILABLE OBJECTS.

The PLAYTHING metaphor calls forth notions of dominance and oppression of one sexual partner over the other (usually the male over the female) as well as passivity in the representation of the woman. Indeed, the implication of considering a woman as a toy or her intimate parts as playthings is that the female partner is seen an object of lust under man's control. In addition, not only is the woman deprived from the capacity to be in control of her own pleasure, but also from any rational capacity. What is more, by virtue of the Great Chain of Being, the woman referred to as a plaything is placed at the bottom of the hierarchy insofar as a human being (a higher form of life) is seen in terms of an object (the lowest form of existence). See how the term *doll* transmits the view of the woman as an object: passive, under man's control and incapable of enjoying the sexual encounter:

(172) He's using you for sex. What he's asking is pretty sick actually. He knows you love him still, but he wants to use you like an object … Feel the way you will feel when you are there, vulnerable, and realize that you may as well be a blow up *doll* for all he feels for you. (TAM, 23 August 2013)

Here the association of women with sexual objects is evident: the woman who posts the message gives some advice on how not to conform to the role of a *blow up doll*, i.e. an inflatable sexual partner created exclusively for male sexual gratification. By considering a woman as a blow up doll, the female partner is equated with an object whose only function is to provide physical pleasure to men.

A different type of DOLL metaphor appears in (173). The Barbie doll, a miniature adult female, offers a portrait of a woman as the male-ideal: an attractive and sexy woman readily available to provide sexual pleasure. In the same posting, the woman is also depicted as cunning and sexually promiscuous by qualifying her as a *sex vixen* through the metaphor WOMEN ARE WILD ANIMALS (see 4.1.1.3). The conflation of the domains of WILD ANIMALS and PLAYTHINGS increases the pejorative value of the metaphorical expression in italics. Also of note is the adjective *hot* as an occurrence of the HEAT metaphor (see 3.1.2):

(173) Man, I'd still fuck her, maybe even more so…the (supposedly) *hot barbie doll sex vixen* stuff makes me cringe actually. (MMSL, 1 November, 2013)

The image of the doll used to conceptualize women as sexual partners in the two postings above highlights the woman's sexual appeal insofar as dolls bring to mind connotations of beauty and attractiveness, especially in the case of Barbie dolls. Although sometimes used as a term of endearment, *doll* evokes the notion of male possession and dominance over the female sexual partner, who is merely considered as a sexual object. This stands as proof of a typical discourse practice that reflects and legitimates hegemonic masculinity. This dominant masculinity is also reflected in the use of 'f-words', like *fuck* in (173). As Coates (2013: 543) argues, 'men's use of taboo language ... performs a dominant form of masculinity'.[17]

The toy-like qualities of sexual partners that this metaphor emphasizes are also observable in the word *plaything*. Although this term does not evoke the notion of the woman as sexually alluring in the same way as *doll* does, the notion of the woman (and her intimate parts) as a possession and as part of the man's game for sexual gratification features heavily in *plaything*. In (174) the poster's wife does not like the idea of possession in reference to her breasts that his husband transmits:

(174) I've been telling my wife she's my favorite possession (and that her various body parts are my *playthings*) for years and years. It started with her saying something like "My boobs aren't your *playthings*, you know" and me just groping them and saying "Wait, whose *playthings* are they, then". (MMSL, 8 August 2013)

However, curiously enough, in the following message a woman refers to herself as her husband's 'plaything'. By doing so, she seems to happily admit the possession as part of the love and respect his husband feels for her:

(175) I'm happy to be my hubbies *plaything* ... because i know he loves and respects me. I don't cry or feel dirty or used EVER [in capitals in the original] after we have sex. I feel loved and sexy. (TAM, 27 August 2013)

The conceptualization that associates sexual partners with playthings is not restricted to females. The compound *toy boy* refers to an older woman's young lover. More specifically, it alludes to a kind of prostitution in which a young man offers sexual favours to mature women.[18] The same connotations of submission and sexual availability that apply to women equally apply to male sexual partners, who are merely considered as sexual objects at women's disposal. *Toy boy* appears in the posting below, in which the four-letter word *fuck* is hidden through asterisks:[19]

(176) At your age you should be f**king him at least twice a week. Alternatively get yourself a *toy boy*, but don't do it secretly – make sure your partner is in on the situation so that you can enjoy and talk about your bit on the side. (FFF, 17 June 2103)

From this perspective, the male prostitute is seen as a sexual commodity whose role is to serve as a product consumed by women: the same as toys, young boys can be bought and sold and have a price. Hence, in the PLAYTHING metaphor the domains of PLAYTHING and COMMODITY conflate to refer to male prostitution: the sexual partner is seen as a product that provides women a sexual service.

4.1.6 TOOLS and MACHINES

Mumford (cited in Murphy, 2001: 17) argues that the cognitive implications of tools and machines are different insofar as 'the tool lends itself to manipulation, the machine to automatic action'. However, both the TOOL and MACHINE domains offer a purely mechanistic view of sex. Let us start by analysing how the TOOL domain conceptualizes sexual issues.

The domain of TOOLS represents the penis in erection and emphasizes, from the male perspective, its active and dominant role in sexual relationships. This domain also applies in the dysphemistic representation of the penis as a mechanical device (see 4.1.1.2). In the following message, the penis is precisely considered as a mechanical device intended to perform a leading function during lovemaking: 'To penetrate to max depth on many females'.

> (177) If I have a *tool*, which has nerves over the entire service which penetrates to max depth on many females, how the hell is another woman going to be able to tell me how the internals are constructed, unless she's a gynocologist? (TAM, 11 July 2013)

Other realizations of the TOOL metaphor for penis put a greater emphasis on the male member as a device intended to dominate over the woman's body. The actions that screwdrivers or drills perform imply a considerable degree of violence and aggression when transferred to sexual relationships. According to Cameron (2006: 156), the use of names of tools as a means to talk about the penis reproduces typical heterosexist views which support the idea that '[t]he phallus must act, dominate, avenge itself on the female body. It is a symbol of authority to which we all must bow down'. In the two postings below, the use of the TOOL domain to refer to penetration of the vagina with a penis implies violence. The female body is evidently attacked by the action of tools which *screw* it in (178) and *drill* it in (179):

> (178) He would get up late, *screw* his wife all morning, go for lunch with the kids, *screw* his wife all afternoon, go for dinner with the kids, get a

babysitter, then go out with the wife to the lounges on board, drinking, dancing, etc... then *screw* his tipsy wife all night. (MMSL, 8 May 2013)

(179) The boy told her, "Shhh... hush, I don't want to hear it. You just sit there, keep whatever it is you'd like me to do with/to you, and hang it tight while I *drill* you like you're a dead fish for an hour". (TAM, 5 August 2012)

In the two messages above the penetration is seen in terms of the actions of screwing and drilling which, we should not forget, would be extremely painful (not to say a torture) if applied to humans. From this perspective, the TOOL domain is linked to the domain of WAR and VIOLENCE in that both domains conceptualize sex as an aggressive and violent activity in which men impose their authority over females (Cameron, 2006: 154).

The TOOL domain impoverishes the conception of sexual relationships at three levels, hence its dysphemistic force: first, it reduces a sexual encounter to the act of penetration by focusing on the action of the penis; second, it considers the sexual encounter from the male perspective, excluding women from any active participation in it; and, third, it leaves aside any affection or sensitivity insofar as it offers a portrait of sex as a purely mechanistic (even violent) activity. Most of these cognitive implications of this domain are also noticeable in the source domain of MACHINES.

The conventional metaphor PEOPLE ARE MACHINES (Lakoff and Johnson, 1980: 132; Johnson, 1987: 98) is a source of praising X-phemistic units: it highlights, on most occasions, male potency, virility and capacity to provide sexual pleasure without limits. This metaphor is based on THE BODY IS A MACHINE (Lakoff, 2003: 103), a metaphor which underlines the notion of functionality of human body. One of the definitions of the term *machine* given by OED3 ('a combination of parts moving mechanically or whose actions have the undeviating precision and uniformity of a machine') provides the conceptual basis for this metaphor: it supports an instrumental and mechanical view of sex, while ignoring the affective side of physical intimacy. Indeed, the focus of the MACHINE metaphor is placed on the mechanics of sexual activity and the function of sexual organs through the conceptualization A LUSTFUL PERSON IS A FUNCTIONING MACHINE (Kövecses, 2003), a reoriented version of the metaphor LUST IS A FUNCTIONING MACHINE (Lakoff, 1987a: 411). The PEOPLE-ARE-MACHINES metaphor presents some conceptual correspondences that characterize it, namely the machine is the person involved in the sexual encounter; the proper functioning of the machine is the proper functioning of the sexual relationship; male sexual organs are mechanical devices; and the person is a device intended to provide sexual pleasure. A great deal of knowledge is derived from these correspondences, as I will explain in what follows.

By virtue of the world knowledge people possess, machines are considered as devices intended to work without rest and in a mechanical and non-reflective way. Such features of machines are transferred to the lover, who is depicted as someone who gets involved in a sexual encounter in a mechanical way. This emphasis on the functional aspects of sex appears in the message below, in which the poster admits not being a sensitive lover in a thread entitled, rather significantly 'I had sex with more than 100 women':

> (180) One time she complained that she hated that I was ejaculating over her body all the time. It is difficult for me. I have systematically trained myself to become a *f**k-machine* and not a sensitive lover – which is what most women are really looking for. (SDF, 1 April 2012)

Here the compound *f**k-machine* offers a view of male sexuality as mechanical and dominant over the female partner and betrays the obsession of male sexuality with power, control and promiscuity as an indicator of virility and culturally acceptable manliness. This praising X-phemistic unit offers a portrait of the man as sexually efficient, which becomes even more evident by the fact that *machine* is qualified by a word from the target domain, *fuck*, euphemistically hidden through asterisks (see note 19, Chapter 4).

Together with these notions of lack of sensitivity and male superiority, the MACHINE metaphor emphasizes the lover's (usually the male's) ability to carry out and consummate sexual intercourse. In fact, the consideration of the man as a machine implies that he will always act with efficiency and mechanical precision. The image of the sexually powerful man is not limited to his sexual organs. In the following message, the man's whole body is depicted as a machine intended to provide sexual gratification. Note how the woman who posts the message praises her lover's sexual ability and endurance, despite his age:

> (181) He kisses all of my body and tells me how beautiful I am, he licks me all over then after working on my breasts for a long time he goes down on me and makes me get off repeatedly and won't stop until i beg him ... Its an endurance test each time, wow. I can't do it every day like he wants to, its too much for me. ... I thought that older guys did not want to do it as much but he is a *machine*. (FFF, 13 April 2013)

The notion of the sexual organs as purely functional and mechanical devices intended to perform a predesigned task ranges, to a greater or lesser extent, all over the manifestations of the MACHINE metaphor detected in the sample. This component of the metaphor is especially evident in posting (182) below, in which the adjective *cumming* specifies the main function of the man considered as a machine: ejaculation. In the advice given in this message, the man is depicted as a device intended to ejaculate (*cumming machine*), to the detriment of his sexual partner's needs. The items that qualify *machine* (*f**k* and *cumming*) contribute to portray the man as sexually powerful from a purely physical point of view rather than as sexually desirable or attractive. In fact, by emphasizing the practical side of male genitalia, a sexual relationship is viewed as a mechanical activity in which the male partner only seeks his own sexual gratification:

> (182) Perhaps try going three days without ejaculating, unless it occurs with a wet dream, and then try to get yourself off. ... Continue the three day intervals until you become a natural *cumming machine* after a few trials. (SDF, August 5, 2011)

By depicting a man as a 'natural cumming machine' the poster's intention is not offensive whatsoever; rather, the metaphor is intended to praise male sexual potency, endurance and achievement – hence its quasi-euphemistic quality. Despite the obvious praising overtones of the MACHINE metaphor when applied to males, the fact remains that the MALE-AS-A-SEX-MACHINE equation is pejorative by nature: the mapping from humans to lower forms of existence (objects) operate in this metaphor as part of the Great Chain of Being, which allows us to comprehend human character traits and behaviour in terms of non-human attributes. From this perspective, males are conceived of as (sexual) objects and, as such, deprived from their capacity to reason and feel.

Not in all the postings consulted does the MACHINE domain represent male dominant sexuality. For example, in (85) the woman is represented as a machine by means of the expression *press the right buttons* with the meaning 'sexually stimulate'. The entailment of the MACHINE metaphor at play here is that the woman is an object with buttons as part of it, and any sexually expert man should know what buttons to press in order to operate the machine. This partial use of the MACHINE domain focuses on the mechanical reaction of the female body to sexual stimulation. In this sense, the MACHINE metaphor supports the stereotype of the active, dominant and experienced man in accordance with the typical discourse of masculinity which ultimately represents women as passive sexual objects. That this is so can be gathered from Murphy (2001: 19):

> Many men still believe, for example, that if they can just master the right technique, they can satisfy women sexually and bring them to orgasm. Men

project upon women their limited view of their own sexuality and assume that with a sufficient number of mechanical strokes anyone can 'come'. This assumption reduces women's sexuality to passive nature while envisaging man's sexuality as instrumental and active.

The use of the MACHINE metaphor also equates a sexual relationship with a machine at work. In (183) the adjective *oiled* emphasizes the fact that the sexual relationship, considered as a machine at a figurative level, is properly functioning: it is 'well oiled' and thus well maintained. This component of the machine as a device that needs maintenance work is mapped onto the sexual encounter to transmit the idea that the sexual relationship being referred to is functioning properly:

> (183) She just loved having him inside of her. she loved his size, his huge loads, and his style of sex. they were totally turned on when they were having sex. i used to watch them, ... it was very exciting and she was very happy, therefore, i loved it too. they were a *well oiled machine* together, but she never loved him. (FFF, 13 April 2013)

The association between a machine in operation and a sexual relationship supports the mechanistic view of sex which characterizes the MACHINE metaphor. The image of a 'well-oiled machine' brings to mind a number of interrelated parts that operate with great precision. This portrayal of lovers passionately engaged in sexual intercourse stands in opposition to the notion of a bodiless sexuality, based on the union of two souls, which has traditionally been represented as 'the purest form of romance' in the Western cultural tradition (Springer, 1998: 487). However, in the posting above it is not the souls that are combined; the emphasis is placed on the utility and functionality of the bodies as sexual devices. In this way, a human relationship is represented as a purely mechanistic activity and therefore dehumanized.

It is worth noting that the highlighting-hiding property of metaphorical naming is at play in all the manifestations of the TOOL and MACHINE metaphors seen. By using the domain of MACHINES to talk about the role of men in sexual relationships, the poster singles out those components of the source which are intended to support a view of males as insensitive, irrational and, above all, sexually powerful. Other aspects of this domain which, if used, had provided a very different portrait of men when engaged in sexual encounters (e.g. machines may break down and fail to operate or become obsolete) are intentionally left aside.

Despite the mechanical view of sex that the domains of TOOLS and MACHINES transmit, there are a couple of significant differences: first, some realizations of the TOOL metaphor present violent and aggressive overtones, which is not the case with the occurrences of the MACHINE metaphor; and second, the source domain of TOOLS does not offer a particularly flattering portrait of males – at least not so obviously flattering as the domain of MACHINES when applied to men.

4.1.7 FLOWERS

Flowers have a symbolic value: they carry connotations of delicacy, softness and beauty. A flower is attractive to the senses: both the sight and the smell participate in the charm of flowers, in their beauty and fragrance. Because of their transient beauty and attractiveness, flowers are associated with decorativeness. Flowers also evoke the idea of purity, innocence and defencelessness; indeed, flowers can be easily torn and damaged and need to be taken care of. People pick out the attributes associated with the domain of FLOWERS to activate various metaphorical entailments which contribute to the judgemental and evaluative property of this conceptualization.

Because of the activation of those qualities associated with flowers in the human mind, flowers have been likened to anything typically feminine and, by extension, to women in general through the metaphor WOMEN ARE FLOWERS, based on systematic correspondences between the domains of WOMEN and FLOWERS that make it possible for different flower metaphors (*lily, daisy, rose,* etc.) to be typically applied to women (Coleman, 1999: 54–64; Wilson, 2011: 198). More precisely, flowers evoke the stereotype of the woman as beautiful, delicate and innocent. Other semantic components which derive from the metaphor PEOPLE ARE PLANTS like youthful vigour and the blossoming of plants (Lakoff and Turner, 1989: 84) are, however, disregarded in the metaphorical reference to effeminacy and, by analogy, to homosexuality. Again, those components of the source domain more apt for insult and disrespect are singled out, which stands as proof of the partial nature of metaphorical projections.

The metaphor WOMEN ARE FLOWERS is reified in order to refer disparagingly to male homosexuals: the association of flowers with effeminacy is used by male heterosexuals with humorous or insulting purposes through the metaphor A MALE HOMOSEXUAL IS A FLOWER, in which female-related attributes of the domain of flowers are mapped onto the target domain of male homosexuality.[20] The fact that from the male heterosexist ideology flowers constitute a symbol of effeminacy, and therefore a synonym of lack of virility (Rodríguez González,

2008a: 229), constitutes the dysphemistic basis for the metaphorical reference to homosexuality. Thus, effeminate men and gays are downgraded by ascribing to them some characteristics that come to be associated primarily with women. In this respect, it is worth noting that the dysphemistic use of the FLOWER domain does not only aim at degrading gays; it also belittles women insofar as females are ready-made material for verbal abuse against another 'marginal' group like that of male homosexuals. This seems to be motivated by the recurrent dichotomy between 'the self' and 'the other', the former represented by heterosexual males and the latter by gays and women. In this regard, the FLOWER metaphor serves to establish male authority, which is reflected in the homophobic labels that this metaphor generates to disparage homosexuals, reinforce stereotypes and impose the ideology of male heterosexuality.

Effeminacy, one of the main stereotypes associated with homosexuality, is used as a source for insult in the two postings below. In (184) the word *pansy* refers disparagingly to a man who does not impose his male authority in bed; therefore he is not playing the role he is expected to play according to heteronormative norms of sexual behaviour. By equating the man to a delicate flower, the poster overtly criticizes his weak and unmanly behaviour, which is associated with female sexuality:

(184) Her husband sounds like a man's man if he is using that word; shutting down his sexuality because he can't call his wife a ***** would make him out to be a silly *pansy*, his wife would lose sexual attraction to him if he acted like such a girly manner. (TAM, 15 February 2011)

Similarly, in (185) *nancy*, another surface realization of the floral metaphor, is not directed towards a male homosexual. It alludes to a weak character, which is associated with effeminacy and, by connection, to gays. In this way, the figure of the male homosexual is indirectly degraded:

(185) My son is starting college in the fall. He is going to be working a few jobs. I need someone to tell me to stop being a *nancy* and quit worrying about whether the jobs will impede his "college experience". (MMSL, 22 August 2013)

In the posting below the connotations of delicacy and softness which are characteristic of flowers are transferred to the target domain of homosexuality. Note that the adjective *little* used to qualify *flowers* reinforces the offence being carried out towards gays. In fact, *little* transmits the idea that gays are weak and easy to handle, a notion which is also used for dysphemistic purposes to talk about women in other source domains already noted, like SMALL FURRY ANIMALS and BIRDS.[21]

(186) I think my favourite part watch watching how all the other "men" at the table cowered and wrinkled up like *little flowers*. (MMSL, 16 October 2013)

As evidenced in the postings provided as examples, the FLOWER metaphor is a useful verbal weapon to attack both gays and 'effeminate' heterosexual males using the stereotypes associated with flowers and homosexuality as the raw material for insult. The hierarchy of entities which is established in the Great Chain of Being helps to explain the offence carried out by means of the FLOWER metaphor: gays are comprehended in terms of a lower form of life, namely that of plants, which, in turn, is implicitly associated with a 'marginal' human group according to the 'macho-type' ideology: that of women.

4.2 Reaching the intended dysphemistic meaning

So far in this chapter we have seen how metaphors are used to provoke offence or discomfort, to insult or to approach sexual topics disparagingly. This deliberate use of metaphors with a dysphemistic purpose on the part of the posters, together with the reader's capacity to grasp the meaning intended, allows for the dysphemistic force of sex-related metaphors in the internet forums consulted. The communicative force and real meaning of the linguistic metaphor in its context of use does not precede the metaphor but is activated in the inferential process of interpretation. When it comes to conventional metaphorical dysphemism, the poster's offensive intention is easy to grasp; in fact, semi-lexicalized dysphemistic metaphors are deliberately used to provoke a face affront and are recognized as such. Hence, in the process of interpretation of dysphemistic metaphors, both the taboo referent and the poster's intention are decoded and identified as such in discourse.

According to relevance-theoretic work, the interpretation of dysphemistic metaphors is an active process of dynamic inferring motivated by the addressee's expectation of relevance which involves encyclopaedic assumptions about the lexically encoded concept and contextual information. In their search for relevance, the participants in the forums are expected to capture the sexual meaning intended by pragmatically adjusting the meaning encoded by the metaphorical utterance. This process leads to the creation of *ad hoc* or pragmatically derived concepts that are communicative relevant, the same as in the interpretation of euphemistic metaphors (see 3.2). Consider the following example:

(187) It is not uncommon for a woman to go from a *tigress* in bed while she is trying to 'win' you ... only to switch over to nun-mode once you're married with children. (TAM, 29 January 2011)

The lexical meaning of *tigress* is a clue to the poster's meaning. The pragmatically inferred concept TIGRESS* constructed by the reader inherits some of the properties of the lexical concept TIGRESS which are applied to the woman. The *ad hoc* concepts constructed and communicated in (187) are broader in some respects and narrower in others. On the one hand, the denotation that is derived in the reception process is broader than that of the linguistically encoded concept because it touches on the domain of WILD ANIMALS and HUMANS; in fact, the metaphorical word *tigress* maps the fierce and aggressive behaviour of the wild feline onto a woman's sexual behaviour as a source of offence and disrespect. As a result of this conceptual association, different meanings are pragmatically inferred for the occasion: the reader understands that the woman is sexually active (*ad hoc* concept TIGRESS*), aggressive (TIGRESS**) and threatening (TIGRESS***). Such characteristics of the wild animal are deliberately used with a dysphemistic purpose and recognized as such in the thread. On the other hand, the *ad hoc* concept is narrower with respect to the lexical concept in that not all attributes which define the lexically encoded concept TIGRESS are applied to the woman; only those which are apt for offence and disrespect are transferred to the target domain, in line with the hiding/highlighting property of metaphorical structuring.

In the inferential approach to metaphor interpretation, the metaphorical item, together with background knowledge and contextual information, gives a clue in the recognition of the poster's pejorative intention and the type of offence intended. Take the use of *chick* in the posting that follows:

(188) P-1: If you are just dating because you're horny and want a *chick* on your arm/bed, then go find those girls who couldnt care less about anything other than physical release. But don't marry them.
P-2: Just an interesting double standard on the guys' part, I'm noticing. Sex before marriage is casual, no big deal, so give it to me before I commit to exclusivity. (MMSL, 14 October 2012)

Chick, a word included in the metaphor WOMEN ARE BIRDS (see 4.1.1.2), triggers an inferential process of interpretation which leads P-2 to move beyond the literal meaning 'young hen' and uncover the real meaning behind the word. The encoding of the metaphor by P-1 does not seem to be arbitrary: it transmits certain attributes of the source domain of BIRDS which are used by the poster for dysphemistic purposes. The meanings derived from *chick* lead to the construction of a wide array of *ad hoc* concepts which depict women as sexual objects at man's disposal: the woman is small and weak (CHICK*); young, attractive and sexually desirable (CHICK**); and a source of nourishment (CHICK***). In this way P-1's intended meaning in (188) is recognized by P-2, a female participant in the thread who does not seem to accept the idea expressed by P-1, judging from the ironical overtones of her reply. Taking *chick* in the posting above as an example, let us see in Table 4.1 (adapted from Wilson and Sperber, 2004: 616) how the inferential process of dysphemistic interpretation occurs.

Some cases of dysphemistic naming seen in this chapter combine metaphor with hyperbole. Hyperbole is a powerful dysphemistic device and a useful strategy of evaluative naming insofar as 'it brings the listener into the perspective of the speaker in a powerful way', as Herrero Ruiz (2009: 50) maintains. The expression of an exaggerated view of reality is used with a specific evaluative and/or ideological aim in mind and reveals an affectively involved attitude on

Table 4.1 Inferential Process of Dysphemistic Interpretation: *Chick*

P-1 has said: 'You're horny and want a chick on your arm/bed'		Embedding of the decoded logical form of P-1's utterance into a description of P-1's ostensive behaviour
P-1's utterance will be relevant to P-2		Expectation raised by recognition of P-1's ostensive behaviour and acceptance of the presumption of relevance in the context of the online interaction
P-2's utterance will achieve relevance by ironically criticizing P-1's comment		Expectation raised by P-1's utterance. Such an explanation would be relevant to P-1
A chick is a small and weak woman	*ad hoc* concept CHICK*	
A chick is a young and sexually appealing woman	*ad hoc* concept CHICK**	Enrichment of the logical form of P-1's utterance plus background knowledge
A chick is a source of nourishment	*ad hoc* concept CHICK***	

the part of the participants in the forums. Given that a hyperbolic utterance transmits meanings that are not explicitly mentioned in it, hyperbole generates a wide range of contextual effects which are evident in the PEOPLE ARE ANIMALS metaphor.

Let us see an example of dysphemistic naming belonging to the FELINE metaphor for women. In (117) *alley cat* is used as part of the criticism against a woman who has had an extramarital affair ('your wife may have the morals of an alley cat', the poster says). The analogy that is established is clearly offensive: the image of a stray cat that frequents alleys in search of food is associated with a woman in search of sex. As part of the reader's cognitive operations during the interpretation process, the reader has to somehow mitigate the exaggeration conveyed by the literal statement so as to make it reasonable via a process of understatement (see 3.2). During this interpretative process, the reader is able to add meaning effects to the lexically encoded concept, which gives rise to different *ad hoc* concepts through which the offence is carried out: namely, the woman is immoral (ALLEY CAT*); desperate for sexually available men (ALLEY CAT**); and likely to transmit illnesses (ALLEY CAT***). In this way, the pragmatically derived concepts which are created out of the lexically encoded ALLEY CAT makes it possible for the reader to establish the connection between an alley cat and a promiscuous woman as part of an obvious exaggeration used for dysphemistic emphasis. In this way, the participant in the thread who reads the posting grasps the poster's intention of overtly criticizing the woman on the grounds of her immorality and lustful behaviour.

It remains to be said that, from the standpoint of RT, the dysphemistic utterances seen above can be said to be *optimally relevant* insofar as they achieve a wide range of contextual effects without any unjustifiable effort on the part of the reader. In fact, the participants in the forums seem to have no difficulty in grasping the intended dysphemistic meaning of the sex-related linguistic metaphors employed and appreciate the metaphorical utterances as relevant contributions to the thread.

4.3 The evaluative function of dysphemistic metaphors

As already commented, many male participants in the forums resort to metaphor as a means to criticize and condemn people who do not conform to conventional gender roles. Although euphemism is also at the poster's disposal to talk judgementally about certain sexual behaviours considered as inappropriate or immoral, as seen in Chapter 3, metaphorical dysphemism is a much more powerful evaluative and persuasive resource. Many realizations of dysphemistic metaphors seen in the postings provided as examples in 4.1 are used as verbal weapons to criticize, discriminate or undermine social groups which, according to dominant male heterosexist ideology, are considered as 'marginal', namely male homosexuals and women. After all, metaphors play a role in the construction of some male participants in the forums as heterosexual beings.

Concerning the role of language in constructing dominant heteronormative discourse, Cameron and Kulick (2006: 165) argue that 'in the heteronormative hierarchy the most favoured norm of sexuality is monogamous (involving marriage or quasi-marital relationships), reproductive (with intercourse penetration of a vagina by a penis – being the preferred sexual practice) and conventional in terms of gender roles (which is to say, based on a norm of men as sexually active/dominant and women as sexually passive/subordinate'. Taking the notion of heteronormative as what is socially considered as acceptable and natural, Coates (2013) demonstrates that heterosexual speakers orient to a dominant heteronormative discourse through different verbal resources. Her findings can be partly applied to the sample consulted. By drawing on metaphor, many male posters in the forums do not only position themselves as heterosexuals, but also display a misogynistic and dominant attitude. This seems to confirm the role of women in heteronormative discourse:

> Women are often absent from male talk, and when they are present they are often referred to in a misogynistic way. Male speakers often draw on misogynistic discourse which reduces women to body parts. (Coates, 2013: 544)

Some conceptual domains seem especially suited for discrimination and offence and clearly reflect an ideological biased view of women and effeminate men as individuals who deviate from 'proper' femininity and masculinity respectively. At the same time, certain domains used to talk about women and homosexuals reflect and reproduce the heteronormative order. To this end, the choice of the source domain is highly significant: language users opt for certain domains in the belief that their message will sound convincing and persuasive, and therefore will provide an effective ideological evaluation of the reality talked about (Deignan, 2010: 361–2). In this sense, following McEnery (2006: 7), evaluative metaphorical language operates in a threefold dimension: the object of offence (a sex-related behaviour or attitude identified as offensive, such as lust or sexual initiative in females and effeminacy in males); the scapegoat categories (the cause of offence, in our case women and male homosexuals); and somebody who does the accusing (the participant in the forum).

The evaluative use of metaphorical dysphemism can be insightfully approached from appraisal theory, an analytical framework concerned with the language of evaluation, attitude and emotion used to express personal views and ideological positions and analyse how speakers use evaluative language for persuasive purposes. Following Martin and White (2005: 1), this framework 'is concerned with how writers/speakers approve and disapprove, enthuse and abhor, applaud and criticise, and with how they position their readers/listeners to do likewise'. From this perspective, sex-related dysphemism is a means through which some of the participants in the forums adopt a negative stance towards the topics and people they talk about. Out of the three domains of appraisal, i.e. attitude, graduation and engagement, dysphemism can be analysed if we consider attitude and graduation; more precisely, attitude as *judgement* (concerned with critical attitudes to people and their behaviour) and *appreciation* (negative aesthetic or functional evaluation of people); and graduation as *force* (concerned with grading according to intensity or amount). Indeed, the use of attitudinal lexis tells the reader how to feel and react in many of the postings seen in this chapter. Let us see how these axes of variation in evaluative orientation apply in some metaphorical items used in the forums consulted.

The appraisal subsystems of attitude and graduation coexist in many of the dysphemistic metaphorical items encountered in the corpus. The choice of a dysphemistic word belonging to a particular conceptual domain expresses attitudinal value assessment by expressing negative evaluation of attitudes and behaviours through emotionally loaded and intense metaphorical language. A good case in point is the use of the ANIMAL domain to criticize certain sexual behaviours that may pose a threat to the dominant male status. In the criticism of the woman's active sexual behaviour dysphemism usually combines with hyperbole: depicting a woman as a *starving lioness* (133) or as a *tigress in bed* (187) involves the exaggerated expression of a negative appreciation of the denotatum: the woman's behaviour is considered as wild and out of control, as that of a man-eater even. By considerably upgrading the negative features of the referent being dealt with, the poster tries to make the participants in the thread agree with his views. In doing so, he reinforces a sense of 'male' in-group identity against what is considered to be a threat to male dominance. The use of intensified lexis – one of the appraisal resources of graduation as force – is a way to adjust the degree of an evaluation in order to show how strong the feeling is (Martin and White, 2005: 37). In this way, metaphorical items expressing attitude on the part of the poster are intensified for dysphemistic purposes, which contributes to criticize an active sexual behaviour as unladylike (i.e. attitude as judgement) and assess sexually active women in terms of men's reactions to them as threatening (i.e. attitude as appreciation).

In Figure 4.1 the different evaluative realizations of attitude and graduation are graphically shown with respect to the linguistic metaphor *starving lioness* 'sexually active woman', included in the conceptualization SEXUALLY ACTIVE WOMEN ARE WILD ANIMALS.

The evaluative function of dysphemism is evidenced in the distinction between those judgements oriented to 'social esteem' and those dealing with 'social sanction'. In *starving lioness* judgements of social esteem are used to condemn the behaviour of certain women (traditional values whereby women are supposed not to take the initiative in sexual encounters), whereas judgements of social sanction focus on negative evaluations of propriety (ethics) to consider the woman as immoral and lascivious. As Deignan (2010: 359–61) argues, the use of metaphors to create entailments constitutes an effective means to talk judgementally about people. Talking of women in terms of predators creates several entailments in the target domain which contribute to the evaluative power of the metaphor: women are condemned for playing an active role in sex and depicted as immoral, dangerous, even out of control, and therefore as a threat to man's sexual hegemony. This stands in sharp contrast with the stereotypical view of the woman as submissive, docile and compliant, traits

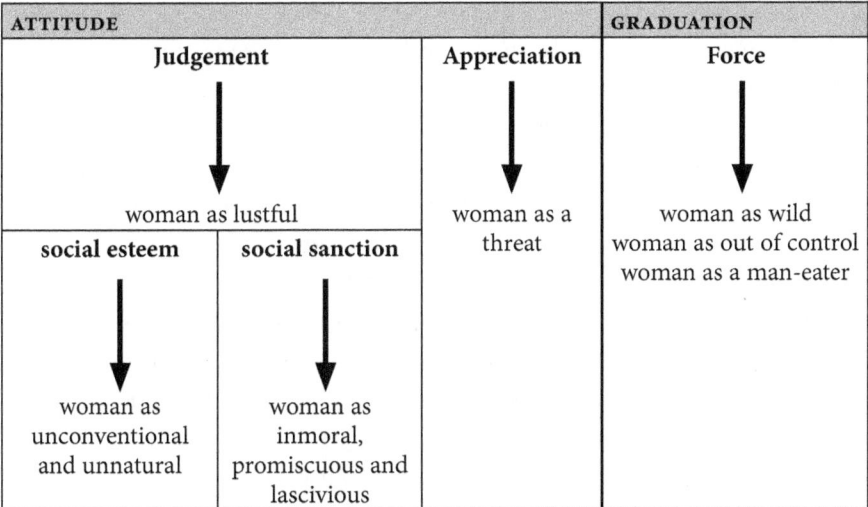

Figure 4.1 Evaluative Realizations in Sexist Dysphemism: *Starving lioness*

culturally considered as feminine. In this regard, by attacking their sexual behaviour, women are deprived of a way to assert themselves in society and in interpersonal relations.[22] Attitudinal meanings of judgement and appreciation have a profound social orientation: they tell us the 'right' way to behave and what is expected of individuals in society by reference to a system of culturally determined values. As Martin and White (2005: 45) claim:

> One way to think about judgement and appreciation is to see them as institutionalised feelings, which take us out of our everyday common sense world into the uncommon sense worlds of shared realm of proposals about behaviour – how we should behave or not.

From this perspective, metaphor is an effective means to condemn behaviours and attitudes which do not conform to social standards.

The attitudinal lexis observed in the corpus also aims at undermining the other 'marginal' group: male homosexuals and effeminate heterosexuals. Posters resort to attitudinal lexis with a view to imposing the dominant male heterosexist ideology and reinforcing stereotypes concerning homosexuality.[23] The term *pansy*, one of the instantiations of the conceptual metaphor A MALE HOMOSEXUAL IS A FLOWER, is a representative example of the way in which homosexuality and effeminate behaviour are evaluated through metaphorical language. In posting (184) *pansy* is used to criticize effeminacy as an inappropriate ladylike attitude in males and transmits a negative image of homosexuals and effeminate men as weak, vulnerable and delicate. Indeed, this metaphor involves the exaggerated expression of effeminacy, which is ascribed to men for an offensive purpose. The idea underlying the metaphor is that homosexuals and effeminate heterosexuals are so weak and delicate that they are flowers rather than men. Consider the evaluative realizations of attitude and graduation in the homophobic label *pansy* in Figure 4.2.

The fact that judgements of social esteem and social sanction coincide in the evaluative realizations of two metaphorical terms considered representative in reference to women and male homosexuals should not be overlooked. As shown in Figures 4.1 and 4.2, they are evaluated as peculiar, odd and unnatural, as individuals who do not conform to social expectations of their assigned sex. This view reflects their consideration as 'marginal' groups according to the heteronormative social order (see note 23, Chapter 4): both women and homosexuals are socially sanctioned as immoral, as people who are not ethical or beyond reproach. This leads us to think of religious and civic observances regarding 'non-standard' sexual practices and preferences which are, at the writing of this

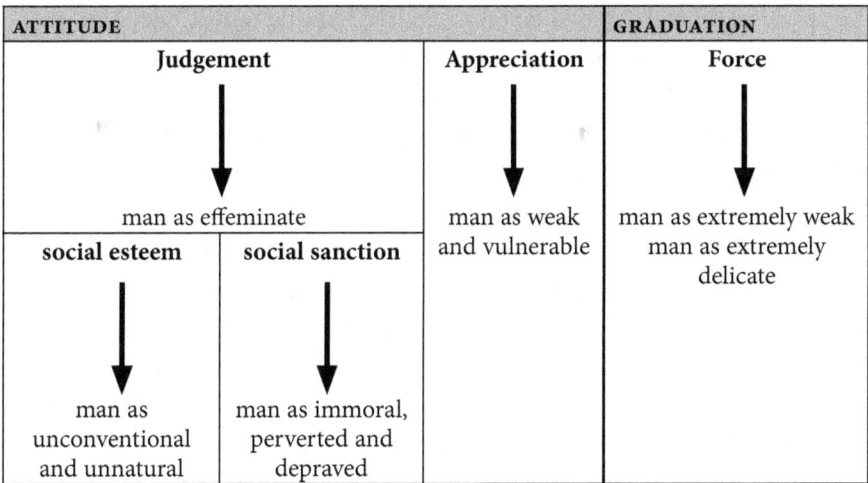

Figure 4.2 Evaluative Realizations in Homophobic Dysphemism: *Pansy*

book, still subject to moral censorship by many in Western countries and even to penalties in Muslim communities. In this respect, the evaluative meaning of nouns like *lioness* and *pansy* is clearly axiological, as they express an evaluation in relation to an ideology and a system of values more or less explicitly codified by the culture that 'normal' people are supposed to adhere to. In fact, male posters give off their heterosexuality in online forums through words that are regarded as explicit references of their heterosexuality in accordance with heteronormative assumptions of masculinity (Cameron and Kulick, 2006; Coates, 2013).

Despite the biased view of women and male homosexuals that many metaphorical terms transmit, it is noteworthy that some of the metaphors analysed imply more than the reproduction of the typical heterosexist assumptions and stereotypes existing in male-dominated culture. In this respect, Cameron (2006: 156) argues that the biased metaphors which men tend to endorse (e.g. those drawing on the domains of ANIMALS to talk about women, FLOWERS to refer to homosexuals or WEAPONS to verbalize the penis) respond not only to a male chauvinistic attitude, but also reflect lexical creativity and a desire to laugh at certain stereotypes and myths. She concludes by saying that, although exaggerated and sometimes humorous, this type of metaphorical language tends to reveal anxieties about masculine sexuality.

In some cases the participants in the forums try to make their message more intense, and therefore their offence stronger, by assembling words which are related from a semantic point of view. The coexistence of dysphemistic metaphors belonging to the same domain is one of the resources by which the appraisal domain of graduation is realized (Martin and White, 2005: 144). For example, in (139) the HUNTING metaphor is linguistically realized by the juxtaposition of different metaphors in the same message whereby women are represented as animals ('you pursued, chased down, hunted for, captured and enjoyed your prey'), while men are depicted as hunters whose aim is to capture the woman, who is ultimately seen as the prey. By the same token, the verbal attack becomes more intense when dysphemistic metaphors drawing on different source domains combine in the same posting, as happens with the verb *devour* (149) in which both the domains of EATING and WILD ANIMALS conflate.

Evaluation does not always take place in the case of dysphemistic labels, as seen so far. The critical attitude and offensive intention of some of the participants in the forums is also realized by means of quasi-dysphemistic references, i.e. those which, despite their socially acceptable disguise, are intentionally offensive. The different realizations of the DIRT metaphor (*dirty, filthy, smutty,* etc.) are typical examples of metaphorical items used to disapprove of certain sexual behaviours (see 3.1.12). Let us see how *flame-throwing*, a linguistic materialization of the FIRE metaphor (see 3.1.2), performs this evaluative function. This metaphorical compound, which touches on the domains of FIRE and WAR, is a derogatory euphemistic label which the poster of message (32) employs to condemn a sinful sexual behaviour (that he calls 'ignorant flame throwing') through an exaggerated and distorted view of reality without any risk of face-affront. The attitudinal meanings of judgement and affect that this word transmits tell us the 'right' way to behave and what is expected of individuals in society according to moral codes and religious principles.

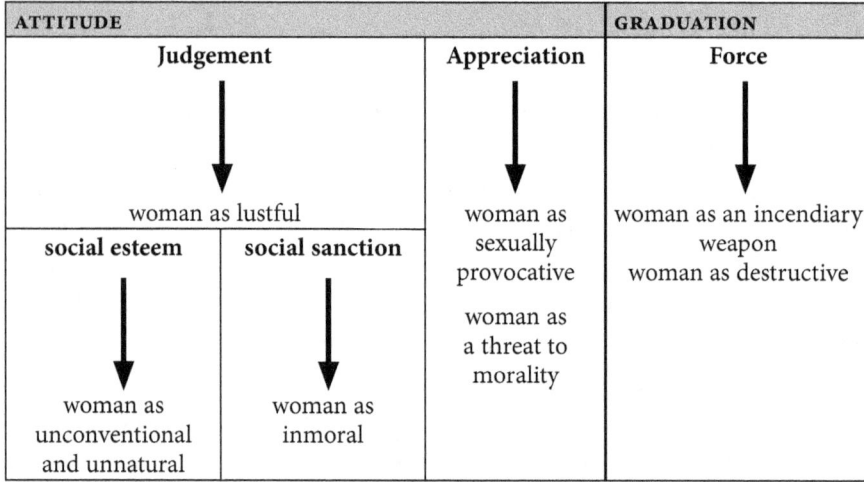

Figure 4.3 Evaluative Realizations in Quasi-dysphemism: *Flame-throwing*

By using the image of a flame thrower the poster resorts to intensified lexis (one of the appraisal resources of graduation as force) which equates the woman to an incendiary weapon capable of destruction and associates fire with the flames of Hell. As for attitudinal meanings, the poster of (32) condemns a lustful behaviour in a woman as unladylike, unconventional in females (judgement as social esteem) and as immoral (judgement as social sanction), and assesses the woman's behaviour as sexually provocative and thus as a threat to morality. From the religious perspective adopted by this forum member, the breach of social sanction is seen as a mortal sin that deserves religious punishment. He warns the woman as follows: '[T]here are some other flames you might want to be considering when you attack the Word of God.' In this sense, the choice of a source domain with a religious significance is not at random: it is a strategy that, apart from the entailments it creates, enables the poster to attract to his views those readers for whom the religious position on sexual issues is important. In this way, this metaphor is intended to perform a persuasive and ideological function in its context.

In summary, granted that the connotative value of lexical units is much more significant than their purely denotative value, to use metaphors to generate particular entailments, to opt for biased evaluative nouns and adjectives or to resort to specific source domains which are especially significant for particular groups of language users constitutes an expression of negative attitudes, moral judgements and emotions encoded in the word chosen to describe women and male homosexuals. In this sense, metaphorical dysphemism stands out as a powerful evaluative resource of language: by resorting to dysphemism the participant in the forum projects a certain attitude and is perceived by the rest of the participants as having taken an explicit sexist, homophobic, religious or moral stance, highly determined by cultural and ideological values.

5

Conclusions and Final Remarks

This book has been concerned with a number of key questions about the relationships between language, taboo and cognition. In order to gain an insight into the conceptual material encountered in a sample of language in internet forums, I assumed that studying metaphors in real-life contexts involves explaining both the role of metaphor in cognition and the use of metaphors in communication. Thus, I considered the cognitive and pragmatic factors that come into play when using and interpreting sex-related metaphors in discourse.

The analysis carried out reveals that participants in internet forums make extensive use of metaphors to discuss sexual topics subject to a greater or lesser degree of interdiction (coition, masturbation, pornography, sadomasochism, etc.). Sex-related online forums are not only a breeding ground for euphemistic metaphors, as can naturally be expected; they are also a fertile ground for sex-based conceptual dysphemism. Indeed, the study has shown that sex is by no means limited to implicit, vague or indirect references: an explicit treatment of this taboo coexists with more or less implicit allusions to sexual issues in online communication.

Evidence from the corpus suggests that the dividing line between euphemism and dysphemism is quite blurred. Indeed, as the relationships between taboo and language are complex and unpredictable in real language use, it is sometimes difficult to establish the axiological value of a given expression with any certainty. This is even more so in the field of sex, as sex-based euphemistic and dysphemistic expressions may easily slide off into slang. Apart from the basic categories of euphemism and dysphemism, other modalities of X-phemistic naming have been detected, namely orthophemism, or direct talking, and quasi-euphemism and quasi-dysphemism as X-phemistic categories in which the form of the language expression is at variance with its illocutionary force.

The analysis provides evidence that different types of metaphorical X-phemistic substitutes, included in the aforementioned categories, are used by the forums' members for a wide range of communicative purposes: to avoid offence (protective); to upgrade and magnify the denotatum (uplifting); to hold interest (provocative); to display group solidarity (cohesive); to defuse the seriousness of the taboo topic (ludic); to praise one's sexual performance (praising); to sexually arouse the partner (dirty); and to provide a socially acceptable criticism in polite contexts (derogatory). Despite the logical differences, these X-phemistic types are the source of preferred (i.e. politic, non-threatening) language expressions to deal with sex-related topics in the context of the online forums consulted. Dysphemism, however, is a face-threatening act *par excellence*: the poster resorts to a dispreferred expression to provoke offence, discrimination or social exclusion.

The examination of the language data demonstrates that our understanding of sex is guided by conceptual metaphors that assimilate the target domain of SEX into concrete source domains. Such different domains as WORK, HEAT and FIRE, GAMES and SPORTS, JOURNEYS, ADVENTURES, CONTAINERS, PHYSICAL FORCES, NATURAL PHENOMENA, FIREWORKS, ILLNESS, INSANITY, HEALTH, DIRT and FALLING are employed to target euphemistically sexual issues. When it comes to dysphemism, the participants in the forums resort to the source domains of ANIMALS, HUNTING and RIDING, FOOD and EATING, WAR and VIOLENCE, PLAYTHINGS, TOOLS and MACHINES and FLOWERS. The diversity of domains used to verbalize sexual topics reflects the rich complexity of human sexuality.

As my discussion has shown, metaphors do not usually perform their X-phemistic function in isolation; rather, linguistic metaphors belonging to different conceptualizations combine and interact in the online threads to deal with the taboo of sex in particular terms. Metaphor also coexists with another conceptual mechanism, metonymy, to verbalize and reason about sex-related topics. All the cases of metonymic expressions found in the corpus belong to the source-in-target type, that involving a cognitive operation of source domain expansion which provides mental access to a more complex scene that includes the taboo target domain.

The analysis reveals a tendency in sex-based metaphorical language to emphasize sexual desire and relationships as a highly intense, even irrational experience over which people have no control. Although one may associate euphemism with mild lexical alternatives to the taboo, the main meaning focus that characterizes the way many sexual issues are euphemistically represented is INTENSITY. In fact, the metaphors that take FIRE, NATURAL PHENOMENA, FIREWORKS or INSANITY as source domains do not really aim at hiding the taboo; rather, they respond to the poster's need to highlight the sexual topic in a socially acceptable way.

This study also proves that the description of metaphors in a sample of naturally occurring language helps to understand the real use of conceptual systems in discourse. As the reader will surely have noticed, the different occurrences of conventional metaphors constitute a potent means of conceptualization of sex-related topics which reflect active schemes of metaphorical thought. For example, metaphorical items like *bunny*, *hot* or *pansy*, despite being deeply entrenched in the language, keep intact their conceptual significance and communicative impact in real discourse. They are deliberately used as metaphors with a conscious X-phemistic purpose that is oriented towards causing a particular effect on the readers of the postings. X-phemistic metaphors therefore may be said to have a special rhetorical status. In this respect, Deignan (1997: 25) insightfully argues that the importance of conventional metaphors in discourse should by no means be underestimated: 'An investigation into the metaphors that are frequently used to talk and write about a topic about can yield insights about the way in which that topic is understood within a culture.' The examination of the metaphors carried out seems to confirm her words.

Furthermore, the analysis reveals that the X-phemistic function of a particular metaphor greatly depends on the components of the source domain that are singled out and mapped onto the target domain for a particular communicative goal. In fact, the highlighting–hiding property of metaphorical projections serves the purpose of euphemism and dysphemism particularly well by emphasizing those aspects of the source domain which are more apt for presenting the taboo in a polite way or for causing offence or disrespect. This implies that only certain components of the source domain are employed in the metaphorical projection from source to target, while the rest remain hidden. And those that are activated in the postings respond to the speaker's communicative intention and reflect the axiological value of the metaphor.

An important conclusion is concerned with the evaluative and persuasive properties of sex-related metaphors. Some of the examples discussed in Chapter 3 and especially in Chapter 4 have shown that X-phemistic metaphor is a powerful evaluative and persuasive resource of language and, as such, potentially ideological. The choice of a source domain that is emotionally meaningful for a particular group of people is one of the mechanisms through which metaphorical evaluation is carried out. To opt for a word belonging to a particular domain expresses attitudinal value assessment by transmitting negative evaluation of attitudes and behaviours, usually through emotionally loaded and intense metaphorical language. By using some of the domains seen in the fourth chapter to target sexual issues, some forums' members project a certain attitude and are perceived by the rest of the participants as having taken an explicit moral, sexist or homophobic stance. Indeed, some male heterosexuals overtly display their heterosexuality in the form of offensive and degrading references to females and male homosexuals and offer a violent and aggressive view of sexual encounters. In this sense, much of the dysphemistic metaphorical language encountered contributes to validate masculinity and reassures heteronormativity insofar as it attacks both males and females who do not conform to the conventional gender roles of the sexually active and heterosexual man and the monogamous and submissive woman respectively.

Another mechanism for framing evaluations found in the corpus is the use of metaphors to create entailments that are likely to present negative value judgements on people or behaviours, mostly on account of their 'immoral' sexual practices. For example, considering women as predators creates several entailments in the target domain which contribute to the evaluative power of the metaphor: they are wild, voracious, dangerous, etc. Obviously enough, the choice of the source domain and the use of metaphors to create entailments are not mutually exclusive; they usually combine in the evaluation carried out by metaphors. In any case, we should not forget that, however offensive or degrading certain source domains may be, metaphors are not dangerous in themselves. As Musolff (2004: 177) puts it, 'what makes them [metaphors] into potential *ignes fatui* [in italics in the original] is the pretence of their users that the analogies based on them must not be questioned'.

The evaluative use of metaphors has also been approached from appraisal theory. The appraisal domains of attitude as judgement (concerned with critical attitudes to people and their behaviour) and *appreciation* (negative aesthetic or functional evaluation of people) and graduation as *force* (grading according to intensity or amount) help to explain how the use of evaluative lexis in the forums tells the reader how to feel and react. The different evaluative realizations of attitude and graduation are usually intensified for dysphemistic purposes through hyperbole, which contributes to overtly criticize people and behaviours considered beyond the limits of conventional sex. Dysphemism is not the only source of evaluation, however. The critical attitude of some participants in the forums is also realized through quasi-dysphemistic metaphors, those which, despite their socially acceptable disguise, are used to disapprove of certain sexual behaviours. In this regard, metaphor has proven to be an effective means to condemn sexual practices and attitudes which do not conform to social and moral standards by reference to a set of culturally determined value systems.

This study has made use of some of the achievements of the relevance-theoretic approach to explain the relationship between the linguistic form and the pragmatic interpretation of X-phemistic figurative language. In the course of the analysis we have seen that metaphoricity is a dynamic process of cognitive activation both at the levels of use and reception. Reaching the poster-intended meaning involves a pragmatic process of *ad hoc* concept construction: the sexual concepts are pragmatically inferred out of lexically encoded concepts during the reception process, which activates the X-phemistic force of the metaphors used in the postings. The X-phemistic nature of the lexical alternative to the taboo is thus recovered by pragmatically constrained inferences which develop the linguistically encoded semantic representation (i.e. the explicature) of the utterance, using contextual information, the logical form of the utterance and the world knowledge the forum member possesses (i.e. his or her encyclopaedic knowledge) as a guide in the interpretative process. In this respect, it is important to note that the identification of the X-phemistic meaning of the concepts encoded requires little processing effort on the part of the participants in the forums; hence, the metaphors employed can be said to be highly relevant in their contexts. After all, in the particular communicative context of online forums devoted to sexual issues, in which the participants are willing to cooperate and help one another, it is not surprising that they find no difficulty in grasping the information behind the logical form of the utterance.

Of course, the study presented here does not exhaust such a rich topic as sex in language and mind. A number of issues require additional linguistic inquiry. First, further research should strive to explore the relationship of metaphor to cultural models and communities by comparing metaphorically motivated expressions in different languages and exploring the way different cultures structure sex-related concepts and the sexist implications that may derive from it. Second, it would be of value to look at how sexual metaphor is used in the language of gay and lesbian communities and see to what extent these groups have a distinctive use of figurative language. By doing so, one could get an insight into the way male and female homosexuality is discursively produced through metaphorical sex-based language, and discover if these language users align themselves with a certain type of discourse. Third, it would be interesting to compare the types of source domains used by men and women to talk about sex and explore to what degree conventional and heteronormative gender roles are challenged or reproduced. I hope that this book will serve as a stimulus for further research in these and other fields.

In summary, the analysis of the messages posted by the participants in sex-related internet forums supports the view that metaphorical language is a vehicle for the public expression of feelings, desires and prejudices. Metaphor pervades the way people reason about sex, leading to a multitude of X-phemistic references to sexual topics, which ultimately demonstrates that the taboo of sex is not only present in people's minds but also in language.

Appendix I: Euphemistic metaphors classified by source domain

Source domain	Source concept	Linguistic realization	Target concept	Posting
ADVENTURE	ADVENTURE	adventure	an extramarital sexual relationship	63
			an exciting sexual experience	65
		adventurous	fond of unconventional sexual practices	64
			fond of exciting sexual experiences	38,155
		sadomasochistic adventure	a sadomasochistic sexual experience	66
CONTAINER	CAGE	come out of one's cage	to get sexually liberated	74
	CLOSET	be out of the closet	to reveal one's homosexual orientation	73
		closeted	a homosexual who has not revealed his/her sexual orientation	72
		come out	to reveal one's homosexual orientation	72
	CONTAINER	backdoor	the anus	67
		cave	the vagina	161
		honey pot	the vagina	69
		pot	a sexually excited woman	68
	PRESSURIZED CONTAINER	explode	to achieve orgasm	85,111
		explosion	an orgasm	71
			sexual excitement	70
DIRT	DIRT	dirty	immoral	100–2
			erotic or pornographic	105
		dirty night club	a brothel	100
		dirty talk	sexually explicit language used to arouse the partner	99, 106,121
		filthy	sexually obsessed, immoral	104
		get nasty	get involved in new sexual experiences	106
		nasty	sexually exciting	106
		smutty	erotic or pornographic	103

Source domain	Source concept	Linguistic realization	Target concept	Posting
FALLING	FALLING	fall for	to become sexually attracted to	107
		head over hills for	sexually attracted to	108
FIRE-WORKS	FIREWORKS	bright lights	relative to orgasm	85
		fireworks	an orgasm	75,85
GAMES AND SPORTS	GAME	adult games	erotic/pornographic games	41
		bed-game	sexual activities	38
		butt play	anal stimulation	106
		finger play	a vaginal stimulation with fingers	45
		foreplay	sexual activity as a prelude to coition	42
		play	to get involved in unconventional sexual practices	39
		play around the anus	to stimulate someone's anus	45
		play away	to commit adultery	46
		play doctor	to get initiated into sexuality (children)	36
		play house	to copulate	37
		play with one's backdoor	to stimulate someone's anus	40
		play with oneself	to masturbate	38,109
		pony play	a sadomasochistic role play involving a trainer and a pony	52
		puppy play	a sadomasochistic role play involving a trainer and a dog	51
		roll	to copulate with	43
		roll in the hay	a casual sexual encounter	44
		toy	an object used to enhance sexual pleasure	45,106
		toy with	to sexually stimulate	57
		sex toy	a person used as an object to enhance sexual pleasure	160
	SPORTS	first base	mouth-to-mouth kissing	49
		play away	to commit adultery	46
		second base	the manual stimulation of erogenous zones	49
		sexathon	a long and intense sexual encounter	48
		sexual athlete	a powerful sexual partner	47
		watersports	a sadomasochistic sexual practice involving urination	50

Appendix I: Euphemistic metaphors classified by source domain   195

Source domain	Source concept	Linguistic realization	Target concept	Posting
HEALTH	HEALTH	*healthy*	moral	97
			relative to conventional sex	98
	LACK OF HEALTH	*sick*	immoral, sexually obsessed	96
		unhealthy	relative to unconventional, potentially harmful sex	93–4, 100
		unhealthy sexual attention	sexual molestation during childhood	95
HEAT AND FIRE	COLD	*cold*	not susceptible to sexual excitement	35
	HEAT	*ardent*	sexually passionate	34
		hot	sexually exciting	20,35, 65,109, 122,127, 132,173
		hottest	sexually exciting	21
		melt	to be sexually excited	33,110
		torrid	sexually exciting	22
		turn up the heat	to sexually excite someone	33,68
		warm-up	sexual stimulation before coition	5
		warm someone up	to sexually stimulate someone	23
	FIRE	*ashes*	lack of sexual desire	76
		light one's fire	to sexually excite someone	26
		on fire	sexually excited	24
		reignite the fire	to sexually excite someone after a period of inactivity	27
		spark	sexual attraction	25
	FLAME	*flame*	sexual excitement	28
		flame-throwing	the act of sexually exciting someone	32
		high-school flame	former sexual partner	31
		old flame	former sexual partner	30
		reignite the flame	to sexually excite someone after a period of inactivity	29

Source domain	Source concept	Linguistic realization	Target concept	Posting
ILLNESS AND INSANITY	INSANITY	crazed	sexually excited	86
		go nuts	to be sexually excited	86
		insane passion	sexual obsession, lust	87
		madly in lust	sexually excited, obsessed	90
		sex-crazed	sexually obsessed	89
		sex maniac	sexually obsessed, pervert	88
	ILLNESS	fever of sensuality	a state of sexual excitement and obsession	92
		sick with lust	sexually obsessed, pervert	91
JOURNEYS	JOURNEY	cruise	to look for casual sexual partners	62
		go all the way	to sexually penetrate	49,61
		journey	a sexual encounter	53,111
	DESTINATION	come	to achieve orgasm	54
		completion	an orgasm	55
		destination	an orgasm	53
		edge	an orgasm	58
		edging	stopping sexual stimulation right before achieving orgasm	59
		finish	to achieve orgasm	56–7
		finish line	an orgasm	56
		get close	to be about to achieve orgasm	57
		get someone to paradise	to make someone achieve orgasm	56
		get someone there	to make someone achieve orgasm	57
		get over the edge	to achieve orgasm	60
		no-comer	a person who cannot achieve orgasm	54
		there	an orgasm	56–7
		walk away	not to achieve orgasm	57
NATURAL FORCES	WATER	ongoing wave of orgasm	the achievement of orgasm	78
		ride waves	to copulate	80
		roller	sexual pleasure preceding orgasm	80
		super awesome crashing wave	an orgasm	80
		torrent of passion	an uncontrollable sexual desire	81
		torrented	sexually exciting	82
		wave of pleasure	sexual pleasure preceding orgasm	79
	WEATHER	storm	sexually attractive	84
		whirlwind	passionate	83

Appendix I: Euphemistic metaphors classified by source domain

Source domain	Source concept	Linguistic realization	Target concept	Posting
PHYSICAL FORCES	ELECTRICITY	crackling sparks	sexual excitement	76
		electric shock type	an orgasm	75
	MAGNETISM	attract	to sexually attract	77
		magnetism	sexual attraction	77
WORK	BUSINESS	business	the prostitution	15
		get down to business	to copulate	5
		go into business	to get involved in an extramarital sexual relationship	4
	COMMERCE	affair	an extramarital sexual relationship	4,19,22
		buy sex	to have sex with a prostitute	16
		buy someone	to have sex with a prostitute	17
		intercourse	a sexual encounter	18,58
		rent someone	to have sex with a prostitute	17
		sell one's body	to work as a prostitute	17
		sell sex	to work as a prostitute	16
	DUTY	duty sex	routine sex	108
		spousal duty	copulation within marriage	13
	JOB	BJ (blowjob)	a fellatio	12
		do a good job	to practise fellatio	11
		finish the job	to make a man ejaculate	9
		handjob	a male masturbation	8,58
		on the job	engaged in oral sex	10
	PROFESSIONS	masseuse	a prostitute	14
		sex worker	a prostitute	7,15
	WORK	do the work	to copulate	6
		work of pleasure	the prostitution	7

Appendix II: Dysphemistic metaphors classified by source domain

Source domain	Source concept	Linguistic realization	Target concept	Posting
ANIMALS	BIRDS	chick	a sexually attractive and available female	122–3, 188
		cock	the penis	2, 124, 126
		cock sucker	a fellator	125
	SMALL FURRY ANIMALS	alley cat	a prostitute; a sexually promiscuous woman	117
		beaver	the female genitals	119
		bunny	a sexually attractive and available female	112
		eager beaver	a lustful woman	120
		playboy bunny	a sexually attractive and available female	113
		pussy	the vagina	121
			a stupid person	118
		pussycat	a sexually attractive and available female	116
		sex kitten	a sexually attractive and available female	114–5
	WILD ANIMALS	cougar	a mature and sexually active woman	132
		foxy	appealing, flirtatious and tricky	127
		horny	sexually excited	21, 137, 188
		lion	a sexually active, dominant man	134
		predator	a lustful man who looks for women in a dishonest way	138
		sexually charged lion	a lustful man in search for sex	141
		starving lioness	a sexually active and dominant woman	133
		tigress in bed	a sexually active and aggressive woman	187
		vamp	a femme fatale	130
			to sexually seduce	131
		vixen	a sexually alluring and tricky woman	128–9, 173
		wolf	a sexually active and aggressive man	135–6

Source domain	Source concept	Linguistic realization	Target concept	Posting
FLOWERS	FLOWER	little flower	a male homosexual; an effeminate man	186
		nancy	a weak and effeminate man	185
		pansy	a male homosexual, an effeminate man	184
FOOD AND EATING	DESSERTS	cheesecake	a sexually attractive and available female	151
		cookie	a sexually attractive and available female	150
		sweetie-pie	a sexually attractive and available female	152
		tart	a prostitute; a licentious woman	153,155
			to behave promiscuously	154
	EATING	devour	to sexually possess	149
		eat cock	to practice fellatio	148
		eat pussy	to practice cunnilingus	147
		full	sexually satisfied	3
		hungry	in need of sex	3,146
		meal	sexual partner	3
		pick up a snack	to have extramarital sexual intercourse	3
		sex-starved	in need of sex	145
	FISH	tuna cave	the vagina	161
	FRUIT	cherry-picker	a womanizer in search for female virgins	157
		pop one's cherry	to lose one's virginity (females)	156
		sugar baby	a young mistress who is provided with benefits by an older man	158
	MEAT	chicken-pot pie	a superficial sexual encounter	146
		piece of meat	a woman as a sexual object	140,160
	others	banquet	an exciting sexual encounter	146
		coffee	a woman as a sexual object	159
HUNTING AND RIDING	HUNTING	capture	to sexually possess	139
		chase	sexual approach; seduction	141
		chase down	to sexually approach; to seduce	139
		hunt for	to search for a sexual partner	139
		hunting days	days of sexual adventures	141
		prey	a woman as a sexual conquest	139–40
	RIDING	mount	to copulate (above position)	142,144
		ride	to copulate (above position)	144
		straddle	to copulate (above position)	143

Appendix II: Dysphemistic metaphors classified by source domain

Source domain	Source concept	Linguistic realization	Target concept	Posting
PLAYTHING	DOLL	barbie doll	a sexually attractive and available female	173
		blow up doll	a woman as a sexual object	172
	TOY	plaything	a woman as a sexual object	175
		playthings	the breasts	174
		toy boy	a male prostitute	176
TOOLS AND MACHINES	TOOL	drill	to copulate with	179
		screw	to copulate with	178
		tool	the penis	177
	MACHINE	cumming machine	a sexually powerful and enduring man	182
		f**k machine	a sexually powerful and enduring man	180
		machine	a sexually powerful, enduring and desirable man	181
		press the right buttons	to sexually stimulate	85
		push the right buttons	to sexually stimulate	58
		well oiled machine	passionately engaged in sexual intercourse	183
WAR AND VIOLENCE	VIOLENCE	bang	to copulate with	170
		beat one's meat	to masturbate	171
	WAR	attack	to sexually assault	140,169
		battle	a sexual encounter	162
		warrior	a lover	163
	WEAPONS	gun	the erect penis	164
		love missile	the erect penis	168
		recharge	to get ready for an additional orgasm	166
		shoot blanks	to be unable to procreate	167
		shoot one's load	to ejaculate during copulation	1,165
		weaponize	to use sex in a hostile way	169

Notes

Introduction

1 The distinction between *taboo* and *linguistic taboo* seems necessary. I understand by taboo the prohibition of certain kinds of behaviour or objects believed to be harmful either for moral, religious or social reasons, whereas the linguistic taboo is the word or phrase to be avoided in public discourse because of the restrictions imposed by taboo topics.

2 Following Allan and Burridge (2006: 47–8), *cross-varietal synonyms* are terms that share the same denotation but differ in connotation. Because of this, they are used in different circumstances with different axiological values with respect to the taboo concept they refer to.

3 This rash of contextual synonyms for sex-related words is a case of what Halliday (1978: 165–6) referred to as the phenomenon of 'over-lexicalization', i.e. an excess of terms for some area of experience or activity considered, for any reason, delicate or problematic in society.

4 Rather surprisingly, the term *euphemism*, and its (roughly speaking) opposite *dysphemism*, are absent from the index of topics in the vast majority of cognitive linguistic studies. For instance, in the seminal book *More Than Cool Reason* by Lakoff and Turner (1989), euphemism is absent from the index of topics, in spite of the fact that the first chapter, entitled 'Life, Death and Time', deals extensively with death-related metaphors, many of which are euphemistic in nature.

5 Rodríguez González's (2008b) dictionary of gay and lesbian verbal usage shows that a considerable number of Spanish words and expressions (many of them of English origin) are used exclusively by the homosexual community. Scholars who studied this distinctive language use, known as 'Gayspeak', assumed that the language used by male homosexuals and lesbians reflected their sexual orientations. For a general overview of Gayspeak, see Cameron and Kulick (2003: 86–98).

6 However, on some occasions, the consideration of euphemism or dysphemism appears to be linked to certain lexical items. As Allan (2014: 2) admits, 'it ignores reality to pretend that ordinary people do not speak and act as if some expressions are intrinsically euphemistic and other dysphemistic – for instance *loo* is euphemistic, whereas *shithouse* is not'.

7 For this reason dictionaries of euphemisms and dysphemisms are never entirely

successful. For example, in Holder's *Dictionary of Euphemisms* (2003) *depart this life* and *gather to God* are considered as euphemisms for dying in the same way as other expressions which have an obvious dysphemistic nature, such as *fall off your perch* or *push up the daisies*.

8   When analysing how metaphors are used with a X-phemistic purpose it is essential to identify the cultural and social values that are attached to the domains on which the linguistic metaphors draw.

1 Cognitive and Pragmatic Issues

1   Whenever I refer to a metaphor like SEX IS A JOURNEY, written in small capitals, I will be referring to the set of correspondences just mentioned.
2   'Image' here is not restricted to visual perception. It refers to all types of sensory and perceptual experience. This helps to explain why Johnson (1987) provides an alternative name for 'image schema' – what he calls 'embodied schema'. This label clearly refers to the fact that metaphorical conceptualization is inevitably linked to perceptual interactions and bodily move.
3   Kövecses's notion of metaphorical utilization is connected with that of different experiential focus, i.e. the process that describes how the embodiment associated with a target domain consists of several components that are given a different priority in different cultures (see 1.2).
4   See the volumes edited by Barcelona (2000a) and Dirven and Pörings (2003) for a comprehensive analysis of the interaction between metaphor and metonymy.
5   As Barcelona (2000b: 17) argues, this view favours the existence of a metonymy–metaphor continuum hypothesis, with prototypical cases of metonymy at both ends of the spectrum, and with metonymy-based metaphors between these two extremes.
6   Kövecses (2010: 8) argues that the cultural context is the combination of the belief system of a person (in which religious beliefs are included) and the physical-cultural environment.
7   Littlemore (2003) conducted an interesting research in which Bangladeshi students were asked to identify the value judgements that some English metaphors expressed. The (mis)interpretations that the students made of the evaluative content of the metaphorical expressions were a consequence of the cultural differences existing. The students' own value systems made them attach connotations to the source domains which were different from those that the metaphors have in English.
8   Grice's theory relies on four basic maxims which underlie everyday interactions – the well-known conversational maxims (quantity, quality, relation and

manner) that people resort to in making sense of what is said. By adhering to these maxims, speakers are expected to be informative (*quantity*), true (*quality*), relevant (*relation*) and perspicuous and brief (*manner*). From this perspective, when an utterance does not seem to make sense at a literal level, and thus a maxim is flouted, the cooperative spirit between the parties involved in the communicative act leads the hearer to search for coherence beyond the surface meaning.

9   Although tremendously influential within pragmatics, Grice's cooperative principle has been explicitly rejected by different authors who have turned to RT to explain the interpretation of utterances in communication. For improvements and replacements of Grice's model, see Carston (1997) and Mooney (2004).

10 Following Ruiz de Mendoza Ibáñez and Peña Cervel (2005: 258), I understand by cognitive operation a 'mental mechanism whose purpose is to derive a semantic representation out of a linguistic expression ... in order to make it meaningful in the context in which it is to be interpreted'.

2   The Cognitive Dimension of Euphemism and Dysphemism

1   Although the mutual preservation of face is an essential characteristic of euphemism, euphemistic use seems to respond fundamentally to the speaker's need to maintain his own *positive* face. In fact, McGlone and Batchelor (2003) carried out an experiment in which they demonstrated that the main motivation for euphemism is the speaker's need to make a positive impression on the audience rather than concern for the addressee's sensitivity (see Foreword).

2   Leech's (1983: 131–9), *politeness principle* is divided into six maxims: tact, generosity, approbation, modesty, agreement and sympathy. These maxims regulate a verbal behaviour oriented towards avoiding conflict and minimizing any potential threat against the individual's social image in communication.

3   However, we should not forget that many standard orthophemisms are metaphorical in origin, like *vagina* (sheath, scabbard), *vulva* (valve), *penis* (tail) or *testicle* (witness), just to mention a few (Allan, personal communication).

4   The classification of X-phemistic types presented here has been partially adopted from that proposed by Burridge (2012: 67–71).

5   Warren (1992) classified 500 euphemistic substitutes according to the different mechanisms of semantic innovation. The results highlight the leading role of figurative language in the generation of euphemism. This author detected 146 metaphorical substitutes, which makes metaphor the most important semantic device for euphemism formation.

6   Langacker (1987: 116–37) proposed a threefold classification of construal

operations: *selection* (i.e. speaker's capacity to highlight some aspects of conceptualizations and disregard others); *perspective* (i.e. linguistic expression of the position from which speakers view an event); and *abstraction* (i.e. speaker's capacity to establish commonalities between different events).

7   For an overview of the linguistic and extralinguistic definitions of euphemism, see Crespo-Fernández (2007: 79–83) and Casas Gómez (2009: 725–33).

8   Herrero Ruiz distinguishes euphemism and dysphemism from other tropes like understatement and overstatement. However, in practical terms, these tropes can be described as euphemistic and dysphemistic resources respectively, in that understatement aims at softening the negative force of the message, whereas overstatement increases this negative force, and, by doing so, tends to magnify the offence. In fact, this author is aware of the fuzzy boundaries between these tropes and X-phemism. He maintains that euphemism and dysphemism 'are derived in the same way as overstatement and meiosis although they work on the basis of an axiological scale' (2009: 265).

9   By referent manipulation I understand the process whereby the language user presents the taboo concept in a particular way, either softening its less acceptable aspects or, on the contrary, intensifying them. Although the referent does not undergo any alteration in itself, it is manipulated by the speaker, and the result of this manipulation is what the receiver notices. For a complete description of this process, see Crespo-Fernández (2007).

10 Lakoff (1987b) distinguishes four types of linguistic metaphors that can be described as 'dead': linguistically dead, conceptually dead, 'one-shot' metaphors and alive conventionalized metaphors. According to Goatly (1997), linguistic metaphors can be classified as dead, buried, sleeping, tired and active. Deignan (2005) proposes a corpus-based classification of metaphorically motivated linguistic expressions including historical, dead, conventionalized and innovative. Muller (2008) distinguishes between dead, sleeping, entrenched, waking and novel.

11 In fact, Gibbs (2011: 532) maintains that many metaphorical expressions that arise from creative metaphorical conceptualizations derive from conventional metaphors: '[M]any novel metaphorical expressions do not completely express new source-to-target domain mappings, but are creative instantiations of conventional metaphors.'

12 The euphemistic basis for this metaphor lies in the fact that death is used to describe the state of unconsciousness that some people have after reaching an orgasm in which they may momentarily lose awareness of time and place. Sexual climax thus implies, to some extent, the dissolution of the individual, 'the annihilation of the self'. As Westley (2008: 70) puts it: 'The annihilation of the self that is inherent to the notion of *jouissance*, makes explicit the association between orgasm (*jouir*) and death.'

13 Yus Ramos (2012: 272) argues that the humorous effects of jokes are sustained in the speaker's prior intentionality, which constitutes a basic feature of jokes. Given that jokes are intentional and seek an effect on the hearer, this scholar considers RT as an appropriate framework to explain how jokes are understood and how they end up producing humorous effects as the result of the hearer's relevance-seeking activity.

14 This bidirectional projection in lexicalized metaphorical units also takes place in Spanish. The coarse word *polla* is, in origin, a BIRD metaphor for penis, now fully lexicalized with the taboo meaning. Its literal, non-taboo meaning, 'young hen', has been virtually abandoned (Crespo-Fernández, 2011). The same happens to other Spanish words from the semantic field of animals, in which the taboo metaphorical sense has overlapped their once neuter meaning like *choto* (literally 'young male goat'/'young bull' and metaphorically 'vagina'). In Spanish the bidirectionality of conceptual metaphorical projections also lends itself to humorous effects, being the source of word play and jokes (see Crespo-Fernández, 2011 and Yus Ramos, 2012 for examples).

15 Following Schmidt and Kess (1986: 2), I understand by persuasion 'the process of inducing a voluntary change in someone's attitudes, beliefs or behaviour through the transmission of a message'.

16 In this vein, Warren (1992: 135) offers a definition of euphemism which is based on the hearer's perception of the speaker's intention to attenuate the taboo: 'We have a euphemism if the interpreter perceives the use of some word or expression as evidence of a wish on the part of the speaker to denote some sensitive phenomenon in a tactful and/or veiled manner.'

3 Euphemistic Metaphors

1 The use of silence as a euphemistic strategy also occurs in the taboo of death. In a previous study on Irish obituaries (Crespo-Fernández, 2006) I found that not only is the direct reference to the subject of death avoided, but also any euphemistic alternative. In fact, in some of the funeral notices analysed the only references to death are the past tense of the verbs employed.

2 Surprisingly enough, the control of public representations that have to do with human sexuality has not totally disappeared from Spanish life, as reflected in the decision to ban the 'Condoms4Life' ads on Madrid transport system during the year's Catholic World Youth Day in 2011.

3 More precisely, *handjob* connotes masturbation of a male by another person (Ayto, 2007: 84).

4 In fact, the term *prostitute* has its origin in the notion of selling. This word first

appeared in the sixteenth century from the Latin verb *prostituere* 'offer for sale' (*OED*3).

5. Kövecses (2000) demonstrated the pervasiveness of HEAT and FIRE metaphors to talk about love and sex. Out of 372 metaphorical items found in a sample of romance novels, 90 are included in these conceptualizations, which makes almost 25 per cent out of the total love-related metaphors encountered.

6. However, according to Lakoff and Turner (1989: 84), for those who are not sexually active, the conceptualization LUST IS HEAT is not grounded in their experience, but in their commonplace knowledge. These scholars argue that the lust-as-heat metaphor does not cohere with the daily experience of these people, but with their knowledge of sex: a sexual encounter involves physical activity which produces heat.

7. Curiously enough, the folk theory of the physiological effects of sex are the same as those of anger, namely increased body heat, increased internal pressure, agitation and inference with accurate perception (Kövecses, 1986: 12).

8. Kövecses (1986: 88) considers that it is romantic love, rather than sexual excitement, that stands at the top of the heat scale: 'On this scale romantic love is conceptualized as an emotion with the highest degree of intensity.' I understand, however, that sexual arousal provokes stronger physiological effects than romantic love, which may be, on many occasions, a less physical emotion, and therefore less intense.

9. The Bible is full of metaphorical uses of fire, as described by Leland, Willhoit, Longman, Douglas and Penney (1998: 377). Fire is depicted as the punishment for the wicked and vicious in Jesus' own words: 'Depart from Me, you cursed, into the everlasting fire prepared for the devil and his angels (Mt. 25.41).' Fire has a healing power: it falls from Heaven and consumes Sodom and Gomorrah (Gen. 19.24). Fire is also associated with Hell. Jesus speaks of the fire of Hell (Mt. 5.22), and the place of final punishment is described as 'a lake of fire' (Mt. 20.14–15).

10. The adjective *ardent* comes from Old French *ardant*, from Latin *ārdens, ārdent-*, from *ārdēre* 'to burn' (*OED*3).

11. It is worth noting that phrases like *play doctor* or *play mums and dads* are not limited to children's initiation into sexuality. They are also used for a wide range of sex-related activities in adults, from masturbation to copulation.

12. In fact, the adjective *adult* has become lexicalized with the meaning 'erotic' or 'pornographic'. This meaning appears in phrases like *adult magazines*, an alternative to the most explicit *porn magazines*, or in the more general euphemistic label *adult entertainment industry*, which refers to the distribution and production of sexually explicit material, including photos, films, video games, etc. Similarly, in the corpus consulted this adjective adds sexual connotations to the name it qualifies, as happens in the phrases *adult dating site* in reference to

those websites oriented to casual sexual encounters, and *adult form of relating*, which alludes to the sexual component of the relationship.

13 This compound may be also used with the meaning 'a sexual act involving the giving and getting of an enema'. The link between water and urination is present as well in other compounds with *water* not related to sex, like *waterworks* 'the urinary system' (Dalzell and Victor, 2006).

14 It is worth noting that in these games the woman commonly acts as the dominant partner and commits violence against the male, as has statistically been demonstrated (Slade, 2001: 987). This seems to contradict the view of the woman as a weak and submissive sexual partner at man's mercy which is present in many sex-related metaphors (see Chapter 4).

15 In these sadomasochistic games the dominant partner takes the role of the trainer or handler of the pony (in *pony play*), the pup or the dog (in *puppy play*) or the cat (in *kitty play*). These practices involve a complete submission on the part of the person who is taking the role of the animal. Accordingly, in pony play the person who takes the role of the pony becomes a *pony slave* in sadomasochist terminology.

16 In Spanish it is also the movement from one place to another that is highlighted in the verb *correrse*, literally 'to run', used as a dysphemistic label for achieving orgasm for both males and females.

17 The scriptural images of Heaven portray it as a magnificent city, far from earthily worries and troubles, built of gold, whose walls are decorated by jewel-gates. Heaven is the symbol of resurrection and eternal life (Leland et al., 1998: 317).

18 Curiously enough, in the figurative language of epitaphs, Paradise is also conceived as the final destination of the journey from earth to Heaven the deceased embarks on (Crespo-Fernández, 2013c).

19 This expression is common in teenage discourse to distinguish full penetration from the intermediate stages of sexual encounters, like caressing, kissing, etc. It appears with this meaning in (49).

20 The CLOSET metaphor has been borrowed by Spanish with the same meaning in the form of calques and the so-called pure anglicisms (Crespo-Fernández and Luján-García, 2013). The word *armario* 'closet', as a calque from the English *closet*, is widely used to refer to homosexuality. It is the origin of expressions like *estar en el armario* 'to be in the closet' and *salir del armario*, 'to get out of the closet', among others. The pervasiveness of the CLOSET metaphor is also reflected in the fact that it is the source of a considerable number of pure anglicisms like *coming out*, *out*, *outing* and *closet* (Rodríguez González, 2008b).

21 One might wonder if a verb like *attract*, well entrenched in the language with the meaning 'sexually attract', can be considered as a realization of a conceptual metaphor or, by contrast, is a case of dead metaphor with no source domain

counterpart. In this respect, Albritton (cited in Lakoff and Johnson, 1999: 84–5) conducted an experiment to prove the degree of activated metaphoricity of *attraction* in 'The attraction between John and Martha was overwhelming'. The results showed that *attraction* is a conventional linguistic metaphor which is cognitively alive and active.

22 However, this is not always the case of WATER metaphors. In a previous study (Crespo-Fernández, 2013b: 101) I demonstrated that linguistic metaphors that evoke natural phenomena like *wave* or *tide* (included in the conceptualization IMMIGRATION IS A NATURAL DISASTER) are dysphemistic in the discourse concerning immigration in the British press. These metaphors make readers believe that immigration will devastate the host societies, as it is – just as uncontrolled water – a dangerous natural phenomenon.

23 The FIREWORKS metaphor has been pervasively used in cinema and television to allude to orgasm. For instance, in the scene of lovemaking between Cary Grant and Grace Kelly in the romantic thriller *To Catch a Thief*, directed by Alfred Hitchcock in 1955, Hitchcock himself admitted having used the pyrotechnic image to allude to orgasm. As an anecdote, Joseph Breen, the director of the PCA (Production Code Administration) at that time, objected to the use of fireworks during a love scene because 'the symbolism was too pointed' (Chandler, 2005: 220).

24 It must be noted that the domain of ILLNESS is very different from the domain of DISEASE. The latter is dysphemistically applied to verbalize social problems like crime, delinquency or immigration with the assumption that these problems are diseases which pose a threat to the community and should be eliminated (see Crespo-Fernández, 2013b: 102–3).

25 For insightful analyses of how HEALTH–ILLNESS metaphors perform an effective persuasive and ideological function in political discourse, see Musolff (2004, 2010) and Charteris-Black (2005).

26 Needless to say, when talking about sex, what is 'normal' for some people may be disgusting or offensive for others. I accept here Deignan's notion of 'normal' to refer to conventional sexual behaviour and practices, leaving aside sadomasochism, sex in group, swinging, sexual fetishes, etc. In the realm of sex it is very difficult to know where to draw the line, especially as far as subjective evaluation of sexual habits is concerned.

27 Turner (1999) argues that the metaphor SEX IS DIRT, closely related with IMMORALITY IS DIRT, plays a crucial role in the discourse of pornography. SEX IS DIRT leads to the emergence of PORNOGRAPHY IS DIRTY, a conceptual equation which evaluates pornography as immoral and depraved.

28 Deignan (2007) carried out a corpus study of the meanings of *heel* and its inflections which consisted on the analysis of 1,361 citations excerpted from the

Bank of English. Interestingly enough, she provided evidence for the fact that the expression *head over heels* is halfway between literal and figurative, metaphorical and metonymic, and word and idiom.

29 Abrantes (2005) adopts Luchtenberg's distinction between the so-called *concealing* (*Verhüllens*) and *veiling* (*Verschleierns*) functions of euphemism in discourse. A euphemistic expression fulfils a function of concealing when a taboo topic is deliberately avoided. The function of veiling, however, takes place when the forbidden topic is manipulated in such a way that it only presents a distorted segment of reality with the purpose of manipulating the hearer.

30 Hereafter the abbreviations P-1, P-2, etc. will be used to refer to the participants in the forums who post messages in reply to others as part of an online discussion within a thread.

31 Table 3.3 does not necessarily show the sequence in which comprehension takes place; in fact, TR claims that comprehension occurs in parallel and not in sequence.

4 Dysphemistic Metaphors

1 The origin of *bunny* can be traced back to eighteenth-century London's 'Cunny House'. It appears that *bunny* was a euphemistic remodelling of *cunny*, a word for rabbits and rabbit tails, as well as a term of endearment for women (Allan, 2012: 25).

2 The sexist connotations of *bunny* led to strong criticisms on the part of some feminine movements during the 1960s. The pejorative force of the BUNNY metaphor, in Levy's (2005) words, 'made feminists want to throw up. They were specifically fighting to be seen as real people, not sudsy bunnies.'

3 Given that the biological family felidae includes animals with very different characteristics and attributes, I decided to focus on more specific domains in this category used to conceptualize women, namely SMALL FURRY ANIMALS (*kitten, pussy, pussycat, alley cat*) and WILD ANIMALS (*cougar, fox, vixen, tigress, lioness*).

4 This stereotype of women is welcome by certain men. Significantly enough, a study carried out by Hall (cited in Fernández Martín, 2011: 69) reveals that that sex-line workers who portray themselves on the phone as being sexually accommodating and submissive earn more money than those who do not.

5 Although *alley cat* applies to any woman of loose morals, it can also designate prostitutes. This usage is motivated by the fact that cats are typically associated with the night – hence the connection between cats, prostitution and illicit sexual encounters (López Rodríguez, 2009: 84).

6 For a comprehensive study on the universality–relativity dimension of metaphor

7   De Corsey (2009) examined the response of some women to the word *cougar* in a discussion thread published in the American web http://www.salon.com (3 Sept. 2009). He found that most of the remarks about the term were negative. Consider the following one: 'When I hear the term "cougar", a sleek, sexy, strong woman doesn't come to mind. Instead, it conjures a tacky, fake tan, fake boobs, fake nails, fake hair, Real Housewives of who-the-hell-cares nightmare; vapid, desperate and pathetic.'

8   It is worth noting that in Spanish the word *loba* 'she-wolf' carries negative connotations. It refers to a woman who, like a wolf in search of food, preys on men to satisfy her sexual appetite.

9   As wild animals are not inherently vicious or lusty creatures, Ruiz de Mendoza Ibáñez and Pérez Hernández (2011) argue for the existence of a metaphorical complex in the ANIMAL metaphor which combines PEOPLE ARE ANIMALS with SEX IS AGGRESSIVE BEHAVIOUR.

10 The phrase *sexually violent predator* (or its corresponding abbreviation *SVP*) is the most common designation for civilly committed sex offenders in the United States legal discourse. More generally, above all in tabloid media, *predator* applies to habitual sexual offenders and sexual psychopaths and, more recently, to internet paedophiles, referred to as 'online predators'.

11 In a corpus consisting of a cross-section of the Bank of English, Deignan (2005: 43) identified 500 citations of *starve/starved/starving/starves*. She found that this word was used metaphorically in 105 citations in which it was qualified by an item from the target domain and included in one of the following three structures: *starv*+of+noun*; *noun+starved*; *starv*+for+noun*. However, the word was used literally if it did not appear qualified in any way.

12 As Bordo (1993: 111–12) demonstrates, the positive view of the man as a 'woman-eater' was exploited by commercials featuring male eaters. Rather significantly, in these commercials men were portrayed 'in a state of wild, sensual transport over heavily frosted, rich, gooey desserts. Their lack of control is portrayed as appropriate, even adorable', whereas women 'are permitted such gratification from food only in measured doses'.

13 This is implicitly transmitted in some realizations of the ANIMAL metaphor: the fact that certain animals, especially young ones, are a source of nourishment may constitute an additional source of sexual desire, as is the case of *chicken* (López Rodríguez, 2009: 89).

14 This phrase seems to allude to the song of the same name by the British post-punk band Sigue Sigue Sputnik. Their song *Love Missile F1-11*, included on their debut

album *Flaunt It*, was released in 1986 and reached number 3 in the UK charts that year.

15 The noun *bang* appears in the compound *gang bang* as a striking image of the violence involved in a sexual intercourse between three or more men with a single willing partner (usually a woman). This compound is commonly (although not exclusively) found in the slang of prostitution and pornography.

16 In fact, in a survey carried out among North American college students, the conceptual schema to refer to the male member as a weapon was totally rejected by the women informants, while it was a very common way to name the penis among the male participants (for the results of this survey, see Cameron, 2006: 151–64).

17 This does not mean, of course, that the stereotype of the pure and innocent female who never swears holds true. Nevertheless, using swearing and graphic taboo language tends to be associated with masculinity rather than with femininity. As Coates (2004: 98) claims, 'the stereotypes of the tough-talking male and the purse, never swearing female are false. However, it does seem to be true that swearing is an integral part of contemporary masculinity.'

18 This compound has been borrowed with the same meaning in Spanish (Rodríguez González, 2008b). However, as a lexical anglicism, *toy boy* does not carry the negative connotations that the English word does. In the host language the foreign word is somehow deprived of its original derogatory overtones and used with a euphemistic intention (Crespo-Fernández and Luján-García, 2013).

19 What we have in *f**king* is the result of the process of *mid-clipping*, i.e. -*uc* is eliminated from the middle of the word, and *quasi-omission*, i.e. each missing letter from *fuck* is replaced in a one-for-one substitution by a non-alphabetic symbol. These morphological deformations, as Allan (2012: 11–12) notes, 'draw attention to the word's being unprintable and thereby mark the obscenity'.

20 This identification between effeminacy and gays is a rather simplistic way of understanding the dichotomy between male homosexuality and heterosexuality. In fact, as Stanley (2006: 51) notes, some gays favour those characteristics associated with extreme masculinity: 'Because our society reward the behaviour assigned to the male, gays also place a high demand on "masculine" behaviour … Masculinity is as highly prized as it is among heterosexuals, and some gay men refuse to associate with other gay men who display any of the characteristics linked to the female role.'

21 It should be noted that the adjective *little* transmits connotations of availability, weakness and delicacy which are used for offensive purposes in *little sex kitten* (114), *little vixen* (128) and *little flowers* (186).

22 Similarly, in patriarchal societies women are not allowed to use bad language because it is supposed that swearing afforded women a chance to empower themselves and not to conform to the ideal of docile femininity (see note 17, Chapter 4).

23 It is worthy of note that sharing values in this area is crucial to the reinforcement of a sense of community, as Martin and White (2005: 52) claim. This leads to the dichotomy 'the self' versus 'the other' (see 4.1.1.2 and 4.1.7), the former represented in this case by the heterosexual, sexually dominant male, and the latter by the lusty and sexually threatening woman.

References

Abrantes, A. M. (2005), 'Euphemism and Co-operation in Discourse', in E. Grillo (ed.), *Power Without Domination: Dialogism and the Empowering Property of Communication*, Amsterdam and Philadelphia: John Benjamins, pp. 85–103.
Allan, K. (1990), 'Some English Terms of Insult Invoking Sex Organs: Evidence of a Pragmatic Driver for Semantics', in S. L. Tsohatzidis (ed.), *Meaning and Prototypes: Studies in Linguistic Categorization*, London: Routledge, pp. 159–94.
—(2009), 'The connotations of colour terms: Colour-based X-phemisms', *Journal of Pragmatics*, 41: 626–37.
—(2012), 'X-phemism and creativity', *Lexis: E-Journal in English Lexicology*, 7: 5–42.
—(2014), 'A Benchmark for Politeness', in J. L. Mey and A. Capone (eds), *Interdisciplinary Studies in Pragmatics, Culture and Society*, Cham: Springer, pp. 1–30.
Allan, K. and Burridge, K. (1991), *Euphemism and Dysphemism: Language Used as Shield and Weapon*, Oxford and New York: Oxford University Press.
—(2006), *Forbidden Words: Taboo and the Censoring of Language*, Cambridge: Cambridge University Press.
Ayto, J. (2007), *Wobbly Bits and Other Euphemisms: Over 3,000 Ways to Avoid Speaking Your Mind*, London: A & C Black.
Barcelona, A. (ed.) (2000a), *Metaphor and Metonymy at the Crossroads: A Cognitive Perspective*, Berlin: Mouton de Gruyter.
—(2000b), 'Introduction: The Cognitive Theory of Metaphor and Metonymy', in A. Barcelona (ed.), *Metaphor and Metonymy at the Crossroads: A Cognitive Perspective*, Berlin: Mouton de Gruyter, pp. 1–29.
—(2003), 'Clarifying and Applying the Notions of Metaphor and Metonymy within Cognitive Linguistics: An Update', in R. Dirven and R. Pörings (eds), *Metaphor and Metonymy in Comparison and Contrast*, Berlin and New York: Mouton de Gruyter, pp. 207–77.
—(2011), 'Reviewing the Properties and Prototype Structure of Metonymy', in A. Barcelona, R. Benczes and F. J. Ruiz de Mendoza Ibáñez (eds), *Defining Metonymy in Cognitive Linguistics: Towards a Consensus View*, Amsterdam and Philadelphia: John Benjamins, pp. 7–57.
Barnden, J. A. (2010), 'Metaphor and metonymy: Making their connections more slippery', *Cognitive Linguistics*, 21(1): 1–34.
Beneke, T. (1982), *Men on Rape: What They Have to Say about Sexual Violence*, New York: St. Martin Press.
Benveniste, E. (1974), 'La blasphémie et l'euphémie', *Problèmes de Linguistique Générale*, 2, Paris: Gallimard.

Blakemore, D. (2002), *Relevance and Linguistic Meaning: The Semantics and Pragmatics of Discourse Markers*, Cambridge: Cambridge University Press.

Boers, F. (1999), 'When a Bodily Source Domain Becomes Prominent: The Joy of Counting Metaphors in the Socio-economic Domain', in R. W. Gibbs and G. Steen (eds), *Metaphor in Cognitive Linguistics*, Amsterdam and Philadelphia: John Benjamins, pp. 47–56.

Bordo, S. (1993), *Unbearable Weight: Feminism, Western Culture and the Body*, Berkeley and Los Angeles, CA: University of California Press.

Braun, V. and Kitzinger, C. (2001), '"Snatch", "hole" or "honey-pot"? Semantic categories and the problem of nonspecificity in female genital slang', *The Journal of Sex Research*, 38(2): 146–58.

Brown, P. and Levinson, S. (1987), *Politeness: Some Universals in Language Use*, Cambridge: Cambridge University Press.

Burkhardt, A. (2010), 'Euphemism and Truth', in A. Burkhardt and B. Nierlich (eds), *Tropical Truth(s): The Epistemology of Metaphor and other Tropes*, Berlin and New York: Mouton de Gruyter, pp. 353–73.

Burridge, K. (1996), 'Political correctness: Euphemisms with attitude', *English Today*, 12 (3): 42–3.

—(1998), 'Euphemism with Attitude: Politically Charged Language Change', in M. Schmid, J. R. Austin and D. Stein (eds), *Historical Linguistics: Selected Papers from the 13th International Conference on Historical Linguistics*, Amsterdam and Philadelphia: John Benjamins, pp. 57–76.

—(2004), *Blooming English*, Cambridge: Cambridge University Press.

—(2010), 'Linguistic cleanliness is next to godliness: Taboo and purism', *English Today*, 26 (2): 3–13.

—(2012), 'Euphemism and language change: The sixth and seventh ages', *Lexis. E-Journal in English Lexicology*, 7: 65–92.

Caballero, R. (2006), *Re-Viewing Space: Figurative Language in Architects' Assessment of Built Space*, Berlin: Mouton de Gruyter.

Caballero, R. and Ibarretxe-Antuñano, I. (2009), 'Ways of perceiving and thinking: Re-vindicating culture in conceptual metaphor research', *Cognitive Semiotics*, 5 (1–2): 268–90.

Cameron, D. (2006), *On Language and Sexual Politics*, Abingdon and New York: Routledge.

Cameron, D. and Kulick, D. (2003), *Language and Sexuality*, Cambridge: Cambridge University Press.

—(2006), 'Heteronorms', in D. Cameron and D. Kulick (eds), *The Language and Sexuality Reader*, Abingdon and New York: Routledge, pp. 165–8.

Camp, E., 'Showing, telling and seeing: Metaphor and "poetic" language', *The Baltic International Yearbook of Cognition, Logic and Communication* 3 (2008), pp. 1–24. http://thebalticyearbook.org/journals/baltic/article/view/20/19 (accessed 27 March 2012).

Carston, R. (1997), 'Enrichment and loosening: Complementary processes in deriving the proposition expressed?', *Linguistische Berichte*, 8: 103–27.
—(2002), *Thoughts and Utterances: The Pragmatics of Explicit Communication*, Oxford: Blackwell.
—(2010), 'Explicit Communication and "Free" Pragmatic Enrichment', in B. Soria and E. Romero (eds), *Explicit Communication: Robyn Carston's Pragmatics*, Basingstoke and New York: Palgrave Macmillan, pp. 217–85.
Casas Gómez, M. (1986), *La Interdicción Lingüística: Mecanismos del Eufemismo y Disfemismo*, Cádiz: Universidad.
—(2009), 'Towards a new approach to the linguistic definition of euphemism', *Language Sciences*, 31: 725–39.
—(2012), 'The expressive creativity of euphemism and dysphemism', *Lexis: E-Journal in English Lexicology*, 7: 43–64.
Cass, V. (2004), *The Elusive Orgasm: A Woman's Guide to Why She Can't and How She Can Orgasm*, Bentley: Brightfire Press.
Chamizo Domínguez, P. J. (1998), *Metáfora y Conocimiento*, Málaga: Universidad.
—(2005), 'Some theses on euphemisms and dysphemisms', *Studia Anglica Resoviensa*, 25: 9–16.
—(2009), 'Linguistic interdiction: Its status quaestionis and possible research lines', *Language Sciences*, 31 (4): 428–46.
Chamizo Domínguez, P. J. and Sánchez Benedito, F. (2000), *Lo que Nunca se Aprendió en Clase: Eufemismos y Disfemismos en el Lenguaje Erótico Inglés*, Granada: Comares.
Chandler, C. (2005), *It's only a Movie: Alfred Hitchcock. A Personal Biography*, New York: Simon & Schuster.
Charteris-Black, J. (2004), *Corpus Approaches to Critical Metaphor Analysis*. Basingstoke and New York: Palgrave Macmillan.
—(2005), *Politicians and Rhetoric: The Persuasive Power of Metaphor*, Basingstoke and New York: Palgrave Macmillan.
Chilton, P. A. (2004), *Analysing Political Discourse: Theory and Practice*, Abingdon and New York: Routledge.
Cienki, A. (2007), 'Frames, Idealized Cognitive Models, and Domains', in D. Geeraerts and H. Cuycenks (eds), *The Oxford Handbook of Cognitive Linguistics*, Oxford: Oxford University Press, pp. 170–87.
Claridge, C. (2007), 'Constructing a Corpus from the Web: Message Boards', in M. Hundt, N. Nesselhauf and C. Biewer (eds), *Corpus Linguistics and the Web*, Amsterdam and New York: Rodopi, pp. 87–108.
Clark, B. (2013), *Relevance Theory*, Cambridge: Cambridge University Press.
Cleland, J. (1985) [1749], *Fanny Hill: Memoirs of a Woman of Pleasure*, Oxford: Oxford University Press.
Coates, J. (2004) [1986], *Women, Men and Language: A Sociolinguistic Account of Gender Differences in Language*, 3rd edn, Harlow: Pearson.

—(2013), 'The discursive production of everyday heterosexualities', *Discourse & Society*, 24(5): 536–52.
Coleman, J. (1999), *Love, Sex and Marriage: A Historical Thesaurus*, Amsterdam and New York: Rodopi.
Corsey, M. de, 'Cougar: Women as Big Cats' (2009), http://open.salon.com/blog/matthew_decoursey/2009/09/24/cougar_women_as_big_cats (accessed 17 February 2013).
Crespo-Fernández, E. (2005), 'Euphemistic strategies in politeness and face concerns', *Pragmalingüística*, 13: 77–86.
—(2006), 'The language of death: Euphemism and conceptual metaphorization in Victorian obituaries', *SKY Journal of Linguistics*, 19: 101–30.
—(2007), *El Eufemismo y el Disfemismo: Procesos de Manipulación del Tabú en el Lenguaje Literario Inglés*, Alicante: Universidad.
—(2008), 'Sex-related euphemism and dysphemism: An analysis in terms of conceptual metaphor theory', *Atlantis: A Journal of the Spanish Association of Anglo-American Studies*, 30 (2): 95–110.
—(2011), 'Conceptual metaphors in taboo-induced lexical variation', *Revista Alicantina de Estudios Ingleses*, 24: 53–71.
—(2013a), 'Words as weapons for mass persuasion: Dysphemism in Churchill's wartime speeches', *Text & Talk: An Interdisciplinary Journal of Language, Discourse and Communication Studies*, 33 (3): 311–30.
—(2013b), 'The Treatment of Immigrants in the Current Spanish and British Right-wing Press: A Cross-Linguistic Study', in M. Martínez Lirola (ed.), *Discourses on Immigration in Times of Economic Crisis: A Critical Perspective*, Newcastle: Cambridge Scholars Publishing, pp. 86–112.
—(2013c), 'Euphemistic metaphors in English and Spanish epitaphs. A comparative study', *Atlantis: Journal of Spanish Association of Anglo-American Studies*, 35(2): 99–118.
Crespo-Fernández, E. and Luján-García, C. (2013), 'Anglicismo y tabú: Los valores axiológicos del Anglicismo', *Estudios Filológicos*, 52: 53–74.
Croft, W. (2003), 'The Role of Domains in the Interpretation of Metaphors and Metonymies', in R. Dirven and R. Pörings (eds), *Metaphor and Metonymy in Comparison and Contrast*, Berlin and New York: Mouton de Gruyter, pp. 161–205.
Dalzell, T. and Victor, T. (2006), *The New Partridge Dictionary of Slang and Conventional English*, Abingdon and New York: Routledge.
Deignan, A. (1997), 'Metaphors of Desire', in K. Harvey and C. Shalom (eds), *Language and Desire: Encoding Sex, Romance and Intimacy*, Abingdon and New York: Routledge, pp. 21–42.
—(1999), 'Corpus-based Research into Metaphor', in G. Low and L. Cameron (eds), *Researching and Applying Metaphor*, Cambridge and New York: Cambridge University Press, pp. 177–202.

—(2005), *Metaphor in Corpus Linguistics*, Amsterdam and Philadelphia: John Benjamins.
—(2007), 'Image metaphors and connotations in everyday language', *Annual Review of Cognitive Linguistics*, 5: 173–92.
—(2010), 'The Evaluative Properties of Metaphors', in G. Low, Z. Todd, A. Deignan and L. Cameron (eds), *Researching and Applying Metaphor in the Real World*, Amsterdam and Philadelphia: John Benjamins, pp. 357–74.
Dirven, R. and Pörings, R. (eds) (2003), *Metaphor and Metonymy in Comparison and Contrast*, Berlin: Mouton de Gruyter.
Epstein, J. (1986), 'Sex and Euphemism', in D. J. Enright (ed.), *Fair of Speech: The Uses of Euphemism*, Oxford: Oxford University Press, pp. 56–71.
Fernández Fontecha, A. and Jiménez Catalán, R. (2003), 'Semantic derogation in animal metaphor: A contrastive study of two male/female examples in English and Spanish', *Journal of Pragmatics*, 35: 771–97.
Fernández Martín, C. (2011), 'Comparing sexist expressions in English and Spanish: (De-) constructing sexism through language', *ES: Revista de Filología Inglesa*, 32: 69–93.
Forceville, C. (2006), 'Non-verbal and Multimodal Metaphor in a Cognitivistic Framework: Agendas for Research', in G. Christiansen, M. Achard, R. Dirven and F. J. Ruiz de Mendoza Ibáñez (eds), *Cognitive Linguistics: Current Applications and Future Perspectives*, Berlin and New York: Mouton de Gruyter, pp. 379–402.
Freud, S. (1967), *Tótem y Tabú*, Madrid: Alianza.
Galera Masegosa, A., 'A cognitive approach to simile-based idiomatic expressions', *Círculo de Lingüística Aplicada a la Comunicación*, 43 (2010), pp. 3–48. http://www.ucm.es/info/circulo (accessed 9 March 2013).
Gibbs, R. W. (2011), 'Evaluating conceptual metaphor theory', *Discourse Processes*, 48(8): 529–62.
Goatly, A. (1997), *The Language of Metaphors*, Abingdon and New York: Routledge.
Goffman, E. (1955), 'On face-work: An analysis of ritual elements in social interaction', *Psychiatry*, 18: 213–31.
Goossens, L. (2003), 'Metaphtonymy: The Interaction of Metaphor and Metonymy in Expressions for Linguistic Action', in R. Dirven and R. Pörings (eds), *Metaphor and Metonymy in Comparison and Contrast*, Berlin: Mouton de Gruyter, pp. 277–349.
Gradecack-Erdelijc, T. and Milic, G. (2011), 'Metonymy at the Crossroads. A Case of Euphemisms and Dysphemisms', in R. Benczes, A. Barcelona and F. J. Ruiz de Mendoza Ibañez (eds), *Defining Metonymy in Cognitive Linguistics: Towards a Consensus View*, Amsterdam and Philadelphia: John Benjamins, pp. 147–66.
Grady, J. (1997), 'THEORIES ARE BUILDINGS revisited', *Cognitive Linguistics*, 8(4): 267–90.
—(1999), 'A Typology of Motivation for Conceptual Metaphor: Correlation vs. Resemblance', in R. Gibbs and G. Steen (eds), *Metaphor in Cognitive Linguistics*, Amsterdam and Philadelphia: John Benjamins, pp. 79–100.
Grice, H. P. (1975), 'Logic and Conversation', in P. Cole and J. L. Morgan (eds), *Syntax and Semantics, Vol. 3: Speech Acts*, New York: Academic Press, pp. 41–58.

Grimes, L. M. (1978), *El Tabú Lingüístico en México. El Lenguaje Erótico de los Mexicanos*, New York: Bilingual Press.

Halliday, M. A. K. (1978), *Language as Social Semiotic: The Social Interpretation of Language and Meaning*, London: Edward Arnold Publishers.

Herrero Ruiz, J. (2009), *Understanding Tropes: At the Crossroads between Pragmatics and Cognition*, Frankfurt am Main: Peter Lang.

Hines, C. (1996), 'What's so Easy about Pie? The Lexicalization of a Metaphor', in A. Goldberg (ed.), *Conceptual Structure, Discourse and Language*, Stanford: California, CSLI Publications, pp. 189–200.

—(1999), 'Foxy Chicks and Playboy Bunnies: A Case Study in Metaphorical Lexicalization', in M. K. Hiraga, C. Sinha and S. Wilcox (eds), *Cultural, Psychological and Typological Issues in Cognitive Linguistics*, Amsterdam and Philadelphia: John Benjamins, pp. 9–23.

—(2000), 'Rebaking the Pie: The WOMAN AS DESSERT Metaphor', in M. Bucholtz, A. Liang and L. Sutton (eds), *Reinventing Identities: The Gendered Self in Discourse*, New York and Oxford: Oxford University Press, pp. 145–62.

Hock, H. (1991), *Principles of Historical Linguistics*, Berlin: Mouton de Gruyter.

Holder, R. W. (2003) [1987], *How Not to Say What you Mean: A Dictionary of Euphemisms*, 3rd. edn, Oxford: Oxford University Press.

Horlacher, S. (2010), 'Taboo, Transgression and Literature: An Introduction', in S. Horlacher, S. Glomb and L. Heiler (eds), *Taboo and Transgression in British Literature from the Renaissance to the Present*, Basingstoke and New York: Palgrave Macmillan, pp. 3–22.

Hughes, G. (2006), *An Encyclopedia of Swearing: The Social History of Oaths, Profanity, Foul Language and Ethnic Slurs in the English-speaking World*, New York and London: M. E. Sharp.

Indurkhya, B. (1992), *Metaphor and Cognition*, The Hague: Kluwer Academic.

Johnson, M. (1987), *The Body in the Mind: The Bodily Basis of Cognition*, Chicago: The University of Chicago Press.

—(1997), 'Embodied Mind and Cognitive Science', in D. Levin (ed.), *Language Beyond Postmodernism: Saying and Thinking in Gendlin's Philosophy*, Chicago: Northwestern University Press, pp. 148–75.

Keyes, R. (2010), *Euphemania: Our Love Affair with Euphemisms*, New York: Little, Brown and Company.

Kittay, E. F. (1989), *Metaphor: Its Cognitive Force and Linguistic Structure*, Oxford: Clarendon Press.

Kleinke, S. (2008), '"I'm sorry, I've no doubt I've offended someone here": Interactional repair in a public message board discussion thread', *Saarland Working Papers in Linguistics*, 2: 73–102.

Kleparski, G. (1990), *Semantic Change in English: A Study of Evaluative Developments in the Domain of humans*, Lublin: The Catholic University of Lublin Printing House.

Koller, V. (2004), *Metaphor and Gender in Business Media Discourse*, Basingstoke and New York: Palgrave Macmillan.

Kövecses, Z. (1986), *Metaphors of Anger, Pride and Love. A Lexical Approach to the Structure of Concepts*, Amsterdam and Philadelphia: John Benjamins.

—(1988), *The Language of Love. The Semantics of Passion in Conversational English*, London: Bucknell University Press.

—(2000), 'The Scope of Metaphor', in A. Barcelona (ed.), *Metaphor and Metonymy at the Crossroads*, Berlin and New York: Mouton de Gruyter, pp. 79-92.

—(2002), *Metaphor: A Practical Introduction*, Oxford: Oxford University Press.

—(2003), *Metaphor and Emotion. Language, Culture and Body in Human Feeling*, Cambridge: Cambridge University Press.

—(2005), *Metaphor in Culture. Universality and Variation*, Cambridge: Cambridge University Press.

—(2006a), *Language, Mind, and Culture. A Practical Introduction*, Oxford: Oxford University Press.

—(2006b), 'Metaphor and ideology in slang: The case of WOMAN and MAN', *Revue d'Études Françaises*, 11: 151–66.

—(2008), 'The conceptual structure of happiness', *Collegium: Studies Across Disciplines in the Humanities and the Social Sciences*, 3: 131–43.

—(2010), 'Metaphor and culture', *Acta Universitatis Sapientiae, Philologica*, 2(2): 197–220.

—(2011), 'Recent developments in metaphor theory: Are the new views rival ones?', *Review of Cognitive Linguistics*, 9 (1): 11–25.

Krajewsky, S. and Schröeder, H. (2008), 'Silence and Taboo', in G. Antos and E. Ventola (eds), *Handbook of Interpersonal Communication*, Berlin: Mouton de Gruyter, pp. 595–622.

Krennmayr, T. (2013), 'Top-down versus bottom-up approaches to the identification of metaphor in discourse', *metaphorik.de*, 24: 7–36.

Kushnick, H., 'In the closet: A close read of the metaphor', *Virtual Mentor*, 12 (8) (2012), pp. 678–80. http://virtualmentor.ama-assn.org/2010/08/mnar1-1008.html (accessed 27 January 2013).

Kyeltyka, R. and Kleparski, G. (2005), 'The scope of English zoosemy: The case of domesticated animals', *Studia Anglica Resoviensa*, 3: 76–87.

Lakoff, G. (1987a), *Women, Fire and Dangerous Things*, Chicago: The University of Chicago Press.

—(1987b), 'The death of dead metaphor', *Metaphor and Symbolic Activity*, 2: 143–7.

—(1993) [1979], 'The Contemporary Theory of Metaphor', in A. Ortony (ed.), *Metaphor and Thought*, 2nd edn, Cambridge: Cambridge University Press, pp. 202–51.

—(2003), 'The Embodied Mind and How to Live with One', in A. J. Sanford (ed.), *The Nature and Limits of Human Understanding*, London and New York: Continuum, pp. 47–108.

Lakoff, G. and Johnson, M. (1980), *Metaphors We Live By*, Chicago: The University of Chicago Press.
—(1999), *Philosophy in the Flesh: The Embodied Mind and its Challenge to Western Thought*, New York: Basic Books.
Lakoff, G. and Kövecses, Z. (1987), 'The Cognitive Model of Anger Inherent in American English', in D. Holland and N. Quinn (eds), *Cultural Models in Language and Thought*, Cambridge: Cambridge University Press, pp. 195–221.
Lakoff, G. and Turner, M. (1989), *More Than Cool Reason: A Field Guide to Poetic Metaphor*, Chicago: The University of Chicago Press
Langacker, R. W. (1987), *Foundations of Cognitive Grammar: Theoretical Prerequisites*, Stanford, CA: Stanford University Press.
Lawrence, D. H. (1986 [1915]), *The Rainbow*, London: Penguin.
Lee, A. P. (2011), 'Metaphorical euphemisms of RELATIONSHIP and DEATH in Kavalan, Paiwan, and Seediq', *Oceanic Linguistics*, 50 (2): 351–79.
Leech, G. (1983), *Principles of Pragmatics*, New York: Longman.
Leland R., Willhoit, J., Longman, T., Douglas, C. and Penney, D. (1998), *Dictionary of Biblical Imagery: An Encyclopedic Exploration of the Images, Symbols, Motifs, Metaphors, Figures of Speech and Literary Patterns of the Bible*, Leicester and Downers Grove, IL: Intervarsity Press.
Levy, A. (2005), *Female Chauvinist Pigs: Women and the Rise of Raunch Culture*, New York: Free Press.
Littlemore, J. (2003), 'The effect of cultural background in metaphor interpretation', *Metaphor and Symbol*, 18 (4): 273–88.
Lizardo, O. (2012), 'The conceptual bases of metaphors of dirt and cleanliness in moral and non-moral reasoning', *Cognitive Linguistics*, 23 (2): 367–93.
López Rodríguez, I. (2009), 'Of women, bitches, chickens and vixens: Animal metaphors for women in English and Spanish', *Culture, Language and Representation*, 7: 77–100.
Marcoccia, M. (2004), 'On-line polylogues: Conversation structure and participation framework in internet newsgroups', *Journal of Pragmatics*, 36 (1): 115–45.
Marsh, J. (1998), *Word Crimes: Blasphemy, Culture and Literature in Nineteenth Century England*, Chicago: The University of Chicago Press
Martin, J. R. (2000), 'Beyond Exchange: APPRAISAL Systems in English', in S. Hunston and G. Thompson (eds), *Evaluation in Text*. Oxford: Oxford University Press, pp. 142–75.
Martin, J. R. and White, P. R. R. (2005), *Language of Evaluation: Appraisal in English*, Basingstoke and New York: Palgrave Macmillan.
McCarthy, M. and Carter, R. (2004), '"There's millions of them": Hyperbole in everyday conversation', *Journal of Pragmatics*, 36 (2): 149–84.
McDonald, J. (1996), *Dictionary of Obscenity and Taboo*, Ware: Wordsworth.
McEnery, T. (2006), *Swearing in English: Bad Language, Purity and Power from 1586 to the Present*, Abingdon and New York: Routledge.

McGlone, M. S. and Batchelor, J. A. (2003), 'Looking out for number one: Euphemism and face', *Journal of Communication*, 53 (2): 251–64.
McGlone, M. S., Beck, G. and Pfiester, A. (2006), 'Contamination and camouflage in euphemisms', *Communication Monographs*, 73 (3): 261–82.
Mooney, A. (2004), 'Co-operation, violations and making sense', *Journal of Pragmatics*, 36: 899–920.
Morris, P. K. and Waldman, J. (2011), 'Culture and metaphors in advertising', *International Journal of Communication*, 5: 942–68.
Muller, C. (2008), *Metaphors Dead and Alive, Sleeping and Waking: A Dynamic View*, Chicago: The University of Chicago Press.
Murphy, P. F. (2001), *Studs, Tools and the Family Jewels: Metaphors Men Live By*, Madison and Wisconsin: The University of Wisconsin Press.
Murray, T. E. and Murrel, T. R. (1989), *The Language of Sadomasochism: A Glossary and Linguistic Analysis*, Westport, CT: Greenwood.
Musolff, A. (2004), *Metaphor and Political Discourse: Analogical Reasoning in Debates about Europe*, Basingstoke and New York. Palgrave Macmillan.
—(2010), *Metaphor, Nation and the Holocaust: The Concept of the Body Politic*, Abingdon and New York: Routledge.
Musolff, A., MacArthur, F. and Pagani, G. (eds) (2014), *Metaphor and Intercultural Communication*, London and New York: Bloomsbury.
Nash, W. (1985), *The Language of Humour: Style and Technique in Comic Discourse*, London: Longman.
Neaman, J. S. and Silver, C. (1990), *Book of Euphemism*, Ware: Wordsworth.
OED3: *Oxford English Dictionary* (2013), Judy Pearsal (dir.), 3rd edn, Oxford: Oxford University Press. http://www.oed.com (last accessed 10 April 2014).
O'Keefe, A. (2012), 'Media and Discourse Analysis', in J. P. Gee and M. Handford (eds), *The Routledge Handbook of Discourse Analysis*, Abingdon and New York: Routledge, pp. 441–54.
Oncins-Martínez, J. L. (2010), 'Shakespeare's Sexual Language and Metaphor: A Cognitive-Stylistic Approach', in M. Ravassat and J. Culpeper (eds), *Stylistics and Shakespeare's Language: Transdisciplinary Approaches*, London and New York: Continuum, pp. 215–45.
Palmatier, R. (1995), *Speaking of Animals: A Dictionary of Animal Metaphors*, Westport, CT: Greenwood.
Partridge, E. (1968), *Shakespeare's Bawdy*, Abingdon and New York: Routledge.
Patthey-Chavez, G., Clare, L. and Youmans, M. (1996), 'Watery passion: The struggle between hegemony and sexual liberation in erotic fiction for women', *Discourse & Society*, 7 (1): 77–106.
Pfaff, K. L., Gibbs, R. W. and Johnson, M. D. (1997), 'Metaphor in using and understanding euphemism and dysphemism', *Applied Psycholinguistics*, 18: 59–83.
Pinker, S. (2002), *The Blank Slate: The Modern Denial of Human Nature*, London: Penguin.

Pragglejaz Group (2007), 'MIP: A method for identifying metaphorically used words in discourse', *Metaphor and Symbol*, 22 (1): 1–39.

Quillian, S. (2009), *The Joy of Sex: The Adventurous Lover*, New York: Octopus Publishing Group.

Radden, G. (2000), 'How Metonymic are Metaphors?', in A. Barcelona (ed.), *Metaphor and Metonymy at the Crossroads: A Cognitive Perspective*, Berlin: Mouton de Gruyter, pp. 93–109.

Rivano Fischer, E. (2011), *Metaphor: Art and Nature of Language and Thought*, Bloomington, IN: AuthorHouse.

Rodríguez González, F. (2008a), 'The Feminine Stereotype in Gay Characterization: A Look at English and Spanish', in M. A. Gómez-González, J. L. McKenzie and E. González-Álvarez (eds), *Languages and Cultures in Contrast and Comparison*, Amsterdam and Philadelphia: John Benjamins, pp. 221–45.

—(2008b), *Diccionario Gay-Lésbico*, Madrid: Gredos.

Romero, E. and Soria, B. (2012), 'Construcción conceptual ad hoc e interpretación metafórica', *Forma y Función*, 25 (2): 217–47.

Ruiz de Mendoza Ibáñez, F. J. (2000), 'The Role of Mappings and Domains in Understanding Metonymy', in A. Barcelona (ed.), *Metaphor and Metonymy at the Crossroads*, Berlin and New York: Mouton de Gruyter, pp. 109–32.

—(2011), 'Metonymy and Cognitive Operations', in R. Benczes, A. Barcelona and F. J. Ruiz de Mendoza Ibáñez (eds), *Defining Metonymy in Cognitive Linguistics: Towards a Consensus View*, Amsterdam and Philadelphia: John Benjamins, pp. 103–24.

Ruiz de Mendoza Ibáñez, F. J. and Peña Cervel, S. (2005), 'Conceptual Interaction, Cognitive Operations and Projection Spaces', in F. J. Ruiz de Mendoza Ibáñez and M. S. Peña Cervel (eds), *Cognitive Linguistics: Internal Dynamics and Interdisciplinary Interaction*, Berlin: Mouton de Gruyter, pp. 249–81.

Ruiz de Mendoza Ibáñez, F. J. and Pérez Hernández, L. (2003), 'Cognitive Operations and Pragmatic Implication', in K. Panther and L. Thornburg (eds), *Metonymy and Pragmatic Inferencing*, Amsterdam and New York: John Benjamins, pp. 23–50.

—(2011), 'The contemporary theory of metaphor: Myths, developments and challenges', *Metaphor and Symbol*, 26: 161–85.

Sánchez Benedito, F. (2004), *Supplement to a Semi-Bilingual Dictionary of Euphemisms and Dysphemisms in English Erotica*, Granada: Comares.

—(2009), *Dictionary of English Euphemisms and Dysphemisms for the Taboo of Sex with Spanish Equivalents*, Granada: Comares.

Santaemilia, J. (2005), 'Researching the Language of Sex: Gender, Discourse and Impoliteness', in J. Santaemilia (ed.), *The Language of Sex: Saying and Not Saying*, Valencia: Universidad, pp. 3–22.

Schmidt, R. and Kess, J. (1986), *Television Advertising and Televangelism: Discourse Analysis of Persuasive Language*, Amsterdam and Philadelphia: John Benjamins.

Semino, E. (2008), *Metaphor in Discourse*, Cambridge: Cambridge University Press.
Shariffian, F. (2009), 'On Collective Cognition and Language', in H. Pishwa (ed.), *Language and Social Cognition: Expressions of the Social Mind*, Berlin: Mouton de Gruyter, pp. 163–80.
—(2011), *Cultural Conceptualizations and Language*, Amsterdam and Philadelphia: John Benjamins.
Slade, J. W. (2001), *Pornography and Sexual Representation: A Reference Guide*, Westport, CT: Greenwood.
Sperber, D. and Wilson, D. (1986), *Relevance: Communication and Cognition*, Oxford: Blackwell.
Springer, C. (1998), 'The Pleasure of the Interface', in P. D. Hopkins (ed.), *Sex/Machine: Readings in Culture, Gender, and Technology*, Bloomington, IN: Indiana University Press, pp. 484–500.
Stanley, A. (1998), 'Women Hold up Two-thirds of the Sky: Notes for a Revised History of Technology', in P. D. Hopkins (ed.), *Sex/Machine: Readings in Culture, Gender, and Technology*, Bloomington, IN: Indiana University Press, pp. 17–32.
Stanley, J. P. (2006), 'When we Say "Out of the Closets!"', in D. Cameron and D. Kulick (eds), *The Language and Sexuality Reader*, Abingdon and New York: Routledge, pp. 49–55.
Steen, G. (2011), 'The contemporary theory of metaphor: Now new and improved!', *Review of Cognitive Linguistics*, 9 (1): 26–64.
—(2014), 'The Cognitive-Linguistic Revolution in Metaphor Studies', in J. R. Taylor and J. Littlemore (eds), *The Bloomsbury Companion to Cognitive Linguistics*, London and New York: Bloomsbury, pp. 117–42.
Stöver, H. (2011), 'Awareness in metaphor understanding: The lingering of the literal', *Review of Cognitive Linguistics*, 9 (1): 65–82.
Szwedek, A. (2011), 'The ultimate source domain', *Review of Cognitive Linguistics*, 9 (2): 341–66.
Taylor, J. R. and Littlemore, J. (2014), 'Introduction', in J. R. Taylor and J. Littlemore (eds), *The Bloomsbury Companion to Cognitive Linguistics*, London and New York: Bloomsbury, pp. 1–25.
Tendhal, M. (2009), *A Hybrid Theory of Metaphor: Relevance Theory and Cognitive Linguistics*, Basingstoke and New York: Palgrave Macmillan.
Terrenoire, D., 'Discussing Uganda: *A Dark Planet*' (2007), http://terrenoire.blogspot.com/2007/02/discussing-uganda.html (accessed 30 August 2011).
Thorne, T. (2005) [1990], *Dictionary of Contemporary Slang*, 3rd edn, London: A & C Black.
Turner, J. (1998), 'Turns of phrase and routes of learning: The journey metaphor in educational culture', *Intercultural Communication Studies*, 7 (2): 23–36.
Turner, R., 'Debating pornography: Categories and Metaphors' (1999), http://www.sensiblemarks.info/debating.html (accessed 19 November 2013).
Verhagen, A. (2007), 'Construal and Perspectivization', in D. Geeraerts and H.

Cuycenks (eds), *The Oxford Handbook of Cognitive Linguistics*, Oxford: Oxford University Press, pp. 48–81.

Warren, B. (1992), 'What euphemisms tell us about the interpretation of words', *Studia Linguistica*, 46 (2): 128–72.

Weber, M. (1958), *The Protestant Ethic and the Spirit of Capitalism*, New York: Charles Scribner's Sons.

Westley, H. (2008), *The Body as Medium and Metaphor*, Amsterdam and New York: Rodopi.

Wierzbicka, A. (1996), *Semantics: Primitives and Universals*, Oxford: Oxford University Press.

Wilson, D. (2011), 'Parallels and differences in the treatment of metaphor in relevance theory and cognitive linguistics', *Studia Linguistica Universitatis Iagellonicae Cracoviensis*, 128: 195–214.

Wilson, D. and Carston, R. (2007), 'A Unitary Approach to Lexical Pragmatics: Relevance, Inference and ad hoc Concepts', in N. Burton-Roberts (ed.), *Pragmatics*, Basingstoke and New York: Palgrave Macmillan, pp. 230–59.

Wilson, D. and Sperber, D. (1990), 'Outline of relevance theory', *Hermes*, 5: 35–56.

—(2004), 'Relevance Theory', in L. R. Horn and G. Ward (eds), *The Handbook of Pragmatics*, Oxford: Blackwell, pp. 607–32.

Yu, N. (1998), *The Contemporary Theory of Metaphor: A Perspective from Chinese*, Amsterdam and Philadelphia: John Benjamins.

—(2008), 'Metaphor from Body and Culture', in R. W. Gibbs (ed.), *The Cambridge Handbook of Metaphor and Thought*, Cambridge: Cambridge University Press, pp. 247–61.

Yus Ramos, F. (2005), 'Attitudes and emotions through written text: The case of textual deformation in internet chat rooms', *Pragmalingüística*, 13: 147–73.

—(2012), 'Strategies and Effects in Humorous Discourse: The Case of Jokes', in B. Eizaga Rebollar (ed.), *Studies in Linguistics and Cognition*, Frankfurt am Main: Peter Lang, pp. 271–96.

Index

Abrantes, A. 127, 211n. 29
ADVENTURE metaphor 102–4
Allan, K. 12–14, 45, 46–7, 59, 67, 143, 153, 159, 161, 203n. 6
ambiguity 54, 56, 58–61, 65–7, 76, 79, 90, 102–3, 127–8, 133
analogy 84, 106, 126, 149, 158, 163, 178
anglicism *see* Spanish, anglicism
ANIMAL metaphor 136–7
   BIRD metaphor 142–4
   SMALL FURRY ANIMAL metaphor 137–42
   WILD ANIMAL metaphor (for men) 148–50
   WILD ANIMAL metaphor (for women) 144–8, 149, 181–2
appraisal (theory) 180, 184–5, 190
axiology 2, 4, 13–14, 46–7, 48, 189
Ayto, J. 58, 72

Barcelona, A. 23, 32, 204n. 5
basis for metaphor
   bodily basis *see* embodiment
   cultural basis 35, 37–8, 72 *see also* culture
   experiential basis 24, 28–9, 32, 37, 119, 122
   metonymic basis 32, 80, 141
Batchelor, J. A. 205n. 1
Beck, G. 52, 58–9
bidirectionality *see* CMT, directionality
Blakemore, D. 40, 134
Braun, V. 105, 161
Brown, P. 45–6
Burkhardt, A. 133
Burridge, K. 2, 12–14, 45, 46–7, 59, 67, 71, 78, 153, 161

Caballero, R. 7, 24, 28, 30, 31
CAGE metaphor 109 *see also* CONTAINER metaphor

Cameron, D. 148, 168–9, 179, 183, 213n. 16
Carston, R. 41, 42, 132–3
Casas Gómez, M. 46, 49, 51, 53, 76, 135
censorship 3–4, 71–2, 182–3, 207n. 2 *see also* taboo, sex
Chamizo Domínguez, P. J. 48, 53, 65–6, 127–8, 132
Charteris-Black, J. 62, 63
Chilton, P. A. 63
Clare, L. 111, 159
Claridge, C. 8, 10
CLOSET metaphor 107–9 *see also* CONTAINER metaphor
CMT (Contemporary Metaphor Theory) 5, 21–4, 49
   directionality 23, 60–1, 207n. 14
   redefinitions 33–5
Coates, J. 64, 167, 179
Coleman, J. 165
cognitive–linguistics theory *see* CMT
conflation 29, 78, 85, 152, 157, 158, 166
connotation 13, 59–61, 63, 66, 124, 128, 157–8, 160, 164–5, 173–4
CONTAINER metaphor 104–7
context 12–14, 41, 49, 55, 66–7
   context-induced (creativity) 55
   contextual effects 40, 42, 49–50, 52, 178
   local context 36
contrast 51–2, 63, 73, 94, 131
Crespo-Fernández, E. 46, 60, 63–4, 207nn. 1, 14, 210n. 22
cross-varietal synonyms 13
CRUISING metaphor 101 *see also* JOURNEY metaphor
culture 35–9, 189
   cultural conceptualization 38, 94
   cultural stereotypes 146, 156, 172, 181–2 *see also* heteronormativity
   cultural variation *see* Spanish, metaphors

Deignan, A. 64, 87–8, 113–14, 124, 125–6, 162, 189, 210n. 28, 212n. 11
DESTINATION metaphor 97–100 *see also* JOURNEY metaphor
diminutive 139, 174–5, 213n. 21
DIRT metaphor 122–5
dirty talk 123, 125, 142, 144
discourse 33–4, 49, 55, 61–2
  heteronormative discourse 179 *see also* heteronormativity
  polite/public discourse 58, 71, 73, 77, 88, 91, 124 *see also* politeness
displacement 52–3, 90–1, 131
domain
  domain expansion 32, 80, 116, 118
  domain highlighting vs. domain mapping 31–2
  source domain 22–3, 25, 48, 63, 72
  target domain 22–3, 25
dysphemism
  colour 159
  conceptual dysphemism 49–50
  conventional dysphemism 56–9, 127
  dysphemism for adultery 67
    breasts 167
    ejaculation 57, 74, 163
    homosexuals 144, 174–5, 182–3
    independent women 147
    intercourse 152–3, 155, 162, 164, 172
    licentious women 146, 157–8
    masturbation 164–5
    men as sex objects 167
    menstruation 159
    oral sex 155
    penetration 168–9
    penis 143–4, 163, 168
    prostitution 140, 157–8, 160, 167
    sexual desire/excitation 149, 154–5
    sexual seduction 146, 151–2
    sexually active men 148–9, 152, 170
    sexually active women 140–2, 145, 147, 155–6, 181–2
    sexually attractive women 138, 145, 166
    sperm 163–4
    vagina 141–2, 161
    virginity 159
    womanizer 157
    women as sex objects 138–9, 141, 156–7, 160, 166

embodiment 24–5, 28–9, 36, 37–8
entailment, metaphorical 26, 64, 77, 82, 87, 101, 103, 109, 151–2, 162–3, 171, 173, 181
euphemism
  associative contamination (hypothesis) 13, 58
  concealing/veiling functions 211n. 29
  conceptual euphemism 49–50
  consolatory euphemism 47
  conventional euphemism 56–9, 127
  double euphemism 108
  euphemism for adultery 93
    anal sex 74, 90, 104
    casual sexual encounters 91–2, 101–2
    exciting sexual practices 102, 155
    immorality 85–6, 121, 123–4, 184–5
    initiation into sexuality 89
    intercourse 79, 89, 91, 93, 97, 99
    lack of sexual desire 110
    masturbation 74, 89, 92, 99, 128
    mouth-to-mouth kissing 94
    obscene language 123, 125
    oral sex 74–5, 94
    orgasm 97–100, 106–7, 110, 112–13, 115, 131–2
    penetration 94, 100–1, 168–9
    pornography 91, 120, 124
    powerful sexual partner 93
    prostitution 74, 76–8
    sadomasochism 94–5
    sexual attraction 111, 114, 125
    sexual desire/excitation 81–7, 106, 114, 116–18, 126, 130
    sexual molestation 120
    sexual obsession 116–17, 124
    sexual stimulation 91, 94, 99
    sexual toys 92, 125
    unconventional sexual practices 90, 103, 120
    vagina 69
  protective euphemism 47, 74, 89, 102, 108, 111
  provocative euphemism 47, 83, 88, 111, 115, 119
  underhand euphemism 47

uplifting euphemism 47, 52, 76
evaluation 49–50, 61–4, 162, 173–4,
    178–85, 189–91 *see also* ideology

face 10, 45–7, 50–1, 54, 58, 71–2, 77–8,
    86, 96, 102, 122, 175, 184, 205n. 1
FALLING metaphor 125–6
Fernández Fontecha, A. 146
FIRE metaphor 82–8
FIREWORKS metaphor 114–15
FLOWER metaphor 173–5, 182–3
folk (theory) 81, 115–16 *see also* knowledge
FOOD/EATING metaphor 153
    DESSERTS metaphor 156–8, 160
    FRUIT metaphor 158–9
    HUNGER metaphor 154–6
    MEAT metaphor 160–1
Forceville, C. 23–4

Galera Masegosa, A. 140
GAMES metaphor 88–92
Gayspeak 203n. 5 *see also* homosexuality
Gibbs, R. W. 34, 67, 206n. 11
Goffman, E. 45
Gradecack-Erdelijc, T. 49–50
Grady, J. 28–9
Great Chain of Being 136–7, 156, 166,
    171, 175
Grice, H. P. 132

Halliday, M. A. K. 203n. 3
HEALTH metaphor 119–22
HEAT metaphor 80–2
Herrero Ruiz, J. 50–2, 177, 206n. 8
heteronormativity 174, 179, 182–3, 190

Hines, C. 156–8, 160
Holder, R. W. 78, 93, 156
homosexuality 107–9, 173–5, 182,
    213n. 20
Hughes, G. 144, 163
humour 61, 91 *see also* X-phemism, ludic
HUNTING metaphor 150–2
hyperbole 83–7, 99, 107, 110, 114–15,
    131–3, 164, 177–8, 180, 190

Ibarretxe-Antuñano, I. 7, 24
ICM (Idealized Cognitive Model) 35–6,
    52

ideology 62–4, 107, 124, 137, 162, 179–80,
    182–3, 189 *see also* evaluation
idiom 16, 84
ILLNESS metaphor 118–19
image schema 24–6
    SOURCE-PATH-GOAL 25, 96–7
    SPATIAL-CONTAINMENT 25, 100, 104–6,
        107
    spatialization of form hypothesis 25,
        107
    UP-DOWN 25, 28
Indurkhya, B. 65
INSANITY metaphor 115–18
Internet forums (as corpora) 8–9

Jiménez Catalán, R. 146
Johnson, M. 22, 24, 25, 27, 31, 97, 98–9,
    122
Johnson, M. D. 67
JOURNEY metaphor 96, 100–2

Keyes, R. 55, 58
Kittay, E. F. 49
Kitzinger, C. 105, 161
knowledge 23, 27
    central knowledge 37, 96
    commonplace knowledge 72–3, 101,
        102, 109–10, 115, 145
    cultural knowledge 34, 37, 39, 132
Kövecses, Z. 25–6, 31, 35–6, 37–8, 55,
    63, 77–8, 80–2, 86, 94, 105–6, 115,
    136–7, 139, 154, 156, 169, 208n. 5
Kulick, D. 148, 179, 183

Lakoff, G. 22, 24–6, 27, 29–30, 31, 53, 58,
    96–7, 98–9, 104, 117, 119–20, 122,
    137, 156, 160, 169, 206n. 10
Langacker, R. W. 49, 205n. 6
Leech, G. 46
Levinson, S. 45–6
lexicalization 53, 59–60
Littlemore, J. 204n. 7
Lizardo, O. 122–3
López-Rodríguez, I. 138, 141, 142, 144,
    149

MACHINE metaphor 169–73
male vs. female talk 167, 213n. 22
Martin, J. R. 6, 180–2, 184

maxim of Quality 132, 134
McEnery, T. 135, 179
McGlone, M. S. 52, 58–9, 205n. 1
meaning focus, main 37, 63, 82, 96, 113, 122, 165, 188
metaphor
  appearance-based metaphor 159
  complex metaphor 38
  conceptual vs. linguistic metaphor 22–3
  conventional metaphor 57–8, 62, 86, 127, 189
  correlation metaphor vs. resemblance metaphor 29
  correspondences, metaphorical 22–3, 25–7, 30, 54, 57, 88, 101, 151, 161, 169–70, 173
  creative metaphor 53–6
  dead metaphor 59, 87, 206n. 10
  deliberate metaphor 34, 42–3, 57, 62, 66, 76, 175, 189 *see also* persuasion
  generic vs. specific level metaphor 29–30
  hiding/highlighting property *see* utilization, metaphorical
  interpretation *see* relevance theory, metaphor interpretation
  lexicalized metaphor *see* metaphor, dead
  mapping *see* metaphor, correspondences
  mapping, central 37
  MIP (Metaphor Identification Procedure) 15, 59
  one-correspondence metaphor vs. many-correspondence metaphor 30
  ontological metaphor 27–8
  orientational metaphor 27–8
  primary metaphor 28–9, 38, 112, 120
  semi-lexicalized metaphor *see* metaphor, conventional
  structural metaphor 27–8
  three-dimensional model 33–4, 62
metonymy
  metaphtonymy 32
  metonymy vs. metaphor 31–3
  metonymy-based metaphor 32
  source-in-target metonymy 32, 80, 116, 141, 188
  target-in-source metonymy 32

Milic, G. 49–50
motivation *see* basis for metaphor
Muller, C. 57
Murphy, P. F. 79, 143, 157, 162, 171–2
Murray, T. E. 94–5
Murrel, T. R. 94–5

NATURAL PHENOMENA metaphor *see* WATER metaphor; WEATHER metaphor
neutralization 51

orthophemism 13, 47, 187

Palmatier, R. 149
Patthey-Chavez, G. 111, 159
PC language 78
Pérez Hernández, L. 28, 41
persuasion 57, 62–4, 179–80, 189 *see also* metaphor, deliberate
Pfaff, K. L. 67
Pfiester, A. 52, 58–9
PHYSICAL FORCES metaphor 109–11
Pinker, S. 13, 58
PLAYTHING metaphor 165–8
politeness 14, 45–7, 78, 86 *see also* discourse, polite/public discourse
  middle class politeness criterion 14, 143
  politeness principle 46, 205n. 2
  politic behaviour 14
Pragglejaz Group *see* MIP

quasi-dysphemism 46–7, 77, 124, 184
quasi-euphemism 46–7, 91, 96, 148

Radden, G. 32
referent manipulation 206n. 9
relevance theory 39–43
  ad-hoc concept 41–2, 127–33, 175–8, 191
  cognition 41–2
  enrichment 42, 129–31, 177
  explicature 41, 191
  implicature 40–1
  inference 40–1, 134, 191
  loosening 42, 129
  metaphor interpretation 39–43, 127–34, 175–8
  optimal relevance 40, 42, 178

relevance principle 39
religion 72, 86, 132, 185, 208n. 9
rhetoric *see* persuasion
RIDING metaphor 152–3
Rodríguez González, F. 108, 174, 203n. 5
Ruiz de Mendoza Ibáñez, F. J. 28, 29, 30, 31–2, 41, 84

sadomasochism 94–6, 126
saliency 25, 28, 150
Sánchez Benedito, F. 53, 65, 127–8, 161
Santaemilia, J. 3
Shariffian, F. 38
slang 95–6, 118
Spanish
   anglicism 209n. 20, 213n. 18
   metaphors 145–6, 207n. 14, 209n. 16, 212n. 8
Sperber, D. 39, 40–3
SPORTS metaphor 92–6
Stanley, J. P. 213n. 20
Steen, G. 33–4, 42, 57, 62
swearing *see* male vs. female talk
symbol/symbolism 28, 107, 138, 168, 173
Szwedek, A. 23

taboo
   abjection 122–4, 161
   ambivalence 2
   death 207n. 1, 209n. 18
   pollution 159, 161
   sex 3–5, 71–2
   silence 72, 207n. 1
   taboo vs. linguistic taboo 203n. 1
Tendhal, M. 34–5
'the self'/'the other' dichotomy 144, 174
Thorne, T. 95, 143
TOOL metaphor 168–9, 173
truth conditions 132–4
Turner, M. 29–30, 97, 137, 160

underspecification 73
understatement 131, 133, 178
unidirectionality *see* CMT, directionality
utilization, metaphorical 25–6, 48, 64, 75–6, 88–9, 93, 101, 110, 154, 172, 189

Verhagen, A. 49, 97
VIOLENCE metaphor 164–5

WAR metaphor 57–8, 66, 161–5
Warren, B. 205n. 5, 207n. 16
WATER metaphor 111–13
WEATHER metaphor 114–15
White, P. R. R. 6, 180–2, 184
Wilson, D. 39, 40–3
WORK metaphor 72–3, 75–6, 79
   BUSINESS metaphor 73–4
   COMMERCIAL INTERACTION metaphor 78–9
   DUTY metaphor 75
   JOB metaphor 74–5
   WORKER metaphor 76–7

X-phemism 14
   artful 53–6
   cohesive 47, 95–6, 188
   complimentary 47
   conceptual 49–50
   conventional 56–9
   derogatory 47, 77, 86, 124, 184
   dirty 47, 142, 144
   explicit 53–4, 59
   ludic 47, 56, 91
   novel 53–6

Youmans, M. 111, 159
Yu, N. 25, 35, 38
Yus Ramos, F. 10, 207n. 13